All the News
Unfit to Print

ALSO BY ERIC BURNS

Nonfiction

Broadcast Blues

The Joy of Books

The Spirits of America: A Social History of Alcohol

Infamous Scribblers: The Founding Fathers and the Rowdy Beginnings of American Journalism

The Smoke of the Gods: A Social History of Tobacco

Virtue, Valor and Vanity: The Founding Fathers and the Pursuit of Fame

Fiction

The Autograph: A Modern Fable of a Father and a Daughter

Play

Mid-Strut

All the News Unfit to Print

How Things Were . . . and How They Were Reported

ERIC BURNS

WILEY

John Wiley & Sons, Inc.

3 1257 01864 1877

Published by John Wiley & Sons, Inc., Hoboken, New Jersey
Published simultaneously in Canada

Library of Congress Cataloging-in-Publication Data:
Burns, Eric.
   All the news unfit to print : how things were ... and how they were reported / Eric Burns.
     p. cm.
   Includes bibliographical references and index.
   ISBN 978-0-470-40523-9 (cloth)
     1. Journalism—Objectivity.   2. History, Modern—19th century.
   3. History, Modern—20th century. I. Title.
PN4784.O24B88 2009
070.9—dc22

                              2008045524

For Dianne, Toby, and Cailin, always, all ways

Contents

PART ONE

Telling Lies

USUALLY WHEN PEOPLE SAY THAT JOURNALISM IS THE FIRST draft of history, they are praising reporters for laying a foundation of knowledge that will last the ages. But there is another way to interpret the sentiment—as a warning to historians to build on firmer ground.

This was especially true in the late seventeenth century and most of the eighteenth, when journalism as we know it today was such a novelty that readers were not quite sure what to make of it. Most Europeans and Americans of the time were citizens of a world that seemed so small it did not encourage curiosity, a world "in which news could not thrive as a commodity because it barely existed as a concept." Which is to say that, the occasional explorer or trader notwithstanding, the lives people lived were narrow ones. They were concerned with their own families, their own farms and shops, their own relationship to the Almighty. What else was there? Of what possible interest could occurrences outside his daily realm be to a man? How could they affect his loved ones, his occupation, his nightly communication with his Maker? And how could a person who worked from dawn until dusk find the time to read a newspaper even if he wanted to? The few moments left at the end of the day for reading would be devoted to the word of God, not the word of a fellow sinner who happened to own a printing press.

It was attitudes like these that were the basis and curse of modern journalism, and it took centuries for them to change, a process so gradual as to be almost imperceptible. And because of these attitudes, many of the men who worked for newspapers in the past did not take their occupation seriously. Put simply, if the readers were not dedicated to the product, why should the writers be? The latter wanted to earn a living, and on occasion have a lark, more than they wanted to provide the historical record on which future generations would depend.

As a result, that record has often been riddled with errors, omissions, and pranks. Historians have had to seek sources other than newspapers in their quest for accuracy: letters to and from the principal figures in a certain event, letters referring to the principals from both supporters and opponents, documents produced by lawmaking bodies, artifacts of various kinds, and archaeological and geological records, to name but a few. And even so, the struggle to know the truth of ages past has often eluded them, and even eluded those living in the past until it was too late for them to respond as they otherwise might have.

We still do not know, and never will, about the precise deliberations of Parliament for a few years under George II, years when the relationship between Great Britain and its New World colonies was just beginning to fray. We still think too harshly of the British for their treatment of Americans that led to the Revolutionary War. We do not, for instance, understand the context of such legislative measures as the Stamp Act, which

Americans found a bellicose provocation but their brethren in England had long accepted.

We were so often presented with one-sided views of early American presidents, either heroes or villains, that until fairly recent times we could not acquaint ourselves with the full range of their humanity. And we have still not discovered the true sentiments of early-twentieth-century presidents on a number of topics, because they forbade reporters to quote them directly, and reporters were only too happy to acquiesce.

Most of us do not realize the role of the press, one news-paper in particular, in leading to the deaths of almost twenty-four hundred Americans in a war that never should have been fought.

By refusing to report on the viciousness of Stalin's rule in the early thirties, a reporter sympathetic to Stalin's goals encouraged those who read him to be sympathetic to his goals as well. As a result, countless Americans were deceived and the entire course of mid-twentieth-century history in our country was altered.

We did not know about the drinking habits of legislators that might have affected their votes on crucial issues, or even their attendance when votes were being taken. We did not know about the extracurricular sex lives of legislators that might have com-promised their integrity and interfered with their commitment to the duties of office.

We cannot even be as certain as we would like about the identity of the kidnapper, or kidnappers, of Charles and Anne Lindbergh's baby son.

But not all journalistic misstatements or cover-ups have had, or have threatened, dire consequences. Some, however inadver-tently, have been the equivalent of practical jokes—the woman determined to fill the colonies with baby colonists, as reported by the most erudite of the founding fathers; the bizarre sight in the Nevada desert, as reported by the man some believe to be the founding father of American literature; the wild man of Baltimore, as reported by the wittiest and most perceptive social critic of the twentieth century; and the three plays reviewed by the great American novelist who didn't see any of them. All of these men, at the time of their falsehoods, were working as journalists.

It is beyond the scope of this book, and beyond the ability of its author, to correct all of the first drafts of history that turned out to be mistaken. What follows are some examples of the sloppiest of those drafts, and analyses of the ways in which Americans, Englishmen, and Frenchmen were victimized, confused, and, on rare occasions, amused by them.

1

How Journalists Got the Idea

THE FIRST LIE EVER TOLD, ALTHOUGH THE STORY cannot be confirmed and therefore might be a lie itself, was uttered for the ears of God. Canadian journalist Bruce Deachman writes that sometime around four thousand years ago, a voice roared through the Garden of Eden, causing tree branches to shake, trunks to quiver, and roots to vibrate. "Who ate my apple?" the voice asked. The question, Deachman reports, "was met by innocent looks all 'round and, eventually, a timid chorus of 'Not me.'"

Then, only a few days later, came the second lie. Deachman tells us that Eve slipped a fig leaf over her midsection, sashayed up to Adam, and asked him whether it made her look fat. "No, dear," Adam replied, "not at all." Eve looked at him dubiously.

Whenever it really happened, it was understandable, even inevitable, that human beings would discover the lie to be an invaluable tactic for interpersonal relationships, a natural reaction when we found ourselves in unfavorable circumstances. Adam and Eve were afraid of God's punishment; why not deny the crime? Adam was afraid of hurting Eve's feelings by telling her she needed a plus-size fig leaf; why not deny the perception? In both cases, self-interest seemed better served by fiction than by fact.

In Aldous Huxley's 1923 novel *Antic Hay*, a young man named Theodore breaks a lunch date with a young woman named Emily. The two have recently made love for the first time, but on this day he prefers not to take the train back to London where she awaits him for a repeat performance. Instead, he wants to meet with another woman, one whose fleshly pleasures he has enjoyed in the past and longs to savor again, the notorious Vivian Viveash. To do so, Theodore must deceive Emily. He sends her a telegram: "Slight accident on way to station not serious at all but a little indisposed come same train tomorrow."

It is not the only lie that Theodore tells Emily, but it is the one that sets off social historian Evelin Sullivan in a volume of her own called *The Concise Book of Lying*. She understands that the reasons for all of Theodore's lies are obvious to readers of Huxley's novel, but she imagines a person opening *Antic Hay* precisely at the point of the falsehood described above and, having no idea of its context, trying to discern its motive. Such a person, Sullivan believes, would find the possibilities limitless, and she illustrates the point with examples that are sometimes intriguing, sometimes ludicrous. Theodore could have lied to Emily, Sullivan tells:

- To get out of a tedious social obligation.
- To blacken the reputation of a business rival.
- To get out of helping a friend move.
- To keep from hurting his parents' feelings.
- To avoid an embarrassing admission of ignorance or lack of money.

- To keep from his wife the truth about a child he fathered before he was married.
- To have an excuse for missing a meeting considered important by his boss.
- To get a woman to sleep with him by claiming to be a marine biologist.
- To keep secret a crime he committed ten years earlier and deeply regrets.
- To protect himself from harm by the thugs of a police state.
- To remain a closet homosexual.
- To keep from his wife the truth about his having an affair.
- To keep his landlord from knowing he has a cat.
- To get a job at a law firm by claiming he graduated from an Ivy League school.
- To conceal from Emily preparations for her surprise birthday party.
- To cover for a teammate who missed practice and has promised to reform.
- To keep his I-told-you-so father from learning that he has been fired.
- To get even with someone who he knows has done him harm.
- To hide his drinking.
- To get a job by claiming he is a veteran.
- To sell as genuine a fabricated account of his childhood, alleging abuse and neglect.
- To save his young sister from the gallows by confessing to a crime he didn't commit.
- To get someone to have unprotected sex with him although he knows he has AIDS [which, given the fact that *Antic Hay* was written in 1923, would make Theodore prescient as well as devious].
- To bring people around to his point of view on something by inventing supporting anecdotes.
- To keep one of his children from learning a distressing truth.
- To sell his romance fiction by using a female pseudonym.
- To pay less income tax.

Sullivan's list is worth considering not because of what it might tell us about Theodore's relationship with Emily, but because it illustrates the vast variety of motives that human beings possess for avoiding the truth. She is, however, just beginning. Several pages later, Sullivan gives even more examples, quoting categories of lies from a long since out-of-print book by Amelia Opie called *Illustrations of Lying, in All Its Branches*. Opie refers to:

Lies of Vanity.
Lies of Flattery.
Lies of Convenience
Lies of Interest.
Lies of Fear.
Lies of first-rate Malignity.
Lies of second-rate Malignity.
Lies, falsely called Lies of Benevolence.
Lies of real Benevolence.
Lies of mere Wantonness, proceeding from a depraved love of
    lying, or contempt for the truth.
There are others probably; but I believe that this list contains
those that are of the most importance; unless, indeed, we may add
to it practical lies; that is, lies acted, not spoken.

Sullivan is still not through. Opie was not detailed enough for her. There are other reasons for truth-bending, Sullivan states:

The fear of losing something—money, a job, a marriage, power, respect, reputation, love, life, freedom, comfort, enjoyment, cooperation, etc., etc.—a better job, admission to a desired school, the chance to hang out with kids our parents tell us to avoid, sexual favors, money, revenge, love, cooperation, respect and admiration, control and power, comfort and convenience, and so forth—is another. Of course, depending on the liar's mental state, the desire for something may appear as the fear of not getting it; the intense desire to marry the adored creature can become the desperate fear of being thwarted, just as the wish for convenience can be the fear of inconvenience—millions have lied to avoid an argument.

The preceding appears on page 57 of *The Concise Book of Lying*. The volume's last numbered page is 334. By that time, "conciseness" has become yet another of the book's countless misstatements.

The first newsmen to lie were probably the first newsmen—the minstrels who sang the news, accompanying themselves with a homemade stringed instrument of some sort, in the villages of medieval Europe. They got their information from the nearby courts, speaking to people who had themselves spoken to the king or duke or baron or lord. Then, as they returned to their villages, they composed their "newscasts" in their heads, almost like stand-up comedians arranging their material to get the biggest laughs.

But surely, one suspects, the minstrels were not concerned with veracity so much as performance. Surely they molded the truth of events to suit the demands of rhyme and the flow of melody. And the more quickly they got back to their villages, the more likely they would be able to stake out positions at heavily trafficked intersections.

And just as surely, the men and women who made up their audience, living lives of isolation as they did, not yet believing that events outside their ken could have any significant effect on their own lives, were only marginally interested in veracity. To them it was the music that mattered, not the lyrics. The news was a show, as it would become once again in the late twentieth and early twenty-first centuries, although this time with much more sophisticated orchestrations.

For hundreds of years, people lied to one another verbally. It was too much trouble to transcribe a mistruth on the rough surface of a hemp-fibered sheet, too time-consuming to scratch out a curse on a clay tablet. Then, in the late 1430s, in the village of Mainz, Germany, on the west bank of the Rhine, a man named Johannes Gutenberg seemed to have had a change of heart. His first goal in life was to be a manufacturer of mirrors. He was fascinated by the way they captured images, the brilliance with which they reflected the sunlight, throwing it off in a hundred different directions. He thought there was a certain magic to the process, and he wanted to associate himself with it.

But for reasons we do not know, he decided against a career in mirrors. Instead, he would invent the movable-type printing press. Actually, the press was a series of three separate inventions: a new means of shaping letters on small pieces of metal that could be easily rearranged into different words; a new kind of ink made of linseed oil that would enable the ink to stick to metal type, previous kinds of ink being insufficiently viscous; and a press that would push the paper onto the inked letters. The latter was probably the most difficult of Gutenberg's tasks, one he could not solve until a carpenter friend suggested building a contraption that resembled a cheese or wine press. In fact, the original Gutenberg printing press might even have contained parts of its cheese- or wine-making predecessors.

"Word of Gutenberg's achievement spread quickly," writes historian Bruce Koscielniak, "and people with interest in printing more books flocked to Mainz to see how this new art of the printing press was accomplished. Hundreds of print shops quickly opened, and soon thousands of different books were in print." But the reading revolution did not begin quite that easily. Gutenberg's first books were produced in a hard-to-read Gothic style of print, meant to resemble handwriting. The closer resemblance was to hieroglyphics: elegant to look at but difficult to comprehend.

"Within a short time," though, Koscielniak continues, "easier-to-read styles replaced the heavy Gothic type. Nicholas Jenson, in Venice, Italy, in the 1470s, designed a Roman alphabet that is still used today. Aldus Manutius, also of Venice, created the well-known slanted *italic* type style." As a result, it took only a few decades for books to become not only plentiful but legible.

Suddenly there was a permanence to the language that had never before existed. Yesterday's lie was today's lie as well, and in some cases tomorrow's. It was the same with the truth. In some cases, especially as the centuries went by and printing presses began to print newspapers, the trick was to tell the two apart, and it was not nearly as easy as it sounds.

2

Journalism from Afar

THE FIRST COLLECTION OF JOURNALISTIC LIES TO SURVIVE
the ages was published in the 1740s. It was written by
perhaps the second most esteemed figure in the history
of the English language, and it did nothing to hurt his reputation. In fact, it seems to have helped. An odd man, as charming
in some ways as he was off-putting in others, he was the result of
a difficult birth. Then he was handed over to a wet nurse whose
milk was tubercular, ensuring that the rest of his life would be no
less difficult.

Of the most esteemed figure in the history of the English
language, William Shakespeare, there are but two authentic
images. One is a portrait on the cover of the First Folio edition
of his plays, the other a statue in the church in which he is buried. But likenesses of number two, Samuel Johnson, abound, and
they reveal a man who appears quite less than dashing, his face

fleshy and his nose overgrown. The truth, however, is worse. In Alexander Pope's words, even as a young man, Johnson was "a sad Spectacle." In fact, he first gained public notice by his appearance, plagued as he was with some kind of neurological disorder, "an Infirmity of the convulsive kind," as Pope put it, "that attacks him sometimes." According to a modern biographer of Johnson, "These obsessional traits took such a variety of forms as to have included almost every major category of tics or compulsive gestures." While walking down the street, Johnson sometimes looked like a marionette whose strings were being pulled by a madman.

What was the cause of this malady? At the time it was thought to be a disease of some sort, physical in cause, like gout, jaundice, or epilepsy. Whatever the problems were,

> they usually tend to have one common denominator: an instinctive effort to control—to control aggressions by turning them in against himself. (As [the painter] Joshua Reynolds shrewdly said, "those actions always appeared to me as if they were meant to reprobate some part of his past conduct.") Or they were employed to control anxiety and reduce things to apparent manageability by "compartmentalization," by breaking things down into units through measure (counting steps, touching posts, and the like), just as he turned to arithmetic . . . when he felt his mind disordered.

And he felt this disordering often. On one occasion he told a friend in confidence that he had "inherited from his Father a morbid disposition both of Body and Mind."

It may be for this reason that Johnson, renowned though he was in his time and venerated as he remains in learned circles, turned out so little creative work in his life. Shakespeare filled the stage, writing eleven tragedies, fourteen comedies, and a dozen histories. His oeuvre also includes five poems and another 154 sonnets. When he was not writing, he was often listening to his words being read during rehearsals or supervising publication of his verse.

Not only was Johnson less prolific, but his works have been less regarded through the ages. He was an eloquent man, a wit, although not quite the stylist Shakespeare was, and certainly not in the same category as an author of drama or poetry. But Shakespeare was not in Johnson's category as a guest at salons. In large part because of his aphorisms, the shortest of literary forms, which Johnson was often able to improvise, his sparkling conversation distracted from his infirmaties and delighted his fellow partygoers. Behind only Shakespeare, Johnson was the most widely quoted man in his native tongue, not only in his time but up to the present as well.

Yet he is far better known for a book written about him than anything he wrote himself. *The Life of Samuel Johnson, LL.D.*, by the Scottish diarist and journalist James Boswell, remains the most famous account of a life ever produced in English; it was as a result of this that Johnson seems to be "one of the most fascinating individuals in history."

The most notable work to which Johnson can lay claim himself was not his alone, but rather a committee's doing, compiled as much as written, and although Johnson headed the committee, he did a minority of the compiling. *A Dictionary of the English Language*, which took Johnson and his clerks a decade to complete, and required them to peruse thousands of books, was the standard volume of its kind for more than a century, until the first edition of the *Oxford English Dictionary* was published in 1884. It was without question a work of scholarship. It was also a work of whimsy, sometimes provided by Johnson's gift for the aphorism, sometimes by his use of quotes from other sources to illustrate the meaning of a word.

Johnson might have done a minority of the compiling, but he provided virtually all of the definitions and quotes. Some of them are as follows:

bear. (1) A rough savage animal.

to bloat. To swell, or make turgid with wind.

The strutting petticoat smooths all distinctions, levels the mother with the daughter. I cannot but be troubled to see so many well-shaped innocent virgins *bloated* up, and waddling up and down like the high-bellied women. Addison, *Spectator*.

a dab. (3) Something moist or slimy thrown upon one. (In low language.) An artist, a man expert at something. This is not used in writing.

retromigency. The quality of staling [making water] backwards.

The last foundation was *retromigency*, or pissing backwards; for men observing both sexes to urine backwards, or aversely between their legs, they might conceive there were feminine parts in both. Browne's *Vulgar Errours*.

tonguepad. A great talker.

She who was a celebrated wit at London is, in that dull part of the world, called a *tonguepad*. *Tatler*.

Johnson also wrote essays, few of them memorable, and a philosophical novel called *Rasselas*, which he produced in one week, supposedly to pay for his mother's funeral expenses, and in which the title character, the prince of Abyssinia, and three companions travel through Egypt looking for happiness. They don't find it. Neither does the reader. At least *Rasselas* has the virtue of brevity; it is so short that in some modern paperback editions the text occupies fewer than 180 pages. Yet, the dictionary notwithstanding, it was Johnson's lengthiest work of prose, and so unmemorable that a person in search of that paperback today will not easily locate it. For so venerated a craftsman of the English language, it seems a remarkably unremarkable output, certainly not comparable in any conventional way to that of Dickens or Hardy, or even Maugham or Forster. Nonetheless, Johnson's name is engraved in the pantheon, and in larger letters than those who were more productive.

*   *   *

The son of a poor bookseller, Johnson was forced to drop out of Oxford University after little more than a year, because his parents could not pay his tuition. He became a schoolteacher, a husband, and the master of an academy that he founded himself near the small town of Lichfield. He did not have problems with overcrowding. His student body, at its peak, numbered three.

In 1777, penniless and pessimistic, Johnson and one of his students, the eventually famous actor David Garrick, set out for London, where Garrick made the rounds of the theaters, quickly winning roles and making a name for himself. As for Johnson, he found employment writing, or rather transcribing, parliamentary debates for a publication called the *Gentleman's Magazine*. These were not debates as we understand the term today. Or perhaps they were, for, more than a genuine interchange of ideas, what they more closely resembled were the quadrennial follies staged by our candidates for the presidency in front of television cameras—the members of Parliament taking turns reciting lines in a manner that did little to enlighten those who came to listen. For that, people would have better advised to watch the debating societies of Oxford and Cambridge in one of their competitions.

Johnson needed the money that the *Gentleman's Magazine* provided. But the thought of actually showing up at the House of Commons, listening to the members of Parliament prattle on day after day, expressing themselves in language so clunky that it made his tics start ticking all the more, was something Johnson could not abide. He would not do it. For more than two years, Johnson was the *Gentleman's Magazine*'s only man on the parliamentary beat. Yet during that time he attended the House of Lords a grand total of once.

Still, from his own sofa or lounging chair or even bed, often wearing only an oversized dressing robe and tattered slippers, he provided daily coverage of parliamentary activity, the only such coverage available to the men and women of London. For instance, in the winter of 1740, Johnson quoted one of the MPs as saying the following about the British war at sea with Spain:

> To encourage our Seamen to do their Duty, and to unite private Men, at their own Expence, to attack and distress the Enemy, must necessarily contribute greatly to a vigorous Prosecution of the War, which, if vigorously prosecuted, cannot be long. . . . [O]ur very Being depends upon bringing this War to a speedy Conclusion. There is a Spirit of late raised among every Nation throughout this part of the World, for improving their Trade, Navigation, and Manufactures. . . . What then shall become of us, if by a languid Prosecution of the War, we allow our Trade to be interrupted by Privateers under *Iberian* [Spanish] colours; whilst our Rivals are carrying on theirs without any Disturbance?

Said another MP one day in 1741, as Johnson tells it, about a proposed bill to protect the citizenry against unethical behavior in Parliament:

> My Lords, a Bill of like Tendency has often been laid before us, I have several times given my Vote against it, and my Reasons for so doing. My Sentiments are still the same, because my Reasons have never been answer'd, nor the least care taken in forming this Bill to obviate any of the Objections to the former.
>
> The Danger of Corruption, my Lords, may be painted forth in frightening Colours, and were it real, I should explode Corruption with as much Zeal and Sincerity I am sure, tho' not with so much Rhetoric, as any Lord in the House; but Corruption, my Lords, ought not, I think, be the Subject of our Debate.

And spoke a third MP in 1742, as the Johnson version has it, in favor of a bill to provide aid for India:

> Let us not add to the Miseries of Famine the Mortification of Insult and Neglect, let our Countrymen, at least divide our Care with our Allies, and while we form schemes for succouring the Queen of *Hungruland* [India], let us endeavour to alleviate nearer distresses, and prevent or pacify domestic Discontents.

If there be any Man whom the sight of Misery cannot move to Compassion, who can hear the Complaints of Want without Sympathy, and see the general Calamity of his Country with employing one Hour on Schemes for its Relief: Let not that Man dare to boast of Integrity, Fidelity or Honour.

Johnson made it up. Every word of it, every punctuation mark, every paragraph break. Every single day that he published his account of the House of Commons, it was just that, *his* account. But he did not make up the positions of the various MPs. He was well enough acquainted with their thoughts on the various issues to know what they would say, and well enough acquainted with their lack of originality to know they were more likely to repeat themselves than reexamine the matters at hand and put forth new ideas.

Despite this, he sometimes employed a young man to eavesdrop on the MPs and then run back to Johnson's rooms with the substance of their comments. But like a movie that is "based on" a book rather than literally following its plot, Johnson's reports were based on the speeches rather than literally rendering them. He did not, to repeat, except for one day, hear a single word from the gallery of the House of Commons.

W. Jackson Bate, Johnson's superb late-twentieth-century biographer, was impressed:

> *The Parliamentary Debates* remain one of the most remarkable feats in the entire history of journalism. . . . When we consider [the debates'] total length, their historical importance (the fact that for so long they were considered authentic speeches by some of England's greatest statesmen), the extraordinary resourcefulness and range of argumentative ability they show, his age (thirty-one to thirty-four) and inexperience, the disadvantages under which he worked [by which Bate presumably means Johnson's failure to attend the events to which he was assigned, certainly a disadvantage to any reporter], and finally the incredible speed with which he wrote them, it is hard to find anything remotely comparable.

But just how accurate was Johnson? Surely there was the occasional member of Parliament who said something the scribe did not anticipate. Surely the occasional topic was raised for which Johnson had not prepared. Surely the young man he hired to listen in on the debates missed something that history would have found worth recording. Surely the estimable Mr. Bate goes too far in his praise, and nowhere at all in offering a cautionary note.

The reason that Johnson's versions of the debates were considered authentic for so long—at least twenty years, and by some even longer—was that Johnson was a much better writer than any of the MPs. They were not about to admit that in the process of being falsified, they were simultaneously being made to appear much more eloquent than they really were.

At first Johnson took pride in the approbation his speeches earned. But after a while pride turned to grumpiness—all that praise directed at so many people, everyone except the person who really deserved it. His anonymity had begun to wear on him, an abrasive to his ego, which became all the more rebellious in response. One night at a banquet, long after Johnson had ceased to write for the *Gentleman's Magazine*, the scholar Philip Francis was addressing the diners and said he had recently come across a speech that William Pitt had given to the House of Lords some years earlier, referring to it as "the best he had ever read." Even Demosthenes, the most famous of early Greek orators, about whom Francis was the reigning British expert, had never written so magnificently.

At this, Johnson's tether snapped. Pitt was in attendance at the dinner, and when the ovation for him died down, Pitt standing at his chair and acknowledging the encomiums with a wave of the hand and the most self-satisfied of grins, a moment of silence filled the dining hall. Johnson ended it by muttering loudly enough so that most could hear, "That speech I wrote in a garret in Exeter."

Pitt's smile vanished in an instant.

And, more than likely, Johnson's doubts began in earnest. The older he got the more he fretted at what he had done, and eventually his reservations were exacerbated by ever-declining health: bouts with bronchitis, pneumonia, catarrh, not to mention blindness in one eye. It was no longer a matter of ego; it was a matter of conscience. He was not a happy person generally, and was specifically annoyed that his replicas of the parliamentary debates were coming to be viewed as the historical record. When he gave up the practice after only a few years, he told a friend that he "would not be accessory to the propagation of falsehood."

But of course he had been, and it is still Johnson's work that is cited in volumes of the British Parliament from the early 1740s. They are, after all, the period's only original accounts.

Six days before Johnson died, still troubled by his creativity as a much younger man, he said to a friend that back when he was crafting the MPs' orations, "he did not think he was imposing on the world." Now, however, he feared otherwise. He had rewritten the truth, and if it is fair to say that he converted it not into lies so much as literature, it is also fair to say that what Johnson wrote was not precisely what the members of Parliament said, in which case *The Parliamentary Debates*, in their hundreds of pages, probably constitute the longest single series of falsehoods ever assembled under the banner of fact in the history of reporting.

Yet that does not seem to be a prevalent view. As previously stated, Johnson's modern biographer toasted him for his ingenuity. His most famous biographer, Boswell, was unconcerned with the *Debates*. This, however, does not tell us as much about Bate and Boswell as it does about the kind of world in which Johnson lived, a world in which, as previously stated, most people had little time for journalism. But when those among the British who did have time—which is to say, for the most part, the upper classes—turned their attention to current events, they preferred to read the works of those who were not paid for their efforts. They trusted men who dipped their pens without remuneration, believing them to be "persons of enlarged views and *unbiased* vision." And, of course, substantial outside income.

As for journalists, like Johnson, who were forced to grasp for every farthing, their publications were often treated with disdain. "Writing for money," states scholar John Brewer, "not only reduced authorship to a mechanical trade but subverted the value of the work. Literature for profit could not be unsullied and unbiased; tainted with lucre, it became a hideous grotesque—distorted, partial and blind."

Brewer goes too far. But his general point, stripped of hyperbole, is accurate. When Englishmen learned of Johnson's duplicity, they became even less trusting of newspapers than before, delaying the eventual acceptance of journalism as a reliable source of information, and contributing to their own ignorance of the world at a time when world affairs were becoming more and more important, and would in fact soon lead the British to a war with their own kin across the Atlantic.

But at least in Johnson's case, if not that of other farthing graspers, the duplicity made for such good reading.

3

A Woman Who Never Was

A FEW YEARS LATER, IN 1747, BENJAMIN FRANKLIN ENTERED THE field of excessively creative journalism. Previously, he had been creative in other ways. The most ethical and erudite of early American publishers, Franklin wanted his *Pennsylvania Gazette* "to expand the very definition of [news]. He wanted to report on '*Algebra*, or the Doctrine of Equations . . . *Analyticks*, or the Resolutions of Problems . . . *Architecture* . . . *Chronology*, or the Doctrine of Time . . . *Mechanicks* . . . *Mineralogy* . . . *Opticks* . . . *Perspective*, or the Projection of Points, Lines, Planes . . . [and] *Pneuumaticks*, or the Consideration of the Air, its Weight, Density, Pressure, Elasticity, &c.'" The *Gazette* told of the latest developments in meteorology, for instance that "the material cause of thunder, lightning, and earthquakes is one and the same." It reviewed the most recently published books from abroad. It did not just publish stories on government; it analyzed the ideas behind various forms and proposals for change. And it did not just publish stories on religion; it contrasted a belief in the Almighty with superstition, "a Monster which has introduced more Misery into the World, than all our natural Evils put together." More than anything else, Franklin said, he wanted to encourage his readers "to join the rationalists of the eighteenth century in pursuit of knowledge and exercise of reason." It was an ambitious list of goals for an eighteenth-century periodical, just as it would be for a periodical of our own century.

But on one occasion, Franklin expanded the definition of news in yet another direction, going even further astray than Johnson. Whereas the latter put his own words into the mouths of real people, Franklin actually invented a person to do the speaking. He did so, however, for reasons entirely different from Johnson's. He was not bored, not shy about being seen in public, not dismissive of those on whom he reported and determined to make them sound more learned. He invented his person because he believed the ruse would serve the public good, better making a point by fictional means than could have been done by the restrictiveness of fact.

Actually, it was not the first time Franklin had done something like this. As a sixteen-year-old apprentice to his older brother James on the *New England Courant*, Franklin found himself longing to write rather than simply set type and clean up the shop after the day's work. But he knew his brother would never accept a submission from him. The two did not get along well; in fact, their relationship was so bad, Franklin said, that on occasion James would beat him. So Franklin, a mere boy of sixteen, began writing letters to the editor of the *Courant* under the pseudonym of Silence Dogood, ostensibly a sixty-year-old widow. And indeed, he managed to sound like a much older person of the opposing gender. "A raging passion for immoderate gain," he wrote in one of his missives, "had made men universally and intensely hardhearted; they were everywhere devouring one another." Just as few teenagers sound like this today, so did few in times past.

The Silence Dogood letters were a big hit with readers. Sales of the *Courant* increased when Silence appeared. But she appeared only eleven times. At that point, it seemed to Franklin, James was beginning to suspect Mrs. Dogood's true identity, and prudence, as well as the author's physical safety, called for him to put her to rest. He was sorry to see her go, but she was not worth another thrashing.

It is the second lady to emerge from Franklin's imagination, however, who concerns us here. Franklin was now in his early forties and found himself becoming more and more upset about the decisions of the Pennsylvania judiciary in cases involving children born out of wedlock. As in the judicial systems of most other colonies at the time, Pennsylvania's judges severely punished the mother while paying virtually no attention to the father, whose name was seldom even mentioned in court proceedings.

Despite having sired a child without benefit of marriage himself as a young man, Franklin found this attitude intolerable. He might have been the beneficiary of the era's judicial hypocrisy, but that did not change the fact that the courts were ruling unfairly, and in his view, men as well as women ought to be punished equally, ought to bear the burden equally, ought to demand reform equally. For his part, Franklin acknowledged his illegitimate son openly.

And so he was moved to write "The Trial of Miss Polly Baker," a charming woman with golden locks and an eye-catching figure, who employed herself as a prostitute in Connecticut. One night, Miss Baker, falling victim to one of the hazards of the profession, conceived a child. And then, later, another. And then a third, a fourth—eventually a fifth. Five illegitimate children from the loins of one wanton woman and the seeds of five different men, none of which she could call husband! As had been the case four times previously, Miss Baker was arrested and put on trial for such defiantly antisocial—or overly social—behavior.

The defendant turned out to be "as sassy a lass as she was prolific." Facing a panel of judges, she said:

> This is the fifth time, gentlemen, that I have been dragged before your court on the same account; twice I have paid heavy fines, and twice have been brought to public punishment . . . I cannot conceive (may it please your honors) what the nature of my offence is. I have brought five fine children into the world, at the risk of my life; I have maintained them well by my own industry, without burdening the township, and would have done it better, had it not been for the heavy charges and fines I have paid.
>
> Can it be a crime (in the nature of things I mean) to add to the number of the king's subjects, in a new country that really wants people? I own it, I should think it a praise-worthy, rather than a punishable action. I have debauched no other woman's husband, nor enticed any youth; these things I was never charged with, nor has any one the least complaint against me, unless, perhaps, the minister, or justice, because I have had children without being married, by which they have missed a wedding fee.

But she was not just doing her duty to the Crown, Miss Baker explained; she was also serving a higher master:

> What must poor young women do, whom custom have forbid to solicit the men, and who cannot force themselves upon husbands, when the laws take no care to provide them any; and yet severely punish them if they do their duty without them; the duty of the first and great command of nature, and of nature's god, *increase and multiply*. A duty, from the steady performance of which, nothing has been able to deter me; but for its sake I have hazarded the loss of the public esteem, and have frequently endured public disgrace and punishment; and therefore ought, in my humble opinion, instead of a whipping, to have a statue erected in my memory.

Whereupon, according to Franklin, Miss Baker took her seat and waited for the judges to leave the room to deliberate.

It did not take long. After but a few minutes, the judges returned, resumed their places behind the bench, and announced their verdict: innocent on all charges. In fact, Franklin reported, so moved was one judge by the defendant's testimony that a few days later he asked Miss Baker to marry him. She accepted, and presumably the two of them went off blissfully—and legally—to provide even more subjects for the king.

The story of Polly Baker's trial first appeared not in Franklin's own paper, the *Pennsylvania Gazette*, but in a journal in London. From there it spread to other papers across the Continent and eventually made its way back to the American colonies, where it was one of the most talked-about, and chuckled-over, tales of the time.

In all likelihood, Franklin did not expect people to take the story seriously. Instead, he believed that he was "teaching a lesson, as did the Bible with its parables and such authors as Chaucer and Boccaccio with their tales of travelers and lovers and others. It was not the facts that were important in such writing, but the moral; it was not the truth as niggling minds defined it, but Truth in the larger sense, as the cosmos recognized it."

Did Franklin teach a lesson? It is impossible to say but tantalizing to speculate. Certainly people talked about Polly Baker and the issue of the male contribution to her state in the aftermath of the trial, but there is no way of knowing how much. Just as certainly no new laws were passed, no new judicial behavior adopted. Few newspapers wrote about women like Polly Baker after Franklin created the original; it was not the kind of topic deemed suitable for journalism at the time.

But as the modern phrase has it, consciousness was certainly raised, however little, however gradually. In Nathaniel Hawthorne's *The Scarlet Letter*, Hester Prynne would have worn an A for her behavior regardless of what had happened to Miss Baker more than a century earlier, but would her lover, Reverend Dimmesdale, have suffered such an excruciating fate? Would God have given him "this burning torture to bear upon my breast"? Would He have brought him "to die this death of triumphant ignominy before the people"? The notion is not preposterous. After all, Franklin was the first to discuss the subject publicly, and surely the conversations became more frequent over the years. By the time Hawthorne took pen to paper in 1850, he might have been reacting to something he had heard that was a distant predecessor of Polly Baker's tale.

At present, there remains more social opprobrium attached to unwed mothers than to unwed fathers. But the latter are catching up, and the laws have already done so, demanding that those who have children, whether married or not, whether male or not, bear at least the financial responsibility for the young one's upbringing.

Again, Franklin was the first to insist to a large audience that such a responsibility was nothing more than the justice that by definition accompanies humanity.

It would be thirty years before Benjamin Franklin finally admitted that Miss Polly Baker, whose story had fascinated so many people over that period, had never drawn a mortal breath. And it's a good thing she hadn't; if she had been the actual living, breathing, procreating creature that so many people suspected, the king might have had more subjects by this time than he had grain to feed them.

4

Lies against the British

I N THE 1760S THERE APPEARED IN NORTH AMERICA A JOURNALIST
similar to Franklin in one way and one way only: he believed
that journalism did not always have to be true so long as it
served a purpose. In fact, it hardly *ever* had to be true if the purpose was separating the colonies from the rule of Great Britain—
legislatively if possible, militarily if not. And whereas Franklin
wrote with subtlety and wit, Samuel Adams wrote angrily, his
style the rejection of whimsy in favor of vituperation that knew
no limits.

Adams told more lies in print than any other figure of his time,
a distinction for which history has not only forgiven but honored him. After all, his lies served one of history's greatest causes,
the creation of the United States of America. As a patriot he was
without peer. As a recorder of events he was without scruple. But

he was motivated in his journalistic assaults on the British Empire by more than just a love of the colonies and an insistence on their rights. There was also something personal, a matter of revenge.

When Adams was a child, his father, Samuel Sr., known to his friends as the Deacon despite being a brewer as well as a church-man, invested some of his money in a land bank, an institution that specialized in real estate transactions. The bank got off to a good start. But to the Deacon and his fellow investors, it was more than just a business. In lending money to local entrepreneurs who wanted to start businesses of their own or expand existing ones, the bank was also providing an invaluable service to a young and growing nation, as it contributed not just to the financial well-being of its individual customers, but to the economic develop-ment of America's leading city, Boston, and its environs.

The British should have been pleased with the enterprise of their countrymen in the New World. Stronger colonies meant a stronger Motherland. Instead, the British were jealous—more than that, vindictive. After but a few months, the Boston land bank was closed by order of Parliament. It seems that "some British banks wanted to offer that same invaluable service to the colonists, perhaps even charging higher interest rates and mak-ing more of a profit, and they had lobbied Parliament to get rid of their American competition. Parliament had acceded to their wishes with little debate."

The Deacon and his partners were stunned. Had they per-haps been misinformed? Was it some other business that had been shut down? When they confirmed it was theirs, they were furious. They did everything they could to reverse the decision, "beseeching Parliament, sending a message to the king, impor-tuning his ministers in North America—all to no avail." Samuel Adams Sr. lost most of the money he had put into the bank, and the family fortunes went into a sharp and lengthy decline. His son, with the exaggerated sense of injustice that the young often feel, was even more enraged than his father, and as he grew older his hatred of the British only grew stronger. It was a hatred that demanded an outlet.

*   *   *

Some years afterward, with relations between the Crown and the colonies having worsened, Adams got the chance he was looking for. The *Boston Gazette*, which had been in business since 1719 without making much of an impression, was purchased by new owners, and the two men, Benjamin Edes and John Gill, not only hired Adams to run the paper, but virtually gave it to him. Editorial policy was his for the formulating, and so heavy-handed were his attacks on the British that those who favored a continued American alliance with the Motherland began to refer to the *Gazette* as the *Weekly Dung Barge*.

On one occasion, Adams wrote a story about Andrew Oliver, the man appointed by the Crown to collect taxes under the Stamp Act in Boston. Oliver had not petitioned for the job, and would in fact rather have served his government in some other way. But according to Adams's article, Oliver lusted after the duties, and furthermore had been one of the men responsible for the existence of the Stamp Act in the first place, a charge that Adams knew to be untrue. Following several paragraphs of undiluted vitriol, Adams closed his piece by suggesting that the good citizens of Boston might want to take matters into their own hands against such a scoundrel. But Adams did more than suggest mayhem; he organized it.

After the *Gazette*'s presses had been shut down for the day, Adams met with some of those good citizens in the paper's offices and gave them their marching orders. The men were known to one another, and to other citizens of Boston who favored independence, as the Sons of Liberty, and to Adams, their father, they could not have been more obedient.

What happened next was exactly what Adams wanted to happen:

Oliver was burned in effigy in August 1765, and then, two nights later, the same mob that had hung the effigy tore its head off as they proceeded to Oliver's office and demolished it with axes before moving on to his residence, where they battered the walls and shattered windows and hurled curses with no less energy or sense of commitment. The rebels demanded that Oliver resign. Fearing for his life, he did.

When the marauders next gathered before Adams, he congratulated them heartily. Toasts were drunk and backs were slapped. In the next issue of the paper, Adams reported the incident with all the impartiality he could muster. There was not the slightest suggestion that the news he disseminated was also the news he incited.

Shortly afterward, a throng of angry Bostonians, jacked up on ninety-proof Sam Adams prose, trashed the house of Thomas Hutchinson, the lieutenant governor of Massachusetts. At first he seemed an unlikely victim. "He was highly regarded in Boston— even the *Boston Gazette* was impressed with him, at least for a time, finding Hutchinson 'a tall, slender, fair-complexioned, fair-spoken, "very good Gentleman," who had captivated "half the pretty Ladies in the Colony and more than half the pretty Gentlemen."'"

But before long, Adams turned on Hutchinson; he was, after all, a servant of the very same Parliament that had treated Adams's family so unfairly in the land bank affair. In a matter of days, the *Gazette* did a complete about-face, now reporting that Hutchinson had been even more of an instigator of the Stamp Act than Oliver. Adams urged the Sons of Liberty to take their revenge.

One night some of them did just that. They were old men, young men, and boys barely old enough to read, and they assembled outside the lieutenant governor's mansion and attacked it as if the structure itself were their enemy. It was a "hellish crew," Hutchinson later said, and it "fell upon my house with the rage of devils." They "split down the door and entered," he went on, and he "was obliged to retire thro yards and garden to a house more remote where I remained until four o'clock."

The hellish crew remained on the premises almost as long, not only wrecking but looting. Hutchinson later told authorities that nine hundred pounds in cash was missing, as well as books and clothing, table settings and jewelry, and perhaps even more. He was in no condition, he declared, to make a dispassionate inventory. For some time, he had been writing a history of Massachusetts, which he seems almost to have finished; the rebels found the manuscript and threw it into the mud in the front yard, ruining it. Hutchinson never had the heart for a rewrite. Of his house, nothing remained, he said, "but the bare walls and floors." Outside, the attackers even cut down the trees.

As Adams knew, but did not reveal when he published his article about the assault on Hutchinson's home, the lieutenant governor had not only *not* supported the Stamp Act, he had pleaded with Parliament to reject it, fearing precisely the kind of reaction in the colonies, especially Massachusetts, that had occurred. But no matter. Hutchinson was a high-ranking official of the Crown in the colonies. Crime enough.

Adams did not always stir up such episodes. Usually it was enough for him just to throw a few more logs on the fires of animosity that were already crackling. And there were times when he could rouse the Sons of Liberty to action without even alluding to rebellion, when his prose was so incendiary that the reader could not help but conclude in the wisdom of an indignant response. For instance, in a regular column alternately called "Journal of Events" or "Journal of the Times," Adams wrote that British soldiers quartered in Boston physically attacked American men on the streets. He wrote that the soldiers insulted and sometimes even mishandled American women. And he wrote that they clubbed American children with the butts of their rifles. He was explicit in his details, insistent on his accuracy. But so far as anyone can prove, none of these events ever happened, or, if they did, they happened much less frequently and with much less severity than Adams had claimed.

The most violent story Adams reported was the Boston Massacre. But he did not just report it; he named it and might also have planned it. The Boston Massacre is a difficult event to understand and explain. Suffice it to say that on one colder than usual night in early March 1770, a crowd of American colonists gathered outside Boston's Custom House, where a single British guard was standing on duty. The crowd apparently taunted the guard. Fearing for his safety, the guard called for reinforcements, and several other soldiers soon appeared around him.

It is not known why the crowd gathered in the first place, nor why it got so much bigger when church bells unexpectedly rang, or who rang them; it was odd for the bells to chime at so late an hour. Nor is it known who pulled the first cudgel or other non-lethal weapon, although chances are it was an American. What *is* known is that it was the British who opened fire, but was the act in self-defense or aggression? Regardless, by the time the shooting was over three colonists had been killed in front of the Custom House and another two died later.

Adams was not there. He learned about the incident from others, and for the most part his account in the *Gazette* reads objectively, almost dryly. Then, suddenly, there is this: "What shewed a degree of cruelty unknown to British troops, at least since the house of Hanover has directed their operations, was an attempt to fire upon or push with their bayonets the persons who undertook to remove the slain or wounded!"

Might the British have attacked in this way? Yes. Is it likely? Not in the least. As even Adams admits, such behavior was not typical of the Crown's defenders in the past and would have been even less typical these days, with Parliament and King George III both having issued warnings to their forces that they were to keep order in the colonies, not foment a rebellion. Sam Adams, one cannot help but conclude, was the one doing the fomenting.

He had done the same thing three years earlier when Parliament passed a series of retributive taxes called the Townshend Acts, which had so angered Americans that they probably led to the Boston Massacre. Adams wrote about the money raised by the acts. He said it was going to officials of the Crown in the colonies, which was true, but he went on to claim that those officials were in turn spending it on "hirelings, pimps, parasites, panderers, prostitutes and whores." There is no reason, none whatsoever, to think that they were.

Other papers began to take their cues from Adams, making the effects of his lies all the more deleterious to whatever slim chances of rapprochement still existed between the colonies and the Crown. In 1774, for example, in response to a new set of taxes from Parliament on the colonies known as the Intolerable Acts, the *Pennsylvania Journal* explained what Parliament was planning to do next:

- It would not allow any British citizen to settle in North America for a period of longer than seven years.
- It would demand that married couples in America pay a tax of fifteen pounds for each male child born and ten pounds for each female. If a child of either gender was born out of wedlock, the levy would be fifty pounds.
- It would impose new taxes on flour and wheat, and more severe penalties on those who did not pay the taxes or did not pay them on time.

And on and on it went, this list in the *Pennsylvania Journal* of proposed laws on the motherland's drawing board. In truth, however, Parliament was not considering *any* of these measures, not a single one of them—and the *Journal* was well aware of the fact. This was Sam Adams–inspired journalism at its very worst.

Even Benjamin Franklin, the most unlikely of colonial journalists to emulate Adams, seems to have done so on one occasion. The year was 1782. Franklin, dispatched by his government to Paris to meet with officials from England and

France, was trying to negotiate the treaty that would bring
the Revolutionary War to a close. But Franklin wanted more
than just an end of hostilities. He wanted reparations. In fact,
he wanted Canada. He reminded Richard Oswald, representing
the British foreign minister Lord Shelburne at one of the meetings, that the motherland had behaved atrociously at times, and
would have to atone for its behavior.

Then, writes John Dos Passos,

> Franklin perpetrated one of the practical jokes he so much
> enjoyed. He had his own printing shop near Passy [on the
> outskirts of Paris] and his slender young grandson Ben Bache to
> operate it. They printed a spurious supplement to a facsimile of
> a number of *The Independent Chronicle* of Boston with a bloody
> tale of bags of scalps captured on their way from the Indians [who
> were allies of the British in the Revolutionary War] to British
> headquarters in Canada: 43 soldiers' scalps, 102 of farmers, 67
> from very gray heads, 88 of women, 193 of boys, 211 of girls big
> and little, 29 of infants "ripped out of their mothers' bellies."
> Copies of the supplement were circulated through Europe
> wherever they would do the most good.

Apparently, they did not do enough good. The colonies did
not get Canada. But Parliament did allow the citizens of the
future United States "indefinite frontiers to the westward," and
American expansion toward the Pacific would come to be known
as Manifest Destiny—the British concession eventually being
regarded by its recipients as a God-given right.

It bears repeating that, as a patriot, a man who put what he
believed to be the best interests of his country above all else,
Sam Adams was beyond reproach, a tireless worker and as self-
lessly dedicated to his ideals as a man could be. In fact, for
all the violence of his prose, it is possible, if not even likely,
that in the long run Adams helped to save lives by inspiring

his countrymen to fight so valorously and tirelessly that the war ended up shorter than it might have been otherwise. Fewer people were killed, fewer injured; there was less disruption to trade and economic well-being for both countries. That was the opinion of some British military officers at the time. It is also the opinion of some historians today as well as the opinion of David Ramsay, perhaps the first man to write a book-length chronicle of the Revolutionary War more than two centuries ago. "In establishing American independence," he wrote, "the pen and the press had a merit equal to that of the sword."

In the hands of Sam Adams, and those journalists who chose to emulate him, the pen was merely a sword of a smaller size.

5

Lies against Americans

ETWEEN THE REVOLUTIONARY WAR AND THE CIVIL War, it was the founding fathers and those of similar stature, most notably Abraham Lincoln, who were victimized more than anyone else by the press. It all started, as did the nation itself, with George Washington.

Washington was accused of wanting to be the first king of the United States, not its first president. Not only did he never have such an ambition, but he was adamant about restricting the power of the chief executive, whatever he was to be called. In fact, when a sculptor once asked him to pose in a cape, he refused on the grounds that it would make him look too regal. But some newspapers did not believe his denials. One accused him of wanting to be *more* than a king. After celebrating one of his birthdays during his presidency, this paper, called the *Aurora*, referred to the observance as a "Political Christmas! What is the idea of this expression, but ranking WASHINGTON with JESUS CHRIST?" Washington did not curse very often. This might have been one of the occasions.

His successor, John Adams, it was said, wanted to start a second war against the British less than a decade after the first one had ended. Several of Adams's advisers urged him to consider such a step, upset, as was the president, that the British were not living up to the terms of the Treaty of Paris. Warmonger, some papers called Adams when they learned of the advice. Tyrant. Dictator.

But a return to arms was never a serious possibility for Adams, and he railed against the newspapers that reported it was. Against some papers he took more drastic action. Under the terms of the Sedition Act, he was entitled to throw publishers and editors into jail if they printed articles deemed harmful to the national interest. And so he did. But Adams defined "national interest" very broadly. His victims were not just those who disagreed with him, but those who used offensive language in so doing.

And then there was Thomas Jefferson, Adams's successor, such a master of ambivalence that he could be attacked in the press, and often was, for any of his positions on any number of issues. Sometimes he favored slavery, and sometimes he favored manumission. Sometimes he defended religion, and sometimes he seemed to advocate atheism. He supported severe restrictions on government spending and yet spent so profligately himself that he died in debt. He defended unfettered academic freedom and yet insisted on passing personal judgment on every professor who was hired, every textbook that a professor proposed to use in class, at his University of Virginia. Since he held such contrasting views and acted so contradictorily on so many different matters, colonial papers were bound to be simultaneously right and wrong anytime they criticized the third president on any of these subjects, as well as several others.

Jefferson was also suspected, during his 1800 presidential campaign against John Adams, of being dead. He had not been seen for several weeks, had written no letters, issued no statements. When it turned out that he was very much alive but simply resting at

Monticello, the *Connecticut Courant* was among the anti-Jefferson papers that had to print sorrowful retractions. The rumor of the candidate's demise, a letter to the editor of the *Courant* concluded, had been started by "some *compassionate* human being" who had "very humanely killed Mr. Jefferson" to lift the spirits of all right-minded voters.

It was with Andrew Jackson's inauguration as the seventh president of the United States that the Virginia-Massachusetts dynasty of "gentleman" politicians ended and the average man moved into the White House. That is what Jackson gave every sign of being. He was a rip-roarin', liquor-guzzlin', pipe-smokin', tobacco chewin', Injun-fightin', frontier-pushin', hard-cursin' fellow who took the oath of office in March 1829. About two months earlier, "Old Hickory," as Jackson was known for his toughness, might also have become the press-hatin'est president Americans had had to that point. To understand why, we must go back almost four decades.

In 1791, Jackson married a woman named Rachel Donelson. She was possessed of a "beautifully molded form, lustrous black eyes, dark glossy hair, full red lips, brunette complexion, though of bril-liant coloring, a sweet oval face rippling with smiles and dimples." She was also possessed of a husband, although she did not want to be and thought she had disposed of him. She and the man she believed was her former mate, Lewis Robards, never seemed to get along. The main problem was that he suspected her of being unfaithful to him, although there is no evidence that she ever was, and because of those suspicions he twice deserted her. The second time, certain he would not return, Donelson agreed to marry Jackson, who had met Rachel when boarding in the Donelson home. She went through all the necessary formalities of obtaining a divorce—or thought she did. Then they became husband and wife.

But two years later, the Jacksons learned that the paperwork for the divorce had not been properly filed, which meant that Rachel's marriage to Robards was still technically valid. Both she and Jackson were embarrassed about the situation, but believing they had done their part as the law required, that the fault for the illegality of their vows lay elsewhere, they felt no guilt. They simply did their part again, this time waiting until they were notified that the Robards-Donelson paperwork had made its way through all of the proper channels, and in 1794, upon being so informed, they once again stood before the preacher and swore their mutual fealty.

Jackson might not have seemed good marriage material, but it was plain to see that he loved his wife and that she reciprocated. Their behavior toward each other in public was respectful and affectionate, and he was always more polite to others when in her company. He did not spit tobacco juice when he was with her, nor did he curse—not as much as usual, at least, although sometimes the actions of his political opponents, of whom there were many, drove him beyond the bounds of restraint. He was almost a gentleman.

The only unhappiness in their union was its brevity. It ended with Rachel's death only six years after it began, a mere two weeks after Jackson defeated John Quincy Adams for the presidency.

In the days leading up to the election, as Rachel's health was failing, the illegitimacy of the Jacksons' first two years of wedlock became a campaign issue. Newspapers claimed that Mrs. Jackson had been a bigamist, which she was, but only by accident, and that Jackson had no respect either for the laws regarding marriage or decency toward women, which was not true.

It was Adams and his supporters who made the misfiled paperwork an issue in 1828, and Jackson berated them for it. But even more he blamed the papers that printed the charges of bigamy, printed them again and again, giving them a sinister cast through repetition. When Rachel Jackson died, the *New Hampshire Statesman and Concord Register*, a pro-Adams paper, reported her passing coldly.

> We are content that newspaper editors should say nothing of the dead, if they cannot speak well—but that they should task their vocabulary, as on the demise of Mrs. Jackson they seem to have done, to furnish out the most high-sounding and superlative epithets to

proclaim her exemplary virtues—and should, as the editors of the Boston Statesman and some other papers have done, dress their sheet in the habiliments of mourning—is at once derogatory to the fearless independence of a free press, and a wanton reflections [*sic*] upon real living worth and excellence. The standard of female character in our country can hardly be thought sufficiently elevated, if Mrs. Jackson, under the known circumstances of the case, is to be spoken of as having the most "exemplary virtues and exalted character" ... "A nation," says the [Washington] Telegraph, "mourns in sympathy with her 'favorite' son. Society has lost one of its brightest ornaments. The friend of the widow and the orphan; the pious Christian, the amiable wife, the consort of Andrew Jackson is no more."

But enough of such flummery. In plain truth, Mrs. Rachel Jackson is dead.

Although strictly speaking Rachel Jackson's bigamy was a fact, many papers used it for the same purpose as a lie: to injure those who were its subject. Rachel was beyond the reach of the press. Andrew was not, and for him the wound of the press coverage would never heal. It was the newspapers, he believed, that killed his beloved wife, adding emotional pain to her physical distress and thus making the chances of recovery impossible. He would not forgive them, not through his eight lonely years in the White House, not through the eight years more that remained to him afterward.

In 1690 there was only one newspaper in North America, and its reign was but a single issue. In it were tedious articles about communal activities, gory articles about murder, and speculation about sexual misconduct among European royalty. It was the latter two that Massachusetts authorities found objectionable, so much so that no sooner did they read the paper than they banned it from further publication. Another fourteen years would pass before Americans saw their second newspaper.

For the next few decades, the growth of journalism was slow, but as relations with the British worsened, more and more papers were founded, and their sales increased rapidly. They continued to increase after the war as Americans debated how to interpret the Constitution, how to respond to the War of 1812, and how far westward their Manifest Destiny destined them to go. By 1857, with James Buchanan in the White House not making very much news, there were 104 regularly published papers in New York City alone. Never before had the numbers been so high, and they would remain that high, and in some cases climb even higher, at the beginning of the next decade.

The same was true in other cities, as the selling of papers became the most familiar of urban scenes. A poorly clad boy would stand on a street corner, screaming out the headlines. Customers would surround him, closing in, nudging their way. Each would hand over a penny or two—the boy would hope for, and usually receive, an extra penny or more for his labors—then take his paper and hurry home or to the streetcar stop or to a stool in his favorite watering hole, where he would slake both thirst and curiosity at the same time. Americans were knowledgeable people, eager and energetic.

As the Buchanan presidency gave way to that of Abraham Lincoln, Americans were frightened. The former might not have been doing much as chief executive, but he should have been, as the country around him was starting to break apart. Several states had seceded from the Union and more were threatening to do so; and when on April 12, 1861, Confederate troops fired on the U.S. military fortress at Fort Sumter, South Carolina, the break was official. The United States was no longer united; the Civil War, brother against brother, American against American, had finally begun. It was for this reason, more than any other, that so many people were now reading so many papers.

At times the papers reported that the North seemed to be winning, at times the South. Among the latter was the spring of 1864, when the Union army suffered that most embarrassing of fates for a military force—running out of men. Most of them had enlisted for three years, and now that their terms were up, their enthusiasm for a second term was down, if not virtually nonexistent.

They were tired of the danger and the filth, the loneliness and brutal sameness of the days, the diseases that struck them down even more often than bullets. Was freedom for Negroes really worth such travail for the white man? Was combat among kinfolk really the way to bind a nation together? Even if the answers were yes, wasn't it somebody else's turn to pick up the weapons and suffer the madness?

Congress tried to encourage reenlistment. It offered bonuses and extra furlough time. It appealed to the men's patriotism and sense of duty. In a few cases local courts even threatened individuals with jail sentences or fines if they laid down their arms, even though they had no legal authority to do so.

Eventually, most of the soldiers were persuaded, deciding on another three years. After all, the war would be raging around them anyhow; why not try to shape its outcome? But a significant minority, perhaps as many as a hundred thousand, refused further service, and the Union could not survive a loss of manpower that great. President Lincoln met with members of his cabinet to decide what to do. Enticement hadn't worked; the threat of punishment had proven equally ineffective—a draft seemed the only choice. None of Lincoln's men was enthusiastic about the idea, but none could think of a better one.

Lincoln mulled it over in that way of his—a faraway look in his eyes but his mind clearly focused, refusing to be rushed. Then, reluctantly, he made his decision: a draft it would be, and the number of call-ups he and his advisers settled on was three hundred thousand. They braced themselves for a public outcry.

It never came. At least not the kind they were expecting. A different kind of outcry, however, even more tumultuous, erupted in its place. Before Lincoln could announce his plans, a proclamation falsely attributed to the president for a draft of four hundred thousand men was published simultaneously by the *New York World* and the *Journal of Commerce*. Lincoln could not believe it.

How did such information find its way to the printing presses? How did journalists know that he was even considering a draft, much less that he had decided on one? Surely none of the men with whom he had conferred would have talked to a newspaperman. Why was the number of conscriptees in the papers so much higher than the actual total? Why had the story been delivered to newsrooms by messenger all over New York City at two in the morning, a time when the papers' top editors, men who might have checked with the White House before deciding to publish, were home in bed, as was the president and other government officials who would have denied the report? And, even so, why did only two newspapers in New York run the story?

One of the results of the news—the desired result, as it turned out—was chaos in the financial community, to whom a draft of 400,000 men could mean only one thing: an acceleration of the war. There would be more death, more destruction, and with it would come more economic uncertainty. Investors reacted in all manner of ways, some of them buying stocks because the prices had dropped, more of them selling to cut their losses; there was "a flurry of speculation on Wall Street."

There was also a flurry of confusion. Some of the buyers sold their stocks the next day; some of the sellers bought again just as quickly. Those who held on to their investments did so, for the most part, out of bewilderment, not confidence.

To the surprise of no one who understood the workings of financial markets, gold proved to be the most stable of currencies in this most unstable of times. In fact, only a few days after the two newspaper stories, its price rose ten percent. And that, as Lincoln would soon learn, was precisely the point. Francis A. Mallison, a reporter for the *Brooklyn Daily Eagle*, and Joseph Howard, the paper's editor, were responsible for the phony proclamation, and produced it without the faintest knowledge that the president had actually decided on a draft, albeit of fewer men, himself.

It was Mallison who wrote the document, doing his best to emulate the stateliness of Lincoln's prose, although falling far short. And it was Howard who arranged for the document to be published under bold headlines in the *World* and the *Journal of Commerce*, whose editors were friends of his. Why did Mallison and Howard make up the news? Why did Howard's associates at the other two papers agree to print it? Because in the angst of others they saw profit for themselves.

In the days before the article appeared, Mallison, Howard, and their cohorts bought all the gold they could get their hands on. They purchased from every source known to them, legitimate and otherwise, emptying their own bank accounts and borrowing from family and friends. Some of them pilfered money from the reserves of their employers to make their transactions. As a result, they became rich overnight—or, if already rich, even richer. It was one of the first cases of insider trading in a country becoming ever more abusive in its capitalistic practices, and ever more brazen in the foolishness of the abusers.

The scam was quickly discovered—then as now, insider training is easily detected from the outside. And once the Lincoln administration learned of the lie and its purpose, it reacted as if the *World* and *Journal of Commerce* were detachments of Confederate troops. Union soldiers "[took] possession by military force" of the offices of the two papers and arrested practically everyone who worked for them in responsible positions. Then, discovering the leadership roles of Howard and Mallison in the scheme, they shut down the *Brooklyn Daily Eagle* and promptly sent the two men to jail, where they spent the remarkably short period of two days. It was long enough, however, to tarnish their reputations permanently.

A few days afterward, Lincoln announced the draft, and the correct number of men it would affect. He did so in tones that Americans found reassuring, telling them that he was simply replacing soldiers previously in uniform, not adding to the total of fighting men and escalating the war. The president also said he did not believe the fighting would last much longer, meaning that the newly drafted would not, like their predecessors, have to serve for three years. In fact, they would not serve even one.

It was not the first time Lincoln had been ill-served by the press, nor would it be the last. Shortly before the Civil War began, the

Raleigh Standard of North Carolina wrote, "We will never permit Mr. Lincoln or his party to touch the institution of domestic Slavery." From the *Vicksburg Whig* of Mississippi: "We do not mean to rebel against the Government because an obnoxious man has been made President." The *Baltimore Republican* referred to "the Despotism of Lincoln and Co." And in Virginia the *Richmond Whig* called the president "Lincoln the beast" and "the Illinois ape." In fact, so brutally did so many papers treat Lincoln, most of them southern, that his secretary of war, Edwin M. Stanton, issued a veiled threat to their continuing operation:

> Newspapers are valuable organs of public intelligence and instruction, and every proper facility will be afforded to all loyal persons to procure, on equal terms, information of such public facts as may be properly made known in time of rebellion. But no matter how useful or powerful, the press may be, like everything else, it is subordinate to the national safety. The fate of an army or the destiny of a nation may be imperiled by a spy in the garb of a newspaper agent.

Of course, nothing of the kind was happening. No Confederate spies were dolling themselves up as Union journalists to pry secrets from the enemy. The president was simply being insulted, in the coarsest of terms, and was getting tired of it—not just for personal reasons, but because he feared that the accumulated weight of the slurs was undermining the authority of his office. Eventually, with Stanton's aid, Lincoln would take action. His administration put a number of newspapers out of business, at least temporarily, and saw to it that their publishers were arrested and jailed. Some historians believe Lincoln rivaled, perhaps even surpassed, the assault on the press conducted at the end of the eighteenth century, when President John Adams wielded the Sedition Act against printers who criticized his administration. Yet Adams was permanently scarred by his actions. Lincoln was not. Historians seem to have sympathized more with the latter than the former for the kinds of abuse directed at him and the crises with which he had to deal.

*   *   *

The recurring strategy of the opposition press was to denigrate Lincoln's substance by mocking his style, a practice going back to his years in the House of Representatives. They criticized his backwoods manners and ridiculed his appearance, everything from his Ichabod Crane–like body to his hollow cheeks to his ill-cut attire. How could a man who did not even fit into his clothes possibly fit into the highest office in the land? How could a man so tall and gangly and in the eyes of many even ugly command the respect of those he purported to lead? How could a man so melancholy by nature possibly give hope to those who heard him speak or read his words in print?

Yet Lincoln often gave hope to his listeners. Once, while campaigning for president against Senator Stephen A. Douglas, Lincoln gave even more hope than usual. In fact, he excited the crowd so much with his sentiments and eloquence of expression that his supporters, giddy with enthusiasm, rushed the podium at the end of his remarks and carried him off in triumph. It was the kind of behavior that a baseball team shows today when it boosts to its shoulders the player responsible for the hit that wins a championship.

The anti-Lincoln papers, though, some of which did not even send a reporter to cover the address, saw it differently. They wrote that Lincoln, so unimposing a physical presence that it was difficult for him to stand at times, had become so weak from the strains of his pompous speechifying that his aides had to rush up and catch him before he collapsed. Then they lifted him from the podium in a supine position and passed him over their heads, one shuttling him back to the other like a railroad tie being sent down the line. Only in this way, went the anti-Lincoln version, could the feeble candidate be removed from the stage and taken to his carriage.

Most appalling were the newspaper stories that reported Lincoln's assassination in 1865. "God Almighty ordered this event," declared the *Dallas Herald*. "Abe has gone to answer before the bar of God for the innocent blood which he has permitted to be shed," said the *Chattanooga Daily Rebel*. And then there were the papers, although few of them, that said nothing at all, treating the deed of John Wilkes Booth as if it had never happened, simply announcing that Vice President Andrew Johnson had assumed Lincoln's duties and would surely carry them out more capably than his predecessor had. It had long been the policy of some journals never to mention Lincoln's name.

It is important to note, though, that not all Southern papers reacted like this. The *Little Rock Unconditional Union*, its title giving its position away, wrote upon the president's death that the "Rebels have slain the best friend they had in the *Republic*." And the *Daily Times* of Leavenworth, Kansas, in describing the town's being decorated with flags draped in black, said, "There was not the outward excitement that characterizes a victory or a reverse; but deep sorrow was depicted on every countenance. A feeling of despair pervaded many hearts."

Still, the Union's sorrow was a celebration for all too many citizens of the Confederacy, and the most ruthless source of high spirits anywhere was the newspaper.

It was about this time that Union general Joseph "Fightin' Joe" Hooker, the grandson of a captain in the Revolutionary War, demanded a crackdown on journalists. The stories about Lincoln troubled him greatly, and they were not the only examples of cruelty and duplicity during the war years. In 1861, a reporter for the *New York Herald*, "the biggest and most powerful newspaper in America," was sent to cover the battle of Bull Run. The paper's account stated that as Union soldiers were dropping their weapons and holding up their hands, Confederate troops ignored the signs of surrender and bayoneted them to death. Like Sam Adams's story about innocents being bayoneted by the British in the previous century, this one was also a complete fabrication.

But the *Herald*'s story went on. It also stated that one Confederate soldier chopped off the head of a foe and began tossing it around with his fellow Southerners as if it were a football. According to historian Thomas Fleming, this did not happen either.

In the Civil War, and in fact going all the way back to early colonial times, decades before the Revolutionary War, newspaper articles had been published anonymously or under a pseudonym. Sam Adams, for instance, was an American and a Son of Liberty; Candidus and Determinatus; Vindex the Avenger and Populus; Principiis Obsta, which means "principal obstacle"; and Decant Arma Togae, a reference to weapons being visible beneath one's apparel—to mention but a few.

From now on, Hooker demanded, those who wrote for the papers were to attach their names to their work. If they did not, they were subject to arrest and loss of employment. It was not that Hooker wanted reporters to be famous. Rather, he wanted them to be accountable. The next time some son of a bitch with ink stains on his fingers and the ruthlessness of Beelzebub in his heart libeled a man of courage and decency, especially on the occasion of his murder, Hooker wanted to know whose wrists to slap the handcuffs on.

But there was nothing official about Hooker's edict, and newspapers were slow to respond to it. Since Hooker was a Union officer, the Union papers were more likely to accede to his wishes than those of the Confederacy. A few seem to have done so promptly, a few more within a matter of months.

Once the practice of granting bylines began, however, there was no stopping it. By the time another half century had passed, some papers allowed reporters to sign their names to virtually anything they wrote. Other papers published bylines only for stories they deemed of particular importance. Still others did the opposite, withholding bylines on the most important stories, wanting to imply that those pieces represented the voice of the entire publication, not a single individual who happened to work for it. Perhaps most common was the use of the byline as a carrot on a stick; once a reporter achieved a certain degree of status at his paper, he was rewarded with his name at the top of the article.

In this way, both the scribes and those who mistrusted them got what they wanted. The scribes got the journalistic equivalent of their name in lights, while government and military officials knew whom to blame, and in some cases whom to seek revenge upon, for stories they believed were contrary to the national—or their own—interests.

6

The Boss

ON WILLIAM MARCY TWEED, "WHO LOOKED LIKE SOMETHING God had hacked out with a dull axe," the cuffs would have been a perfect fit—although not for the reasons Joseph Hooker advocated. In fact, Tweed probably did wear a set of handcuffs a time or two in his life as he was taken off to jail on this charge or that. To look at him, though, was to wonder whether there was a cell anywhere in New York that could contain him.

"A craggy hulk of a man," writes biographer Alexander B. Callow Jr., "he was nearly six feet tall and weighed almost three hundred pounds. Everything about him was big; fists, shoulders, head (which sprouted receding reddish-brown hair, like weeds growing from a rock, carved into a mustache and closely cropped whiskers); eyes, blue and friendly; the diamond, which 'glittered like a planet on his shirt front.'"

Between 1852 and 1867, Tweed, a Democrat, was elected to the United States House of Representatives, the New York State Senate, and the New York City Board of Advisers. He was also appointed the city's commissioner of public works, all of which meant that he was uniquely qualified to hold that most uniquely American position: big-city political boss. He was, in fact, commonly known as Boss Tweed, and many of the people who dealt with him thought it was his given first name, so perfectly did it suit his station in life. Tweed may have been the most powerful such creature in any city in the United States in the nineteenth century, and his power came not from the ballot box but from the contacts he had made in politics, favors he had done for elected officials, which translated into favors now owed. He was Cardinal Richelieu without a Louis XIII looking over his shoulder.

Tweed kept regular office hours, although not every day and not all day long—long enough, though, for a parade of supplicants to file by his desk almost without end, hands folded in front of them, heads bowed. They pleaded for jobs on the city payroll, help with medical expenses, a better apartment to live in, or a good word to immigration officials so that a relative from abroad could stay in the United States a few extra weeks or months and maybe one day become a citizen.

The Boss usually granted their wishes. All they had to do in return was hand over some cash if they could spare it, or provide some special service for the Boss depending on their vocational skills—and, oh yes, vote for whomever he told them to. They were always happy to comply.

Tweed's other duties included managing most of the city services and deciding how much they would cost, and bribing policeman so they wouldn't look into those costs. Sometimes, you see, they were a bit high. For instance, when a county courthouse was constructed behind City Hall, it was Tweed who purchased many of the items needed for the interior of the building: "The cuspidors . . . were priced at $190 apiece. Thermometers totaled $7,500. There were $404,347 worth of safes. Brooms and other 'articles,' as they were categorized, cost $41,190. A rug expert estimated that for the amount spent on carpeting the county courthouse, all 8.25 acres of City Hall Park could have been covered three times over." The difference between the normal prices of these goods and the amount that appeared on invoices went directly into the Boss's pockets.

Another of Tweed's cons involved the assistance of city officials. According to historian Oliver E. Allen, "A fictitious resolution would be introduced [before New York's Board of Aldermen] threatening some merchant or trade, whereupon the alderman would go to the aggrieved party, commiserate with him, and say, 'Give me $250 and I'll make sure it's killed in committee.' The merchant would pay, never dreaming he'd been had." The alderman was happy to hand over a percentage of the take to the Boss.

And, of course, there was the usual graft involved in the awarding of all city contracts. The winning bidder for a franchise to build a new streetcar line on the east side of Manhattan had to pay $18,000 to Tweed and various city officials for their compliance, without which the contract would have gone elsewhere.

The Boss and his henchmen, known as the Tweed Ring, were in a sense the forerunners of the Mafia, except more civic-minded and less violent. As such, they were a perfect target for newsmen. For the most part, though, the press ignored them—or praised them, whatever Tweed desired. In most cases, it was the former. He simply did not want attention to be called to him, especially for his various methods of operation, few of which could have withstood journalistic—or legal—scrutiny. But since most reporters who covered the workings of city government at the time were on Tweed's payroll, he had nothing to worry about.

It was common for the Boss to invite reporters to lavish banquets and give them presents of liquor, champagne, and fine cigars. Many of the reporters at the banquets did not recognize many of the others. "I never saw so many people claiming to represent the newspaper profession," one of them wrote in his column.

At Christmas, the Boss would give legitimate members of the press gifts of as much as two hundred dollars. At other times of the year, the amounts could get much higher, as the Tweed Ring also subsidized reporters on nearly all the city papers with fees of $2000 to $2500 to exercise the proper discretion when it came to writing about politics. There was the reward of patronage for the especially deserving: Stephen Hayes, on the *Herald* staff during the high days of the Ring, was rewarded with a sinecure in the Marine Court ($2500 a year) and Michael Kelly, also of the *Herald*, received positions in both the Fire Department and the Department of Public Works. Moreover, reporters from various newspapers of the country, from a Cleveland newspaper to the *Mobile* [Alabama] *Register*, were hired to write favorable notices of the Democratic administration in New York. And if a firm went too far and tried to print a pamphlet exposing the Ring, it might find its offices broken into by the Ring's men and the type altered to present a glowing account of the Ring's activities—as did the printing company of Stone, Jordan and Thomson.

Adding to the unwillingness of reporters to find wrongdoing in the workings of municipal government was the fact that New Yorkers were living in relatively prosperous times, many able to afford dinner at a fancy restaurant, a night at the theater, tickets to concerts and the occasional sporting event—and the Tweed Ring had a lot to do with it. The Boss padded the city payroll with lackeys and paid them well. He saw that some of his ill-gotten gains were dispersed to local businessmen, a purchase of loyalty rather than goods. In addition, Tweed devised a new and more democratic charter for the city, although he ignored its provisions when he found them personally bothersome; brought to a close the long-delayed construction of Central Park for New Yorkers to enjoy in all manner of ways; and even worked to make the city's water supply cleaner and healthier. It was hardly the right time for the press to dig into the Ring's more corrupt practices and demand that something be done about them.

In fact, only two publications of note in the city opposed the Tweed Ring. One of them was the *New York Times*, which ran a series of anti-Tweed editorials without really having any evidence, or public groundswell, to support its charges. George Jones, one of the founders of the *Times*, paid dearly for his editorials, finding himself ostracized for his campaign against the Boss. According to Tweed biographer Kenneth D. Ackerman, Jones "could barely leave his home on West Thirty-Seventh Street these days without getting cross looks and cold shoulders—from his club friends at the Union League, his fellow newsmen on Park Row, or city workers he passed on Broadway or Chambers Street. Even his own *New York Times* staff, the clerks, writers, and typesetters, seemed to doubt him." Jones was no longer invited to the annual New Year's reception at the mayor's manse. "Is it a hopeless fight?" the *Times* asked in an editorial shortly after one of the receptions in 1871. "Even those who are anxious to see us continue the struggle profess to be in very low spirits concerning the probable results."

The other anti-Tweed publication was *Harper's Weekly*, which employed the brilliant editorial cartoonist Thomas Nast. Nast's drawings, it has been said, showed their subject to be "a gross, half-comic character done in quick sure black line, a figure of corruption incarnate, leering, lecherous, Falstaff with a stickpin." Tweed hated the cartoons. He knew their impact. As he explained one day to a friend who was making light of the cartoons, "I don't care a straw for your newspaper articles, my constituents don't know how to read, but they can't help seeing them damned pictures."

Eventually, though, it was not the pictures that brought the Tweed Ring to justice; it was a variety of factors, perhaps most important the inevitability of economic cycles. When, for a number of reasons, the good times began to fade away in New York, so did tolerance for the underhanded methods of the man who ruled the city. The press turned on Tweed because he could no longer afford such generous stipends for their obedience, and the public turned on him because he could no longer afford his previous levels of civic largesse. He was finally arrested and charged with trying to maintain his high-rolling lifestyle by stealing hundreds of thousands of dollars from taxpayers and the Democratic Party tills. Sentenced to two separate jail terms, he was released from the first one after serving but a single year of a mandated fifteen.

After a brief hiatus, he was incarcerated for his second term, but he escaped and fled to Cuba, then to Spain, where he was captured by Spanish authorities, who recognized him from one of the Nast cartoons. They handed him over to the Americans, and Tweed was returned to confinement in New York in 1876. It did not agree with him. He began coughing, struggling for breath, losing weight. He would never be a free man again, much less a powerful one. Two years later he died behind bars, the largest man of his time in more ways than one.

It is remarkable that bribery has played so small a role in the history of journalism. One would think that more people profiting by nefarious activities would, as Boss Tweed did, offer money to reporters to keep quiet about them; one would think that more reporters would be receptive to the increased compensation. One would also think that members of the press who were themselves on the nefarious side would seek a quid pro quo to tailor their stories for the benefit of those who could pay. And it did happen from time to time, as the next chapter will reveal.

But there are no other tales of bribery in American journalism on the scale of the Tweed Ring. The closest came early in the twentieth century when a fellow named William d'Alton Mann began publishing *Town Topics: The Journal of Society*. Among Mann's scurrilous practices was to pay butlers, maids, and other members of the staffs of New York's social elite for gossip about the sexual and financial peccadilloes of their employers, as well as their ostentatious displays of wealth before people too poor to afford an issue of *Town Topics*. The elite's horror was Mann's delight.

But an even more profitable venture, Mann decided, would be to gather the information and *not* print it. "If a story was particularly damaging," writes Greg King in *A Season of Splendor*, "[Mann] would have it typeset and print up a copy—which in fact he never intended to publish, then discreetly let the person known he was set to print damning information and wanted them to read it first and correct any errors."

It was, of course, an invitation to bribery, almost always accepted. Once Mann's victims had collected themselves, and then gone out and collected little portions of their fortunes, they would pay a call on him in his offices later in the day. Invariably, we are told, "a check changed hands, marked down as a loan or stock purchase or perhaps an advertising contract, the offending item was removed from next week's edition, and the visitors retired, sighing the long sigh of the reprieved."

Mann was not candid about his methods but was perfectly open about his goals. "My ambition," he once said, "is to reform the Four Hundred [the most elite of New York's social elite] by making them too deeply disgusted with themselves to continue their silly, empty way of life. I am also teaching the great American public not to pay attention to these silly fools." He was publishing *Town Topics*, he said, "for the sake of the country."

Mann failed in his quest. Americans not only continued to pay attention to silly fools, but at present pay attention to even sillier ones. He had, however, a wonderful if thoroughly unscrupulous time trying.

The last we hear of bribery to any significant extent is in the 1960s, when it was common practice for boxing promoters to offer hookers to the journalists assigned to bouts. The sexually sated journalists responded, for the most part, by ignoring the seamier side of the sport, treating an obviously fixed fight as if it were the real thing, an obviously decayed sport as if it were cricket before the queen and her court. Columnists got the girls for free, reporters at a discount. Copy boys, one assumes, had to pay full price.

But we are getting ahead of our story.

7

The Epoch of the Hoax

SAMUEL LANGHORNE CLEMENS DID NOT CHANGE THE NAME HE affixed to his newspaper articles, and to the rest of his life, to Mark Twain because of General Joseph "Fightin' Joe" Hooker. No one really knows why he did it. But in creating a new identity for himself, Twain was in a sense formalizing a lie, and would eventually be one of the great American advocates of deception, producing it for newspapers long before he turned out his wondrously inventive fiction in books.

But there was a kind of deception Twain did not advocate. It was the kind perpetrated by governments, such as the government of the United States in carrying out what he thought to be the heartless dictates of Manifest Destiny, adding territory to the country regardless of the wishes of the people who lived in that territory. Nor did he care for the deception of the Confederate government in trying to defend the indefensible institution of slavery. He was troubled by the deception of dictatorships overseas and unfeeling corporate interests at home. "When whole races and peoples conspire to propagate mute lies in the interest of tyrannies and shams," he said late in his life, "why should we care anything about the trifling lies told by individuals? Why should we try to make it appear that abstention from lying is a virtue? . . . Why should we without shame help the nation lie, and then be ashamed to do a little lying on our own account? Why shouldn't we be honest and honourable, and lie every time we get a chance?" The questions undoubtedly represent some of Twain's most deeply held feelings. They also provide the footholds for a lifetime of falsehoods.

Twain claimed that he could not recall his first lie; he had been too young at the time. His second lie, however, he remembered "very well. I was nine days old at the time, and had noticed that if a pin was sticking in me and I advertised it in the usual fashion, I was lovingly petted and coddled and pitied in a most agreeable way and got a ration between meals besides." He continued, harkening back to his ninth day: "It was human nature to want to get these riches, and I fell. I lied about the pin—advertising one when there wasn't any." And he went on lying—one supposes he is telling the truth here—about one thing or another all the way through childhood.

But he didn't stop there. He was still lying in his early days as a reporter for the *Virginia City Territorial Enterprise* in Nevada, where his first duty was to report on local news, the kind of local news that doesn't even interest people in the locality: comings, goings, shipments of new merchandise arriving in stores, engagements, weddings, births that people already know about, deaths they have already mourned.

Twain grew bored quickly. Not yet mature enough to write about Tom Sawyer and Huck Finn, he decided instead to give free reign to his immaturity. In October 1862, less than thirty years old and still known as Sam Clemens, mustachioed and with bushy hair, although not yet white, his eyes sometimes twinkling, sometimes narrowed in something close to malice, he wrote a story for the *Territorial Enterprise* about the discovery of a "Petrified Man":

> Every limb and feature of the stony mummy was perfect, not even excepting the left leg, which had evidently been a wooden one during the lifetime of the owner—which lifetime, by the way, came to a close about a century ago, in the opinion of a savan [*sic*] who has examined the defunct. The body was in a sitting position . . . ; the attitude was pensive, the right thumb resting against the side of the nose; the left thumb partially supported the chin, the forefinger pressing the inner corner of the left eye and drawing it partly open.

Clemens went on to say that this "strange freak of nature created a sensation in the vicinity," and several people volunteered to remove him and bury him. A Judge Sowell, however, refused to allow the bones to be taken away, fearing that to disturb them would be to damage them. "The opinion expressed by his Honor . . . was eminently just and proper," Clemens stated. "Everybody goes to see the stone man, as many as three hundred having visited the hardened creature during the past five or six weeks."

To Twain biographer Justin Kaplan, the tone was obviously that of a hoax, the excess of detail giving away the ruse. Historian Peter Charles Hoffer has written that "for a lie to work—for it to fool us—it must wear the mask of truth." In this case, Kaplan believed, it did.

Most people who read the article, however, thought just the opposite, finding that the detail provided the ring of authenticity. Nobody could make up the right thumb against the side of the nose. Nobody could make up the left thumb supporting the chin. The story was reprinted by other papers in Nevada, as well as some in California, and people wrote to the *Territorial Enterprise* demanding to know the exact location of the petrified man so they could pay a visit. How long would it take to get there? Did one have to pay a fee to see him?

The responses forced Clemens to explain that he had only been kidding, and the nature of the piece was such that most readers enjoyed it once they knew it had been meant for their entertainment, not their enlightenment. But there is an important distinction here; Clemens was explaining, not apologizing. More than likely he was bemused by the readers who were foolish enough to believe so exaggerated and unlikely an account.

This was, after all, the Old West. Tall tales, both written and spoken, were one of the primary forms of amusement: one fellow telling another that he knew of a man who could put a chokehold on two bears at the same time and when he was done with them they would scamper back into the woods whimpering; the listener responding that he knew of a man who could whip a whole regiment of soldiers single-handed, without even using a weapon. And then the first storyteller seeing the second one and raising him, exaggeration topping exaggeration until the pot was so full of blarney it could hold no more. Sometimes listeners copied down the tall tales for later retelling. Sometimes they just made a point of remembering. And so the stories spread and lived on, and Clemens must have hoped the same would happen to the petrified man, which had already been committed to the relatively long life of print.

Further evidence of Clemens's lack of contrition is that he wrote another fake story for the *Territorial Enterprise* six months later, this one about "five Indians [being] smothered to death in a tunnel back of Gold Hill." And then, six months after that, yet another hoax, this one causing much more of an uproar than either of its predecessors.

The mining business was the most important industry in the West in those days. It was what drew the majority of settlers to that part of the country, as well as most of the businesses, which were set up to provide the miners with goods and services. The boom had started in earnest with the California gold rush of 1849, which itself proved to be the source of a number of hoaxes. "The whole country," read one of the first reports, in a newspaper called the *Alta California*, "from San Francisco to Los Angeles, and from the seashore to the base of the Sierra Nevada, resounds to the sordid cry of *gold! Gold!! GOLD!!!*" The paper went on to lament that "the field is left half planted, the home half built, and everything neglected but the manufacture of shovels and pickaxes." It was, to say the least, a false lamentation. The last paragraph in the *Alta California*'s story notified its readers that it was going out of business for a while. Its entire staff was heading for the mines.

That particular article was not a hoax. But so many people gave up their previous lives to search for precious ore that after a few years there wasn't nearly enough gold left to make the trip west worthwhile for them. Yet in the East, papers continued to publish accounts of riches in the mines. And sometimes the papers reported that it wasn't even necessary to dig them out; you could just pick up pieces of gold from the ground or pluck them out of a stream.

In many cases, the papers knew nothing whatsoever about conditions in the so-called gold country. The stories they printed did not come from correspondents in gold country but from swindlers in cities like New York and Boston, who paid the papers to have their stories run—more bribery. The con men wanted to encourage a continued migration toward the Pacific so they could sell the gold-seekers transportation, lodging, supplies, and perhaps even land on which, the swindlers assured their marks, there was gold galore, just waiting to be removed and toted off to the assayer's office. The newspapers, well compensated for their lack of integrity, collaborated in the fraud without reservation. What they did not do was publish stories about the families without number who had headed to California, lost their nest eggs within a few weeks, and were now begging either for a job or a means to return to the homes from which they had departed so recently and hopefully.

In one type of scam, speculators would buy a worthless mine and "salt" it, in other words, scatter gold dust on the floor and walls, in the hope of attracting investors who believed there was more wealth to be found once they started hacking away with picks. In other cases, speculators, through means too complicated to explain here, would appeal to their potential clients by creating false dividends to make the mines seem more profitable than they really were.

The speculators were Clemens's target—although not, it seems, clearly so—in one of the first and vilest pieces he wrote under his new name, "A Bloody Massacre Near Carson":

> It seems that during the past six months a man named P. Hopkins, Philip Hopkins, has been residing with his family in the old log house at the edge of the great pine forest which lies between Empire City and Dutch Nick's. The family consisted of nine children—five girls and four boys. . . . About ten o'clock on Monday evening Hopkins dashed into Carson on horseback, with his throat cut from ear to ear, and bearing in his hand a reeking scalp from which the warm, smoking blood was still dripping, and fell in a dying condition in front of the Magnolia saloon. Hopkins expired in the course of five minutes, without speaking. The long red hair of the scalp he bore marked it as that of Mrs. Hopkins. A number of citizens, headed by Sheriff Gasherie, mounted at once and rode to the Hopkins house.

There, Twain says, they found Mrs. Hopkins's scalpless corpse, with "her right hand almost severed from her wrist." Six of the children were discovered in a bedroom. "Their brains had evidently been dashed out with a club."

Particularly important to the story, though not nearly as riveting as the preceding, was Twain's description of Hopkins's employment before he committed his dastardly crime: "He had been a heavy owner in the best mines of Virginia [Nevada] and Gold Hill, but when the San Francisco papers exposed the game of cooking dividends in order to bolster up our stocks he grew afraid and sold out, and invested an immense amount in the Spring Valley Water Company of San Francisco."

Soon, however, the dividends were cooked on his new property as well, the water drying up and the investment worth nothing. "It is presumed," Twain says, "that this misfortune drove him mad and resulted in his killing himself and the greater portion of his family."

None of it ever happened—not the scalping, not the throat cutting, not the dividend cooking. Not in this particular case. It was simply Twain's way of calling attention to the practices of real-life crooks like the imaginary Philip Hopkins. Once again, he admitted the truth promptly. This time, though, at least at first, it did little good, as "a storm of denunciation raged about him, from editors and readers who had been taken in by the hoax. Rival newspapers denounced that fountain of lies the *Enterprise* and that lunatic Mark Twain." Friends told him he had gone too far; even strangers approached him on the street and asked him how he could make up a tale so grisly in its details. Why not simply describe the practices of real-life speculators? Why cut Hopkins's throat? Twain's bosses thought about firing him; he thought they had a point and considered resigning.

But the storm died down almost as quickly as it had arisen. After all, Ben Franklin and several others over the years had published hoaxes in newspapers for the purpose of giving their opinions on important issues, and Twain believed that the plague of speculation in gold mines was precisely that, a disease that ate away at the financial health of decent, hardworking Americans. And, he said, the more dramatically he made the point, the more likely people would be to remember it.

As had been the case previously, Twain was not apologetic. Like a lot of humorists since, he had an edginess to him, a deep-seated pessimism. He did not think much of his fellow human beings on the whole, or most of their institutions. "To find a petrified man," he said several years later, "or break a stranger's leg, or cave an imaginary mine, or discover some dead Indians in a Gold Hill tunnel, or massacre a family at Dutch Nick's, were feats and calamities that we never hesitated about devising when the public needed matters of thrilling interest for breakfast. The seemingly tranquil ENTERPRISE office was a ghastly factory of slaughter, mutilation and general destruction in those days." He was pleased to have had a role in making it so.

A few years later, having moved to New York, Twain turned the office of the *Buffalo Express* into a ghastly place of a different kind. This time it was not a hoax that he perpetrated, but a corrupt and complete dismissal of the truth. And he did it not to make a point for society's benefit, but to try to solidify his personal gain.

It all had to do with the price of coal, which was so high around Buffalo at the time that consumers formed a citizens' cooperative to try to fight the coal companies. It was the companies, not the marketplace, that had set the prices, having formed a cartel whose sole purpose was to squeeze every last penny of profit out of people in desperate need of their product. Today, such actions would be illegal. In fact, once Theodore Roosevelt got to the White House they would be illegal through most of the twentieth century. But this was the nineteenth, and capitalism was all too often unbridled.

For some time, the position of the *Buffalo Express* was, as it should have been, in favor of the citizens' cooperative. Twain's position was the same; he had in earlier days blasted monopolistic practices in private industry, and this was monopoly at its most corrupt. But after a while, he received a promotion and became the editor of the paper's editorial page—and all of a sudden, with no explanation to anyone, he took the opposite view. In that moment, the man of the people became the man of the cartel. Those who knew him and knew what he had long stood for, including his superiors at the *Express*, were aghast.

Jervis Langdon was one of Buffalo's richest citizens. Among his many sources of income was a coal company that he had purchased well after having amassed a fortune in lumber. Langdon has been described as a "stout, good-looking man of medium height

[who] carried his achievements lightly. Unlike his daughter, he had a sense of humor. As a host, he was generous and hospitable." As a coal baron, however, he was as grasping and uncaring as the rest of them. Pay up or freeze was his motto—if never overtly stated. For Twain to take his side was, on the surface of it, unthinkable, a form of mental illness.

Yet one day in 1870 Twain published and prominently displayed a letter from John Slee, Langdon's sales manager, placing it next to an editorial Twain had lifted from the *New York Evening Post*. Both pieces defended the cartel. They insisted that it was not, as charged, manipulating prices; the high price of coal was the result of "unreasonable demands" by consumers. It was also the result of a miners' strike some months earlier, which had adversely affected production and forced the companies to raise their rates.

Langdon, who because of his prominence had become the face of the opposition, was mentioned several times by both articles and vigorously exonerated. "Although he is wealthy and a member of a corporation," Twain wrote in the *Buffalo Express*, "he has a soul of his *own* and his liberality is not confined to the city in which he resides." It is true that during this period Langdon donated fifty tons of coal to the Buffalo General Hospital, but that is the only example of a soul of his own that he demonstrated during the entire strike.

The two articles provided a comprehensive, if totally unconvincing, defense of the cartel. What they did not do, however, what the *Express* never did—not until the day after the nuptials, that is—was mention the marriage plans of Olivia Langdon, Jervis's daughter, the one with no sense of humor. As it happened, she was engaged to one of the town's leading journalists, the editorial page editor of the *Buffalo Express*, Mark Twain, he of the most prominent sense of humor, who was afraid that to take issue with his future father-in-law would cost him his bride. And so to all being fair in love and war, he added for his own selfish interests, and the gross disservice of his readers, all being fair in journalism as well. This was not a humorist with the cheery nature of his successor, Will Rogers.

Twain might have been the leading practitioner of the hoax in nineteenth-century newspapers, but he was not responsible for the grandest of them, the one that foreshadowed the more extreme hoaxes of the future, the stories that would captivate millions of grocery shoppers midway through the twentieth century, in supermarket tabloids. That distinction goes to the *New York Sun*, which, in 1835, the year Twain was born, presented one of several whoppers it would print over the period of the next few years. What it published, in fact, was an epic: a six-part series on the discovery of men, or some kind of similar creatures, on the moon. The series claimed that a new telescope, the most powerful ever invented, had recently been erected in Africa at the Cape of Good Hope and had allowed scientists to see living beings that

> averaged four feet in height, were covered, except on the face, with short and glossy and copper-colored hair, and had wings composed of a thin membrane, without hair, lying snugly on their backs, from the top of their shoulders to the calves of their legs. The face, which was of a yellowish flesh color, was of a slight improvement upon that of the large orang outang, being more open and intelligent in its expression, and having a much greater expansion of forehead.

The series also reported that of conventional animal life there was only one example on the moon, "an elegant striped quadruped about three feet high, like a miniature zebra."

Those who wanted to believe the series were free to do so, and they reacted with awe. Those who did not believe it derived their own enjoyment from the articles, laughing at both their excesses and the gullibility of those who thought they were reading the truth. Edgar Allan Poe, among others, was a fan of such writing in general and the series about the moon in particular. "From the epoch of the hoax," he wrote, "the *Sun* shone with unmitigated splendor."

Almost a decade later, Poe, now a newspaper reporter himself, wrote about some men who crossed the Atlantic in a balloon in just three days. It was "ASTOUNDING NEWS," declared the *New York Sun*'s headline, and Poe picked it up from there:

> The great problem is at length solved. The air, as well as the earth and the ocean, has been subdued by Science, and will become a common and convenient highway for mankind. *The Atlantic has actually been crossed in a Balloon*; and this too without difficulty— without any great apparent danger—with thorough control of the machine—and in the incredibly brief period of Seventy-five hours from shore to shore!

It was as factual as "The Fall of the House of Usher."

The eastern half of the United States was not terribly civilized when the *New York Sun* was making up the news. The English writer Frances Trollope, mother of the even more distinguished writer Anthony, was visiting America in 1828 and decided to take a steamboat trip in Ohio. She found her seat, made herself comfortable, and then looked down at the carpet. It was covered with the dried spit of tobacco juice. She tried to muffle a shriek and then said, "Let no one who wishes to receive agreeable impressions of American manners, commence their travels in a Mississippi steamboat; for myself it is with all sincerity that I declare, that I would infinitely prefer sharing the apartment of a party of well-conditioned pigs to the being confined in its cabin."

The most famous English writer of the century, Charles Dickens, came to America in the early 1840s. Ironically, he and some friends were riding in a carriage along Broadway in New York City and were astonished to see pigs sharing the street with them, occasionally so many of the animals that the carriage had to stop to allow them to pass.

Like Trollope, Dickens too was appalled by tobacco chewers. They spit indiscriminately, sometimes onto their own shoes, sometimes into their own beards. In rare instances, women would also chew and spit, the muddy brown substance landing on their boots or the hems of their dresses. Neither gender seemed to mind.

The other side of the Mississippi was no more civilized a few decades later when Twain was making up the news. Pigs were not the only animals that roamed and relieved themselves freely in the streets of the West, nor were they the only threat to safe and sanitary living. Lawlessness was rampant, drunkenness even more common, violence a daily occurrence, and salubrious living conditions of interest to virtually no one, especially those men who stumbled out of saloons and urinated and defecated in the streets.

The press could not help but be as untamed as the society on which it reported. There was little respect for niceties, and truth is a nicety. There was little reverence toward institutions, either civil or sacred, and accuracy is a form of reverence. There was little regard for restraint, and a man who is afraid to wiggle a fact or two is not really a man at all. It is also fair to say that newspapers, although not new in America, were new enough so that they had not yet established the tradition of integrity upon which they pride themselves, if often abuse, today.

"Therefore," said Mark Twain, who deserves the final word on this subject, "the wise thing is for us diligently to train ourselves to lie thoughtfully, judiciously . . . to lie firmly, frankly, squarely, with head erect, not haltingly, tortuously, with pusillanimous mien, as being ashamed of our high calling."

There is no reason to think he was kidding.

8

Furnishing a War

WILLIAM RANDOLPH HEARST, PUBLISHER OF THE *New York Journal*, transcended the hoax. While Mark Twain and Edgar Allan Poe and others made *up* events, Hearst actually *made* an event, or at least was one of its principal architects. His building blocks were real people, real countries, real grievances, real armaments, and real battleships.

Hearst did not create the ill will that led to the event, but that he exacerbated it beyond all reason cannot be disputed. Would the event have happened had it not been for Hearst's journalistic ferocity? Almost certainly not in the form that it finally took. And almost certainly not as quickly. He was, thus, in the curious position of reporting the truth about circumstances of his own manufacture, which therefore should have been a lie because they should not have happened in the first place. He was Sam Adams all over again, except with a less relevant cause and, perhaps, if such a thing is possible, even less regard for truth.

Hearst was born into wealth in a relatively poor part of California during the Civil War, much more his mother's son than his father's. When he was four years old, Phoebe Hearst, a former schoolteacher, said proudly of her boy, "He likes his books, you would be astonished to hear him spell and pronounce words of three letters, can count 100, and knows what country, State and City he lives in. Also who discovered America and about the world being round." His father was less impressed and spent far less time with the boy than did his mother.

Hearst was a willful child, with a temper to match his intellectual precociousness. Once, he and a pal skipped dancing school and were discovered by a friend of Phoebe's, who ordered them to go. Hearst refused and stuck out his tongue at her. When the woman scolded him for the gesture, he grabbed a hose lying at his feet and turned it on her, ruining her dress and causing her to run into the house screaming. Sometime later, showing his continued distaste for the dancing lessons upon which Phoebe insisted, he led a group of similarly dissatisfied terpsichoreans to the school and they bombarded it with rocks.

So it was that at a very early age Hearst demonstrated he was no one to trifle with. At a later age, his demonstrations would be all the more vivid, and in one case deadly.

For many years, the United States had hoped to acquire Cuba, if not as a state, at least as a possession. Part of the reason was to add more territory to the country, America manifesting more of its destiny. Another part was that the Spanish ruled Cuba and we were wary of what might turn out to be an enemy presence only ninety miles from our shores. And a third part was that we were unhappy with the way the Spanish were treating the citizens of the tiny island nation, restricting their freedoms and taxing them beyond endurance. Cubans were punished for even the most minor of offenses by their overlords and more severely than common sense could justify. It is believed that some four hundred thousand Cubans were being held in Spanish detention camps in and around Havana at one time and that half of them eventually died in their confinement.

In 1895, conditions grew so bad that Cuban rebels formed an army to try to overthrow the Spanish. They won some battles and took back some land, but they were too few in number to accomplish their goals, being neither strong enough to put down their oppressors nor irresolute enough to give up the struggle. So the fighting went on, as did the Spanish oppression, in a kind of stasis.

In the United States, though, interest in Cuba, already high, was increasing. This was especially true among two newspaper publishers, Hearst and Joseph Pulitzer of the *New York World*. Their concerns were sincere. They worried about the Spanish proximity and genuinely sympathized with the Cuban plight. Nonetheless, they found visions of increased circulation dancing in their heads.

William McKinley, who had become president in 1897, was also wary of the Spaniards. At the urging of several cabinet members, he persuaded them to grant Cuba a limited form of self-rule, hoping it would satisfy the rebels. It did not. In fact, the limited self-rule only encouraged the Cubans to increase the violence and the Spaniards to increase their counterattacks. McKinley now began to worry about the safety of Americans living on the island.

To protect them, he ordered the battleship *Maine*, all 6,682 tons of it, armed with twenty-five guns and four torpedo tubes, to proceed to Havana harbor. It docked on January 25, 1898, under strict orders from the president. The *Maine* was not to open fire, not to instigate or engage in any kind of aggressive action, unless specifically approved by the White House. The warship was simply to act a kind of sentinel: large and dark and foreboding—but for the time being, at least, inactive.

The Cubans were glad to see the ship, knowing American sympathies were with them. The Spanish found the ship's very presence an insult, a deliberate taunt, and the Spanish minister in Washington wrote a letter, which he thought would be private, to a friend in Madrid that was critical of McKinley's decision to employ the *Maine*. Actually, some of the language in the letter was more than critical; it was bellicose.

Unfortunately for both sender and recipient, the letter was stolen and news of its contents eventually reached the press room of the *Journal*. For Hearst, it was like a birthday present. The next day's headline, a detonation of hyperbole probably written by the publisher himself, read:

THE WORST INSULT TO THE UNITED STATES IN ITS HISTORY

and the article beneath it urged war, something that was on Hearst's mind at this point much more than on the president's.

For three weeks, duty aboard the *Maine* was something of a vacation for the 250 or so men stationed there. The fighting on the mainland had decreased; there seemed no immediate danger to Americans; and the sun shone down brightly on calm Caribbean waters day after day. The men kept the ship clean and functional, slept more than usual, and acquired healthy, golden-brown tans. They played cards on deck and looked more longingly than usual at the wrinkled pictures of girls back home that they had brought with them. If only they could leave the ship for a few hours, a few beers, a few of the Cuban women who were probably looking for ways to show their gratitude.

The reporters on the island were idle too, but they didn't want to be. Supposedly, *Journal* correspondent and illustrator Frederic Remington was so bored with the inactivity that he telegraphed Hearst, asking for permission to return to New York. "Everything is quiet," the telegram read. "There is no trouble here. There will be no war. I wish to return." Hearst wired promptly in response: "Please remain. You furnish the pictures and I'll furnish the war."

On February 15, 1898, the sun was a little hazier than on previous days, the temperature perhaps a degree or two lower. There was no sign of military activity ashore, not even any activity that could be called out of the ordinary. Still vacation, still, as Remington had written, "no trouble here." The water remained placid; a few seabirds hovered and flew away. Maybe they sensed something, because a few minutes later the idyll ended for sailors and reporters alike.

Late in the morning, the USS *Maine* exploded. Everyone on board was killed. The cause of the explosion was not known at the time and is not certain to this day, but to some Americans there could be no doubt: the Spaniards, those filthy curs, who had been biding their time until this very moment to blow up so peaceful a symbol of American sovereignty.

Three days later, fearing reprisal, the Spanish sent a warship of their own, the *Vizcaya*, to roost in the waters of New York harbor, although she flew her colors at half mast in honor of the Americans who had been killed aboard the *Maine*. Still, it was one more provocation to those who believed the worst of Spain.

President McKinley was not one of them. But he knew that he had to do something, had to prove that Assistant Secretary of the Navy Theodore Roosevelt was wrong when he described the president as a man with "the backbone of a chocolate éclair." Even though he would soon come to believe that the destruction of the *Maine* was caused by an accidental explosion of its own magazines, a conclusion that would be verified shortly afterward by a naval court of inquiry and that most historians would find plausible, if not definite, McKinley could not help but be carried away by the *Journal*-fueled zeitgeist.

Hearst printed his paper in black and white. He painted his portrait of Spaniards and Cubans in the same colors. The former were vicious, savage, subhuman beings who would not stop at destroying an American battleship and continuing to misrule a small island off the U.S. coast. One day they would attack the United States as well, hungry as they were in their barbaric way for world domination. The latter were harmless, peaceful, deeply religious tillers of the soil who represented the highest, if not the most sophisticated, form of God's creatures on earth. The Americans were the only people both powerful and virtuous enough to defeat the forces of evil and elevate the simple forces of good to their proper place in the world order. It was thus their duty to do so. "Anyone advocating peace was a traitor or a Wall Street profiteer," wrote Hearst biographer W. A. Swanberg, paraphrasing his subject's sentiments, "probably both."

Two days after the *Maine* blew up, the *Journal* reported that there was "undoubted proof of Spanish treachery and hostility." It stated unequivocally that "American sailors were deliberately sacrificed." It claimed to have found "other proofs in plenty of Spanish treachery and duplicity. The most villanous [*sic*] paper in Havana, the Diario del Ejercito, appeared in deep mourning, and in obedience to official instructions expressed deepest sympathy. But it is the organ of the army, and from one end of Havana to the other there is no feeling among the Spaniards save delight at the sinking of the Yankee vessel."

And somehow, the *Journal* knew exactly what the Spaniards were saying. "'She has gone to the bottom,' they shout. 'Serves her right after coming here to insult us by lying fairly under our noses.'"

It was journalism as a blunt weapon. "Hearst's coverage of the *Maine* disaster," says Swanberg, "still stands as the orgasmic acme of ruthless, truthless newspaper jingoism. As always, when he wanted anything he wanted it with passionate intensity. The *Maine* represented the fulfillment not of one want but two—war with Spain and more circulation to beat Pulitzer. He fought for these ends with such abandonment of honesty and incitement of hatred that the stigma of it never quite left him, even though he still had fifty-three years to live."

In the days following the explosion, "Remember the *Maine*" became the nation's battle cry. Hearst printed it. Pulitzer printed it. Banners hanging from buildings proclaimed it. Americans spoke it to one another on the street and in their workplaces; to some it became almost a form of greeting. And the *Journal* kept the ship's name alive in headlines that rang out almost daily, the print seeming to enlarge and darken with each succeeding edition:

CRUISER MAINE BLOWN UP

THE WARSHIP MAINE WAS SPLIT IN TWO BY AN
ENEMY'S SECRET INFERNAL MACHINE

THE WHOLE COUNTRY THRILLS WITH THE WAR
FEVER

HOW THE MAINE ACTUALLY LOOKS AS IT LIES,
WRECKED BY SPANISH TREACHERY, IN HAVANA BAY

HAVANA POPULACE INSULTS THE MEMORY OF THE
MAINE VICTIMS

And in case someone didn't get it the first time:

THE MAINE WAS DESTROYED BY TREACHERY

After almost two months had passed, with the United States still not having decided to send in troops to avenge the treachery, the *Journal* went for the heartstrings:

SUICIDE [VICTIM] LAMENTED THE MAINE
Aged Mrs. Mary Wayt Enhaled Gas through a Tube.
GRIEVED OVER OUR DELAY
"The Government May Live in Dishonor," Said She, "I
Cannot."

By this time the *Journal* had even gone to the preposterous length of making up something it called the "Game of War with Spain," to be played with a conventional deck of cards by four people. "Two contestants would portray the crew of the United States battleship *Texas*, doing their best to 'sink' the other two, who manned the *Vizcaya*." One shudders at the thought of what

Hearst might have done if the technology for computer games had been available to him in those days.

A few days after it published the rules for the card game, the *Journal* wrote that it "can stake its reputation as a war prophet on this assertion: There will be a war with Spain as certain as the sun shines unless Spain abases herself in the dust and voluntarily consents to the freedom of Cuba." Spain did not, and Hearst was right. On April 25, 1898, he was finally able to publish the headline toward which he had been aiming all along:

CONGRESS DECLARES WAR

A few days later, not as a headline but as a banner running at a diagonal in both upper corners of the paper, framing the masthead, Hearst asked:

HOW DO YOU LIKE THE JOURNAL'S WAR?

But something like this was too tasteless even for New York's most tasteless publisher, and after two days he dropped it.

Theodore Roosevelt, by reputation an advocate of virtually any war, was supposedly delighted with the *Journal*'s, so much so that he expressed his glee to a *Journal* reporter. The paper quoted the future president on the front page: "It is cheering to find a newspaper of the great influence and circulation of the *Journal* tell the facts as they exist and ignore the suggestions of various kinds that emanate from sources that cannot be described as patriotic or loyal to the flag of this country." But according to Roosevelt, he said nothing of the kind. The entire *Journal* interview was an "invention from beginning to end," the future president complained. "It is difficult to understand the kind of infamy that resorts to such methods."

Previously, there had been other inventions. The naval court of inquiry that would agree with McKinley that the *Maine*'s demise was an accident announced the results of its investigation on March 28, 1898. The *New York Journal*, however, couldn't wait that long. It announced the results of the naval court's investigation more than two weeks earlier, when there *were* no results to announce. Nonetheless, engraven on the *Journal's* front page was the news that the court "finds that Spanish government officials blew up the *Maine.*" It was the gaudiest, most transparent of lies, so brazen that when other papers pointed it out in their next editions, the *Journal* did not bother to apologize or defend itself or even acknowledge its fabrication. What could it say? It knew the lie would be revealed within hours of the story's hitting the streets and exposed all the more when the naval court finally did come to its decision. No matter. The *Journal* only wanted to improve its circulation for a few hours, and it did—-a few teaspoonfuls of success before a few more gushers of opprobrium.

When the naval court of inquiry ruled that "the *Maine* was destroyed by the explosion of a submarine mine, which caused the partial explosion of two or more of the forward magazines," and when it further stated that it had no idea how long the mine had been in place, nor who had put it there, the *Journal* was ready. It ridiculed the court's finding, charging it with suppressing evidence that conclusively proved Spanish guilt and denouncing it for being riddled with agents of the Spanish government, whose ultimate goal was Spanish dominion over the entire world. In other words, the *Journal*, in the *Journal's* version, had been right after all, and right the hard way—in the face of all logic and reason. Hearst must have popped the buttons of his vest in pride.

It is surprising, at least in retrospect, that there was so little opposition to Hearst's practices from those who worked for him. True, they wanted to keep their jobs, especially in the difficult economic times that lingered from the Panic of 1893, but, just as true, many of them were appalled by the lengths to which they had to go to do so, and they spoke often of their dissatisfaction to one another. Only one man, however, seems to have ever defied Hearst, a remarkable man by any standards, and someone who was not really an employee.

Richard Harding Davis was the era's most famous reporter, and one of the few in any era to whom the adjective "swashbuckling" might justly be applied. A successful novelist and playwright as well as a globe-trotting correspondent, he covered the Greco-Turkish War of 1896–1897, World War I, and virtually every conflict in every corner of the globe in between. But he knew how to keep fiction and fact apart and took pride in so doing. His renown never affected his integrity. As one of his fellow journalists commented, "His powers of observation were the most remarkable I have ever known. . . . In addition, he possessed a remarkable nose for news. He seemed to have a natural instinct for picking out the right point to make for [sic] when in search of a really good story."

Davis also knew that "a star reporter must not only observe but be observed." Which is to say he was one of the first journalists to realize that his occupation could bring public notice as well as a regular paycheck. And he realized that being seen in the right places, in the company of the right people, attired in the right manner, was an important part of the process. "His costume was an ulster and yellow gloves in his youth, English tweeds and khakis in his maturity." He was also known, at a formal gathering, to enter wearing a cape, remove it with a flourish upon passing through the front door, and present it to the butler with a slight bow.

Davis's good looks would have been obvious even without his clothier's assistance. His jaw was square, his eyes magnetic, his hair slicked back, his collar starched, his voice "an aristocratic drawl"; so striking a figure did he cut that the artist Charles Dana Gibson, who created the famed Gibson Girl, often drew her on the arm of a man clearly modeled after Davis. No ink-stained wretch, he.

The effect that Davis had on women can be imagined. His effect on men was no less electric. Writers of all sorts, not just journalists, seemed especially drawn to him. To read F. Scott Fitzgerald is to conclude that he described the dress and behavior of many of his heroes with Davis in mind. The American author (not the future British statesman) Winston Churchill wrote a novel based on Davis called *The Celebrity*, and even Sinclair Lewis, in *Dodsworth*, has one of his characters, an ambitious college student, cite Davis as he effuses about his plans to travel the world. "Certainly like to see Europe some day. When I graduate, thought I'd be a civil engineer and see the Brazil jungle and China and all over. Reg'lar Richard Harding Davis stuff."

Booth Tarkington, the Indiana novelist, never wrote about Davis, who could not easily fit into a novel set in the adventure-starved towns of the American Midwest. But in his own college days, he found himself with some friends in New York's Waldorf Hotel during a school break, "and Richard Harding Davis came into the Palm Room—then, oh, then, our day was radiant! That was the top of our fortune; we could never have hoped for so much. Of all the great people of every continent, this was the one we most desired to see."

Even in a war zone, Davis could be the center of attention. According to his biographer, Arthur Lubow, Davis refused to turn his back on amenities, no matter how close he was to the front lines. He was "the reporter who brings a folding bathtub and dinner jacket to the front so that he can dress properly in the evening."

Hearst was no less transfixed by Davis, his exploits and his aura, than were the others. More than a year before the *Maine* exploded, but with fighting between the Cuban rebels and the Spanish increasing at the same time that interest at home was decreasing, Hearst offered Davis the unheard-of sum of three thousand dollars, plus all expenses, to cover the battles for a single month. Stories by Richard Harding Davis, Hearst reasoned, would ratchet up both the passions of the populace and the circulation of the *Journal*.

At first Davis did not even respond to the offer. He was dubious about Hearst and had little regard for the *Journal* and thus no desire to see his byline on its front page. Then Hearst repeated the offer and Davis began to find the notion of so much money for so little time irresistible. Finally he accepted. But for a variety of reasons, some of them involving Hearst's difficulties in arranging transportation for him to Havana, Davis became almost immediately disenchanted with his employer and let him know about it. Rather than being upset by Davis's attitude, Hearst was almost obsequious. He apologized, pleaded for another chance, and spent an additional thousand dollars to charter a boat to get the reporter to his destination.

Davis arrived in Cuba only a little later than he had anticipated and began to file stories immediately. But when he found out that Hearst had changed one of them, making Davis's balanced account more pro-Cuba and anti-Spain than he believed circumstances warranted, he quit on the spot. Hearst pleaded with him once more and promised it would never happened again. Davis would not listen. No one, he told Hearst, tampered with his prose. It was the same thing as tampering with his reputation, and that was unforgivable. He took a boat back to the United States four days before his month was to end and never again dealt with the publisher of the *New York Journal*.

As for Hearst, who had by this time armed his personal yacht and loaned it to the navy for the duration, he eventually went to Cuba himself to write a few stories. The *Journal* "ran reports on the front page in large type under enormous headlines with insistent mention of his name." They assured readers that war was certain. They predicted the Hearst yacht would play a significant role in defending U.S. interests.

Hearst was capable of occasional drippings of charm. So was Joseph Pulitzer, but less often. Author Theodore Dreiser described him as "undoubtedly semi-neurasthenic, a disease-demonized soul, who could scarcely control himself in anything."

As a young state legislator in Missouri, Pulitzer found that he could not control himself in the company of a certain lobbyist. So he pulled out a gun he should not have been carrying in the first place and shot the man. It was just a flesh wound, however; the lobbyist staggered out of the state capitol and, after getting treatment from a nearby doctor, continued with his career. Pulitzer, fearing he might not have the temperament for politics, got out of the field, and several years later he headed east to become the publisher of the *New York World*, which he turned into one of the city's more respected sources of news.

Pulitzer himself was less respected. On his bad days, his temper could be vicious. One of the worst was when he found out that his brother Albert, who owned the *New York Journal*, had sold it to Joseph's soon-to-be bitter enemy, William Randolph Hearst. Pulitzer thought Hearst represented the worst in journalistic excess. Albert thought he was exaggerating, and besides, he said, he needed the money. Pulitzer screamed at his him, berating him for what seemed virtually an act of treason. It was years before the chasm between the two brothers closed.

The gap between Pulitzer and Hearst never did, and was reinforced as soon as Hearst bought the *Journal* and started stealing Pulitzer's employees, including many of his top reporters and editors. He offered them salaries that Pulitzer could have matched but would not, believing them to be, as they were for the time, outrageous. There was another reason Pulitzer might have lost employees to his foe. He treated them miserably. In a letter to relatives in London, his secretary described Pulitzer as "a coarse, bloated millionaire, who thinks that by paying people he can buy immunity from the little self-restraint that comes natural to most people (thank goodness)."

He was no kinder to his family. When his fourteen-year-old daughter Lucille had throat surgery, she lost so much blood that she fainted. A second operation was necessary, and afterward she had to be given a form of morphine because the pain was so intense. Pulitzer's wife seldom left her bedside, and there was fear for a time that she would die. As for Pulitzer, he made not a single appearance at the hospital. When his wife came home one night for a quick dinner, she asked why. Had he no pity for his daughter? "Pity Lucille!" he screamed. "No! I'm the only one to pity—has no one any pity for *me*!—does no one realize what I suffer!" Kate Pulitzer, stunned speechless, hurried back to her daughter's room, having no idea what her husband was talking about, no idea what he might do next, wanting only to be out of his reach.

As a newspaper publisher, Pulitzer was more admirable—most of the time, at least. When the *New York Tribune* published a front-page story about a six-year-old girl being sexually molested by two boys only a few years older than she, he criticized the *Tribune* in his own pages, claiming that the *World* was also aware of the story but would not stoop to print such filth. In explaining his reason for this and similar decisions, Pulitzer stated that in his opinion,

> a newspaper should be scrupulously accurate, it should be clean, it should avoid everything salacious or suggestive, everything that could offend the good taste or lower the moral tone of its readers; but within these limits, it is the duty of a newspaper to print the news. When I speak of good taste . . . I mean the kind of good taste which demands that frankness should be linked with decency, the kind of moral tone which is braced and not relaxed when it is brought face to face to vice.

But when he came face to face with Hearst over the Spanish-American War, Pulitzer blinked.

A few years before the Americans entered the war, Pulitzer's *World* started covering the events that led to the conflict in a relatively objective and restrained manner. It was a decision he would later come to regret, for as Hearst turned the story into a national sensation, the *Journal* became the "official" paper of the Spanish-American War and remained so throughout the fighting. Pulitzer could never catch up.

He certainly tried. Well before the *Maine*, with Hearst already inflaming his readers, Pulitzer began to slide down the slippery slope of sensationalism. A *New York World* headline predicted the effect that Spanish mistreatment would have on the Cubans:

THE RIOTS IN HAVANA MEAN REVOLUTION

The day after the *Maine* blew up, despite the *World*'s view in an editorial that "nobody outside of a lunatic asylum" believed Spain had deliberately destroyed the ship, the paper's headline for the lead story seemed to indicate that someone from the asylum had escaped and gotten his hands on the *World*'s type tray.

MAINE EXPLOSION CAUSED BY BOMB OR TORPEDO?

In fact, by this time, Pulitzer, as he was later forced to admit, had abandoned his journalistic principles and his coverage had become roaringly, and in some cases irresponsibly, anti-Spain. In one edition of the *World* he went so far as to write that the *Vizcaya*, which had done nothing since it arrived in American waters but float, would soon begin an offensive against the United States. "While lying off the Battery," the *World* predicted, "her shells will explode on the Harlem River and in the suburbs of Brooklyn."

Yet it was not until almost two months after the *Maine* exploded that the *World* published its first pro-war editorial. Pulitzer's tone, apparently, was meant to make up for lost time, and part of the editorial was meant to chastise the *Journal*:

> Spain is a decaying, ignorant and well-nigh bankrupt nation. No Spanish ship could stand an hour before the Americans. Havana is at our mercy and this is a nation that talks of war with the United States. Now fifty-four days have passed since the Maine was destroyed by a stationary mine. God forbid that The World should ever advocate an unnecessary war! That would be a serious crime against civilization. The first duty of the President and Congress is to order the navy to proceed to Cuba and Puerto Rico without delay. No declaration of war is necessary. Send the fleet to Havana and demand the surrender of the miscreants who blew up the Maine.

Apparently not believing the war was unnecessary, and not believing that he was guilty of a crime against civilization, Hearst did not respond.

At one point in the war, however, the *Journal* did take on the *World*. A few days earlier, in one of its articles, the *World* had written critically of New York's 71st Regiment, saying that many of its members had lost heart and, instead of fighting the Spaniards, had fled from them—this at the same time that Colonel Roosevelt, who had resigned as assistant secretary of the navy, was leading his Rough Riders up San Juan Hill. The story was true; the men of the 71st were in fact running away from the Spanish aggressors, afraid of coming under attack. Nonetheless, Hearst, having no information to contradict the *World*'s account, sprang to the men's defense:

SLURS ON THE BRAVERY OF THE BOYS OF THE 71ST
The *World* Deliberately Accuses Them of Rank Cowardice at San Juan.

But Hearst was not yet done taunting Pulitzer. Not long afterward, the *Journal* published an article about the death of Colonel Reflipe W. Thenuz, supposedly a famed European artillery officer, who had been killed while fighting for the Cubans. The *World*, not knowing anything about the incident, was forced to rely on the *Journal*'s story and published its own version the next day. As W. A. Swanberg tells us:

Joy was unrestrained in the Hearst newsrooms. The Journal disclosed that Colonel Reflipe W. Thenuz was its own invention and rearranged the letters of his name into "We pilfer the news." For a time the World's encounter with Colonel Thenuz was given almost as much space in the Journal as the war news from Cuba. It published a poem, "In Memoriam," honoring the colonel. It published a fanciful cartoon of him, captioned "specially taken for the *World*, by the *World*'s special photographer." . . . The Journal kept it up for more than a month while the mortified World preserved a pained silence.

A British journalist visiting the United States during this time was appalled at the war between the two newspaper publishers. It seemed to him "a contest of madmen for the primacy of the sewer."

* * *

In his will, Pulitzer would leave two million dollars to Columbia University to establish awards for journalism and the arts that are today among the most prestigious in those fields. Nothing that appeared in the *New York World* during the Spanish-American War would have even qualified for a nomination.

Yet, as biographer Denis Brian points out, after the war the *World* "regain[ed] its former glowing reputation," which it kept, and for the most part deserved, for the rest of Pulitzer's tenure as its owner. The Spanish-American War was something of an aberration in U.S. foreign policy, and something more of an aberration in the journalistic career of Joseph Pulitzer, who, having vowed not to let Hearst egg him on to irresponsible excess anymore, once again felt free to make his paper what he had always wanted it to be.

Their sympathy for the Cubans and their animosity toward Spain notwithstanding, the real struggle for both Hearst and Pulitzer was with each other. Shortly before American soldiers landed in Cuba, one issue of the *Journal* sold more than three million copies, probably an all-time high for any newspaper at any time anywhere in the country. That, however, was far from the norm.

As the war began, both the *Journal* and the *World* were selling about 1.3 million issues a day, still more than either paper had ever sold before on a regular basis. The two publications stayed at that approximate level throughout the fighting, although the slight edge in sales went to the *Journal*, despite the *World* having been the more popular paper in earlier years. The war might not have done much for the *Journal*'s image, but it did wonders for its visibility.

Some of the credit, if that is the proper word, probably goes to the newsboys who sold the *Journal* on the streets of New York. They were a feisty lot who would often plant themselves within a few feet of the *World*'s young salesmen and simply outyell them. The *Journal*'s headlines were usually exaggerations of one sort or another; the newsboys would exaggerate them even more, bellowing Armageddon so loudly that a person could hear it from one end of the block to the other, if not farther.

From time to time the purveyors of the two papers would resort to fisticuffs, dropping their papers and flailing at each other, sometimes rolling into the street in a violent embrace and coming up stained with dirt and grime and horse droppings. Their customers were forced to wait until one or the other had surrendered before they could make their purchase, in the meantime cheering on their favorite. Usually it was the *Journal* boy. Bellicose prose, bellicose kids to hawk it.

The irony for both papers was that with increased circulation came decreased profits. The costs of covering the war were immense, more than either Hearst or Pulitzer had anticipated. Reporters could not file their reports electronically in those days. In most cases they wrote them out longhand and made arrangements for them to be transported from Cuba to the United States like any other kind of merchandise: on muleback to the docks, by boat to southern Florida, by train (or sometimes, if there was a good connection available, by phone) to New York. As mule owners, sailors, and railroad officials saw how important the cargo was to the *Journal* and the *World*, as well as to the other papers covering the war less bombastically, they raised their rates. And then raised them again, and again. Eventually, things reached such a point that, added to the other costs of coverage, each issue that Hearst and Pulitzer sold meant a slight loss for them. Both men could afford it; neither was happy about it.

Fortunately for the two journalistic combatants, the war ended after less than a year, and in another ten months Spain officially granted Cuba its independence. A total of 385 Americans had lost their lives in the fighting. More than 2,000 died as a result of disease and other causes related to the war, and another 1,660 were injured. Neither they nor the surviving members of the families liked the *Journal*'s war at all.

But it was a more consequential event than the casualties, which were small for an armed conflict, suggest. For one thing, the

Spanish-American War fueled our country's desire for expansion in warmer waters and nations. Professor Jeffrey Bass of Quinnipiac University refers to a "spate of U.S. interventionism in Latin American countries, most notably Cuba, Haiti, the Dominican Republic." The noted diplomatic historian William Stueck Jr. picks up the theme. "It is highly unlikely," he wrote, "that the United States would have acquired the Philippines without the war, and it's possible that we would not have annexed Hawaii without it (there had long been pressure to annex it, but it was only after the war started that Congress finally acted)."

That long-existing pressure, directed not just at Hawaii but at the other nations just mentioned, had come largely from American business interests that wanted new markets for their goods. The *New York Journal's* reporting on the Spanish-American War roused the captains of American industry as well as the rabble who were its more frequent readers. Stueck also believes that the U.S. State Department became a much more professional organization after the war. No longer would amateurs like William Randolph Hearst be able to exert such influence over the conduct of the nation's foreign policy.

Two decades later, Hearst had still not learned his lesson—although that is a misleading way to put it. Hearst was not the kind of man who was open to lessons, who conceded that other people or events might have something to teach him. He was the kind of man who *taught* lessons. If people did not listen, he simply taught them louder. If his lessons proved wrong, he either ignored them or found someone to blame, in either case moving on to the next lesson. Shy and full of himself at the same time, easily able to bend people to his will, he was tall and well-built, his broad shoulders somewhat stooped. His physical presence dominated a room, and you could sense that presence on the pages of the *Journal*, a kind of energy that respected no limits. He wanted the people who worked for him to be similarly hard-driving, unwilling to be deterred, except in their dealings with the

Chief, as Hearst was sometimes known. In those cases they were to keep their conversations brief and their behavior obsequious.

When World War I broke out, Hearst let it be known that his sympathies were with the Germans and that if the United States ever got involved in the fighting, despite President Woodrow Wilson's denials that such a thing would happen, he hoped America would align itself with the kaiser.

Of course, the United States finally did enter the war, with the Germans as foes, not allies. Nonetheless, Hearst announced that the *Journal* would cover the fighting fairly and extensively, that it would in fact provide the best coverage of any paper in the nation. Heading up the reporting team would be five of his very best men: John C. Foster and Lawrence Elston in London, Frederick Werner in Berlin, Franklin P. Merrick in Paris, and Brixton D. Allaire in Rome.

Executives of other New York papers shook their heads. They had never heard of any of them.

They've been overseas, getting the lay of the land, Hearst replied, in effect. Don't worry, he said, you'll hear of them. These men will get to the truth of the fighting and the reasons behind it and capture it, every single day on the pages of the *Journal*. Of course, the *Journal* did not give bylines to its war correspondents (although it certainly would have given one to Richard Harding Davis), but when you see the dateline, you'll know the man.

Hearst's competitors were suspicious. Wrote an editor at *Harper's*, "Brixton D. Allaire, dear reader, is not a romantic figure in khaki, braving untold dangers in the field of battle, but simply a common ordinary, contemptible Hearst fake."

It was true. The other four reporters were also fakes. Take the following article, which appeared in the *Journal* late in the summer of 1917: "Paris, August 23.—More than 8,426 German prisoners, 200 machine guns and twenty-four cannon have been captured by the French on the Verdun front since the French drive opened on August 20, the War Office announced to-day. Of the total number of prisoners taken—186 were officers. All but 600 of the captives are unwounded."

It reads like a wire service dispatch or, worse, a press release. It might have been either. Or it might have been written for the *Journal* by a burned-out old desk man in London or New York—if New York, he might have been sitting within a few feet of Hearst himself—with the Paris dateline the only thing in the entire article even remotely resembling reportorial enterprise.

And it was not the first time the Chief had done such a thing. Occasionally, during the Spanish-American War, dispatches from Cuba would be delayed a day or two. In that case, Hearst assigned the stories to more hacks, either in Miami or New York, and they crafted precisely what the Chief wanted to hear, forgetting their early dreams of a noble career in the newsroom, and then drowning their sorrows of self-recrimination at the neighborhood saloon after work. They had not taken the world by storm as they had hoped in younger days. They were approaching the end of the line, and what they were taking was dictation.

William Randolph Hearst died on August 14, 1951, at the age of eighty-eight. His last public crusade was for the illegalization of marijuana, which helped lead to the passage of the Marijuana Tax Act of 1937. As for his legacy, Martin Lee and Norman Solomon describe it concisely and accurately in their book *Unreliable Sources.* They point out that Hearst "routinely invented sensational stories, faked interviews, ran phony pictures and distorted real events." The world always remained a dancing school to him, and over the decades he had become much more sophisticated in his ways of throwing rocks at it.

Most notably, as far as some people were concerned, Hearst served as the model for *Citizen Kane,* the title character in the movie that is the consensus choice of critics as the best American film ever made.

It is only fitting that William Randolph Hearst would make more of a contribution to fiction than he ever did to the world of fact.

9

L'Affaire

A FEW YEARS BEFORE THE *MAINE* EXPLODED, THERE WAS AN explosion of a different sort in France, one that the French had been building up to for many years and which resulted in perhaps the most shameful episode in the nation's history. The principal villains were the military and the press, especially a newspaper called *La Libre Parole*—the free word. We know the episode as the Dreyfus Affair.

At the age of thirty-five, Captain Alfred Dreyfus looked like a soldier even when he wasn't in uniform. He might have been strolling with his wife, Lucie, for whom his love never wavered; might have been playing with his children; might have been enjoying the company of his brother—he still carried himself almost as if at attention: head back, shoulders back, chin jutting forward proudly, some would say haughtily. And he spoke in crisp tones, as if he were addressing one of his superiors. He was not an unapproachable man, just brusque on the surface; the warmer man beneath the surface was known only to those closest to him.

As an artillery officer in the French army, Dreyfus had a spotless record and a great deal of promise. Especially impressive was his grasp of military strategy. So too was his dedication; he had joined the army in the first place because he was "saddened and angry" about a previous French defeat by the Germans and wanted to do his part to see that nothing like that ever happened again.

It could not, then, have been more ironic. For in 1894, with no warning whatsoever, the exemplary Captain Dreyfus, this man who could have modeled for a recruiting poster, was arrested and charged with passing military secrets to the very same Germans.

Dreyfus was aghast, sad, and angry. He had not passed military secrets to the Germans or to anyone else and could not believe that anyone who knew him would believe such a thing. He was completely dedicated to the interests of his homeland, where his family had long lived and prospered in the textile industry.

Yet there were people who could not help but wonder: what really *was* his homeland? The Dreyfus textile factory was located in the hard-to-categorize province of Alsace, which over the centuries had been ruled by both France and Germany and whose citizens, at present, were officially governed by the former despite speaking primarily the latter's tongue. Perhaps young Alfred had somehow managed to develop the wrong allegiance and had intended to be a spy all along. And then there was his father, who upon retiring from the textile business had moved to a village that because of recently rearranged borders, was now in Germany.

In terms of evidence, there was nothing against Dreyfus worthy of the name. The prosecution's case was based largely on a type of document called a *bordereau*, which contained information that would in all likelihood have been helpful to the Germans. The bordereau was found in a wastebasket by a cleaning woman who was also a French spy, and the specific information it contained, about a new howitzer the French had developed called the

Modèle 1890 120mm Baquet, seemed to implicate an artillery officer. That was one reason to suspect Dreyfus, although numerous other artillery officers possessed the same intelligence. Another cause for suspicion was that he paid yearly visits to his father, who was now dying. Who knew what else the captain did in Germany, what he said and to whom he said it?

But no one had ever seen Captain Dreyfus in the company of a German, in either country. No one had ever heard him utter a word that indicated his loyalty to France was anything less than it seemed. No Frenchman had ever had any reason to doubt his loyalty. And there was widespread disagreement about whether the handwriting on the bordereau was in fact Dreyfus's. Most experts thought it probably was not. No matter. Captain Alfred Dreyfus was found guilty of treason by a military tribunal in December 1894, a mere two months after his arrest. He was sentenced to solitary confinement for the rest of his life on Devil's Island, which was little more than a big, inhospitable rock measuring thirty-four square acres and located less than ten miles off the coast of French Guiana.

Upon hearing the verdict, Dreyfus did not move. He could not move. He could barely breathe. Members of his family in the courtroom began to sob, but it is doubtful that Dreyfus heard them. It was all he could do to remain conscious.

Initially, Dreyfus had thought he was the victim of circumstance or some sort of terrible misunderstanding. But the manner in which the tribunal had acted against him, its refusal to admit exculpatory evidence, the unwillingness of the judges even to meet his eyes on the few occasions when they condescended to speak to him, confirmed his worst fears; he was in truth the victim of a conspiracy. The bordereau had not only been written by someone else, but had been planted in the wastebasket for the specific purpose of being found to implicate him. Perhaps it was supposed to have been turned up by the cleaning lady who doubled as a French spy and would hand it over to the proper officials, who would identify Dreyfus as the author. Perhaps it was to have been discovered by a fake agent for the Germans, who would have been arrested and, as part of the sham, would claim that Dreyfus had left it for him.

But why? Why had Dreyfus been chosen as the victim of so insidious a scheme when he was such an exemplary soldier? Not because he knew about the specifications of the howitzer. Not because he was now an annual visitor to Germany. Not because his father's textile business had made him wealthier than his fellow officers, rousing envy among many of them. Not even because he had a "reserved, highly controlled public manner seeming, at times, like arrogance." No, Captain Alfred Dreyfus was, to the majority of Frenchmen, military and civilians alike, guilty of something much worse than any of the previous offenses: he was a Jew.

He was, in fact, "an agent of international Jewry," according to the Catholic newspaper *La Croix*. Two other papers, *Le Temps* and *Le Matin*, claimed that he had been seduced into treason by an Italian noblewoman, who in fact Dreyfus had never met or heard of. And *La Libre Parole* was one of three papers calling for his execution, this before he even stood trial. It wrote that Dreyfus "entered the army with the premeditated plan of committing treason against it. As a Jew and as a German he detests the French. . . . German by taste and education, Jew by race, he does their work and nothing else."

If anything, the name Devil's Island understates the isolation and gruesomeness of the place, which at the time of Dreyfus's sentencing was a leper colony—home not to the Almighty's rejects but the Earth's.

Tending goats and picking wild tomatoes and coconuts, the community of eighteen lepers had been housed in a small complex of ramshackle huts. Dreyfus, "whose hideousness," according to Commandant Bouchet, the prisoner's warden, "was a thousand times more frightening than that of the wretches who had preceded him" on Devil's Island, had to wait for colonial officials to transfer the lepers and burn the remnants of their colony—to "purge it of its vermin."

In addition to Bouchet, there were five guards assigned to Dreyfus duty. They were not needed. There was no way to escape from Devil's Island except to tumble down the sheer cliff walls and smash oneself to death in the descent, or to leap into the ocean and drown. Even if there were a survivable means of escape, Dreyfus was not in any condition to try. While incarcerated in Paris, awaiting his transfer, he had lost weight, becoming pallid and listless, his eyes not always able to focus, his mind—perhaps in self-defense—not able to grasp the dimensions of the tragedy of which he was now in the midst. He was no better when he arrived at the former leper colony. In the diary that he kept beginning his second day on Devil's Island, he wrote, "Until now, I made a cult of reason. I used to believe in the logic of things and events. Finally, I used to believe in human justice! Whatever was bizarre, out of the ordinary, penetrated my brain only with the greatest difficulty. Alas, what a total collapse of all my beliefs, of all my sound faculties of reason!"

Even so, the French colonial minister thought Dreyfus to be a threat of significant proportions and, at the urging of the anti-Semitic press, issued an order to Commandant Bouchet. If the prisoner tries to escape, he said, "Blow his brains out." Not taking any chances were the Frenchmen, so concerned were they with how a single, virtually paralyzed man might compromise the security of their nation.

The only way Dreyfus could get through his days was to sink himself into the mindlessness of routine. He woke up most mornings at five-thirty and boiled the dried vegetables he would eat later for breakfast. At eight, a guard would bring him the food for his other meals. He would do so with saying a word to the prisoner. The guards never spoke to him. They were under orders not to. If Dreyfus asked them a question, they were not even to shake their heads yes or no. Once in a while Dreyfus asked anyhow, just to hear his own voice. It began to seem less and less familiar to him.

Dreyfus would do whatever he could to protect the food he had been given from turning rancid in the tropical heat. It was not easy. Usually he put it on the stove so that it would not spoil as quickly, but there was no way to slow the spoilage for more than a few hours.

At nine he ate his vegetables, making of the water in which he had boiled them an odd-tasting tea. Then he cleaned his quarters, chopped wood for the next day's fire, and did his laundry. He wrote in his diary and wrote a letter to Lucie.

By midafternoon, not permitted to be out of his hut alone, he would stroll around the tiny island in the company of a silent guard. He might exercise in an area set aside for that purpose, but barely large enough to accommodate his movements. Afterward, he would sit for a while on a bench and stare across the ocean in the direction of France, watching the perpetual motion of the waves, listening to them slap against the rock he could not bring himself to call home. Then it was back inside the hut for dinner, another entry in the diary, and another letter to his wife. He received mail in return twice a month, although none of it was allowed to refer to his "affair," and if for some reason the correspondence was delayed, his desperation, always close to the surface, reached a peak. On one such occasion, when a ship unloaded some goods at Devil's Island without any mail from Lucie, he wrote in his diary, "My heart bleeds so that everything is a wound for me. Death would be a deliverance."

Sometimes before going to bed he would read Shakespeare or the essays of Montaigne. The editions were so old and tattered that he had to turn the pages carefully so they would not rip. There were nights when tears fell on the pages, making them even more fragile.

The routine kept him from completely losing his sanity, but it did nothing for his physical health. Still pale and listless, he now began to suffer from a fever that did not allow him to sleep and robbed him of what little energy he had left. "When occasionally he did sleep," writes biographer David L. Lewis, "it was only because of immense exhaustion, and when he awakened, the dreams of the night—of Lucie and the professional triumphs of the past—pursued him cruelly."

It took more than a month for his fever to lift. His spirits did not. Sometimes as he sat on his bench in the late afternoon and looked out at the ocean, he would not just watch the endless expanse of water but would hope it would begin to roil. "When storms stirred up the sea and the waves thundered against the rock," writes another biographer, Nicholas Halasz, "he took advantage of the sound to give vent to shrieks of despair. He waited for the storms because he did not want anyone to hear him." The guards and their commandant might not have. They would not have cared if they did.

But at other times, sitting in the same place, Dreyfus would keep better control of himself. He would wonder about his family and friends at home. Had they given up on him, or were they still working to clear his name and earn his release?

The answer was the latter, and no one was working harder than Mathieu Dreyfus, who had begun to think about what role the newspapers might play in vindicating his brother. Perhaps the press could do more to free Alfred than either the military or the judicial system. Mathieu was about to make a terrible mistake.

By this time, Dreyfus had been a prisoner on Devil's Island for a year and a half, and Mathieu was afraid that people had forgotten him. There was no longer conversation about the Dreyfus Affair in coffee shops and salons, no longer stories about it in the newspapers. Paris hummed with activity, with elegantly dressed ladies and refined gentlemen going to the theater and concerts, with garish displays of electric light along the Champs-Elysées and other boulevards, with the constant bump and rattle of carriages proceeding to and fro, clogging those same boulevards. Emile Zola had not yet written "J'accuse," his brilliant and widely circulated polemic against Dreyfus's mistreatment, but his novels were the talk of some Parisian circles. Paul Verlaine's poetry was the talk of others. Alfred Dreyfus had become old news, and until he was once again on the minds of Parisians his chances for vindication were nil.

Mathieu was distraught. He had found new evidence that he believed would exonerate his brother and was trying to persuade French authorities to order a new trial. But he was having no luck. The authorities, who had once been willing to meet with him, would no longer do so. Nor would they admit the possibility that the military tribunal had made a mistake. The French army was, after all, the nation's pride, and many of those refined gentlemen stepping out of their carriages into the Parisian night-life had once served in it, or still did.

Mathieu, then, had to find a different way to pressure the government. He had to get his brother back into people's minds, back into the public discourse, and hope that this would provide the necessary momentum for a second trial.

He decided to turn to the press, but in an unusual fashion. A friend of his arranged for the publication of a story in a Newport, Wales, paper called the *South Wales Argus* that Dreyfus had escaped from Devil's Island. It was pure fiction, as was the name of the ship on which he supposedly escaped, the *Non Pareil*, and the man in charge of the vessel, Captain Hunter. But news of the escape soon became the "hot word"; Alfred Dreyfus, the Frenchman who had tried to sell his country to the Jews or the Germans or some combination of both, was supposedly free now somewhere in England.

The *London Daily Chronicle* was next to run the story, and afterward virtually every paper in France carried it. Although many of them, especially in Paris, were to one degree or another anti-Semitic, no paper gave the "escape" more space, darker ink, larger type, or more steaming vitriol than *La Libre Parole*.

Founded in 1892 by Edouard Drumont to advance the already advanced cause of Jew-hating, the paper immediately became one of France's most popular and influential. Drumont wanted to make "real" Frenchmen aware of the "savage energy of Jewish invaders." He referred to them as a "hooknose tribe" and as "dirty kikes." He wrote of "Galician kikes with their curly forelocks, who, come together for some ritual murder, laugh with one another while, from the open wound of the victim there runs pure and crimson the Christian blood for the sweet bread of Purim." With notions like this in the background, it is no wonder that *La Libre Parole* found Jews responsible for most of France's problems in the present.

Since its inception, the paper had run a column called "Les Juifs dans l'Armée" (Jews in the Army), libelous portraits of individuals whose service records, like Dreyfus's, were for the most part beyond reproach.

Some of the Jews in the service simply ignored the paper. They had been living with anti-Semitism all their lives in France; defamation from Drumont and his ilk was to be expected. Others, however, were so upset about the articles that they challenged their authors to duels. One of them was actually fought; the Jew, a Captain Mayer, was killed, and *La Libre Parole* rejoiced in so just a settling of accounts.

When the paper's editors got news of Dreyfus's alleged escape, they were furious. They blamed it on a cabal of people who, they believed, were the direct descendants of Satan. They indicted every Jew in France, especially those in the army, as a potential Dreyfus. Then they sent their "special correspondent" to get an exclusive interview with the fictitious Captain Hunter. He did. *La Libre Parole* published it, praising itself for being the only paper in France with the connections to arrange a meeting with the captain. The article no longer exists, but considering the venomous diatribes that the paper printed from real-life human beings, one can only imagine how foul an interview it created with a nonexistent being. Captain Hunter's words made anti-Semites in France even more enraged at Captain Dreyfus. *La Libre Parole* could not have been more delighted at the reaction to its special correspondent's work.

Other French journals joined in the hostilities, one of them revealing details of the plot to free Dreyfus. Reports historian Michael Burns, "'Stirring up emotions in Paris,' as *L'Éclair* reported, it described a sensational scenario that included

Lucie Dreyfus ('obviously well furnished with money') arranging the escape from her base in Cayenne [the capital of French
Guyana]."

Officials of the French government did not believe any of it.
To them it was all a misunderstanding of some sort, or perhaps a
ruse. Escape from Devil's Island simply could not happen. They
cabled Commandant Bouchet and, learning that the prisoner was
still there, still under twenty-four-hour-a-day watch, immediately announced that the story was a lie. Mathieu Dreyfus also
denied his brother's freedom, something he had planned to do
all along. All he wanted was the attention, and he knew that the
anti-Semitic press would give it to him. For the time being he
was satisfied. He believed his plan had worked. His brother was
back on people's minds again, back in the public discourse, and
perhaps now momentum would build for a new trial.

Mathieu could not help being pleased with himself.

To Mathieu's brother Devil's Island now became the fiery depths
of perdition itself. With the issue of escape having been raised,
however unreasonably, the men in charge of guarding Dreyfus
became alarmed. Maybe he really *could* escape. They would have
to take greater precautions, to make what was already impossible
become even less likely.

Dreyfus was confined to his hut twenty-four hours a day, not
allowed to step outside to glance at the ocean for a single moment.
Actually, he could not even see it from indoors, as a new wall was
built around the hut, rising higher than its roof. When Dreyfus
looked out his window, he could see only the wall—not the water,
perhaps not even the sky.

At night, a double *boucle*, a kind of manacle similar to what the
Puritans used to punish sinners in the public square, was attached
to his feet. Further, "an iron band was stretched across the foot
of the bed. To it two iron bands were fastened and, when Dreyfus
retired to sleep, his ankles were locked into the bands." In his
diary, Dreyfus wrote, "The torture was hardly bearable during

those tropical nights. Soon the bands, which were very tight, lacerated my ankles."

In addition, French officials put an end to mail deliveries to Devil's Island, and Dreyfus's guards, as he said, "received orders to report every one of my gestures and even the changes of expression on my face." If he had so much as uttered the word "escape," he would have been bound and gagged, blindfolded and beaten.

It would be several weeks before Dreyfus was allowed out of the hut, longer before he could see the Atlantic again. He walked around the island now with a limp, his frame having become skeletal and bent, his clothes ragged. He was losing his hair. He could almost feel his eyes sinking into his head.

The new evidence that Mathieu had uncovered would eventually lead to the arrest of Major Ferdinand Walsin Esterhazy, although it has never been clear why he wrote the bordereau. True, he had achieved the remarkable feat of being one of the worst Jew-haters in the late-nineteenth-century French army, but that alone does not seem to explain his actions.

He might have written about the howitzer to distract the Germans from looking into the development of other new French weapons, in which case it is possible that he was acting for the good of his country, if not the good of Captain Dreyfus. But this theory is unlikely. He might have written about it in the hope that German officials would be tempted to offer him money for more details, in which case he was acting as a spy, a more possible explanation, as it is known now that Esterhazy had committed other acts of espionage previously. When they were discovered, as Esterhazy knew they would be, he wanted a Jew already fattened and tenderized to take the rap for him. He never imagined that the Jew's friends would fight so long and hard and successfully to vindicate him. He never imagined that in the process of fighting as they did, they would shine a brighter, more unsparing spotlight on French anti-Semitism than ever before. He never imagined that he would do far more damage to France's standing in the world community as an anti-Semite than he had ever done, or could have hoped to do, as a spy.

In 1899, Alfred Dreyfus got his second trial. Had it taken place a century later, it would have been a skit on *Saturday Night Live*. The judges, civilians this time, would hear no evidence against Ester-hazy, nor any new evidence in favor of Dreyfus; the proceedings were even worse than the military tribunal. They simply rehashed the charges that had led to Dreyfus's initial conviction, and he was convicted again, although this time his sentence was reduced from life to ten years. In that sense it was a small victory for justice.

But too small for French president Émile Loubet. A short and kindly man, proud of his peasant stock, he thought the trial a travesty and the verdict a perversely anti-Semitic joke. Dreyfus had been confined no more than a day or two, await-ing a return voyage to Devil's Island, when Loubet intervened, granting him a full pardon. Alfred Dreyfus was, as he always should have been, a free man.

The French press protested, denouncing Loubet's interference, insisting that he change his mind for the good of the republic. He refused. Not until 1906, though, would Dreyfus be officially exonerated. It was then that the Court of Cassation, the French equivalent of the U.S. Supreme Court, overturned the verdict in Dreyfus's second trial. He was now officially innocent of all charges. The French press seethed, accusing the court of being a bunch of Jew-lovers.

Dreyfus had long since returned to active military duty, explaining to those who thought him foolish, or worse, that it was a simple matter of his being a soldier and a Frenchman. The army was where he belonged. What could he do? He was not received warmly by his comrades in arms, but he did not expect to be. If he could survive four years, two months, and five days on Devil's Island, he could certainly survive an indifferent home-coming. After the Court of Cassation's ruling, Dreyfus was pro-moted to the rank of major.

The French press ranted, accusing the army of having become infiltrated with Jews, which would certainly lead to defeat the next time it was called on to defend the nation in battle.

In 1918 Dreyfus was promoted again. He was now a lieutenant colonel and, to his great pride, a member of the Legion of Honor. In World War I, he was assigned to command one of the forts that had been erected to defend Paris. He carried out his duties flawlessly and was cited for his valor and strategic brilliance, helping to lead his nation not to defeat, as *La Libre Parole* and others had predicted, but to victory in battle.

The French press, on this occasion, this rarest of all occasions, neither seethed nor ranted nor accused. Rather, it said not a single word about the French hero Lieutenant Colonel Alfred Dreyfus.

10

Speeding Up a War

H. L. MENCKEN WAS A FEW YEARS TOO YOUNG TO HAVE written about Captain Dreyfus and the outrageous behavior of so many French journalists. It is certain that the affair would have interested him. Everything of importance interested him, and a number of topics that did not seem significant to others suddenly took on surprising relevance when he turned his attention to them. There has never been anyone like Mencken in an American newsroom, and given the nature of journalism today, with its appeal to base emotions, simpleminded analysis, and a slobbering passion for the trivial, it seems certain that there will never be again.

Despite a minimum of formal education, Henry Louis Mencken was the most erudite journalist and critic the United States has ever known, and stylistically he is not only unique but indescribable; one need read only a few lines of his work, on any subject, to know

who was pounding the typewriter keys, and to delight in the ram-
bling cadences, baroque vocabulary, ingenious metaphors, and
exuberant, if pointed, sense of humor.

Mencken on political conventions:

> There is something about a national convention that makes it
> as fascinating as a revival or a hanging. It is vulgar, it is ugly,
> it is stupid, it is tedious, it is hard upon both the higher cerebral
> centers and the gluteus maximus, and yet it is somehow charming.
> One sits through long sessions wishing heartily that all the
> delegates were dead and in hell—and then suddenly there comes
> a show so gaudy and hilarious, so melodramatic and obscene,
> so unimaginably exhilarating and preposterous that one lives a
> gorgeous year in an hour.

Mencken, who never partook of higher education, on those
who preside over its classrooms:

> The college professor, as I have often argued . . . is almost devoid
> of any true critical sense. The stupefying training that he has to go
> through, and the atmosphere of pedagogic pish-posh surrounding
> him, make him anesthetic to all those fine qualities which distinguish
> a work of art, and particularly to those delicate and unfamiliar qualities
> which enter into what we call originality . . . but when it comes to
> embalming and laying out, so to speak, what is accepted—when
> it comes to what may be called the morphology of criticism—when it
> comes to arranging the specimens in the museum, then the peculiar
> talents of the super-sophomore have their chance, and he performs
> a necessary and unstimulating office with admirable industry, and
> even with a touch of passion. Thus stand the true critic and the true
> professor, the one fit for aesthetic obstetrics and the other specially
> gifted for aesthetic autopsies.

It was Mencken who famously described President Warren G.
Harding's oratory as "a string of wet sponges; it reminds me of
tattered washing on the line; it reminds me of stale bean-soup,
of college yells, of dogs barking idiotically through endless nights.
It is so bad that a sort of grandeur creeps into it."

And it was a different, more mellow Mencken, on the perfect experience with a woman. It is hard to believe that a man capable of such heights of imaginative bombast was also capable of such candlelit tenderness:

> It is the close of a busy and vexatious day. . . . I have had a cocktail or two, and am stretched out on a divan in front of the fire, smoking. At the edge of the divan, close enough for me to reach her with my hands, sits a woman not too young, but still good-looking and well-dressed—above all, a woman with a soft, low-pitched, agreeable voice. As I snooze she talks—of anything, everything, all things that women talk of: books, music, the play, men, other women. No politics. No business. No religion. No metaphysics. Nothing challenging and vexatious—but remember; she is intelligent; what she says is clearly expressed. . . . I observe the fine sheen of her hair, the pretty cut of her frock, the glint of her white teeth, the arch of her eyebrow, the graceful curve of her arm. I listen to the exquisite murmur of her voice. Gradually I fall asleep—but only for an instant. . . . Then to sleep again—slowly and charmingly down that slippery hill of dreams. And then awake again, then asleep again, and so on.
>
> I ask you seriously: could anything be more unutterably beautiful?

Mencken was, in the words of one admirer, "the nearest thing to Voltaire that America has ever produced."

He was born in Baltimore in 1880, died in Baltimore seventy-five years later, and lived his entire life in Baltimore, all but five years of it—when he was married to a woman who broke his heart by dying of meningitis—in the same house. When he was a child, he and his father once dropped in at the newsroom of a local paper. Fascinated by what he saw, Henry asked his father for a printing press for Christmas. Before the start of the new year, he was publishing a newspaper of his own and distributing it throughout the neighborhood. We do not know what it said. We are probably safe in assuming that at least some of the neighbors were enraged by at least some of the articles.

But Mencken was not supposed to grow up to be a journalist. He was supposed to follow his father, August, into the family's cigar business and had made up his mind to do so, unhappily but without complaint, seeking solace from a future in commerce with several hours of reading each night: the ancient Greek philosophers and playwrights, and such historians as Herodotus and Thucydides, Tacitus and Livy. Mencken was close to his father and would not think of contradicting him, no matter what his personal yearnings. When August died unexpectedly of a kidney infection early in 1899, Henry was as sad as any son would be in such a circumstance.

But a few days later, though admittedly with a heavy heart, he headed straight for the offices of Baltimore's papers and begged for jobs. He was turned down everywhere. He came back the next day to be turned down again. But he kept returning, often sitting in a corner of the newsroom for hours at a time, staring so intently at what was going on around him that he might have been memorizing every person's duties.

Finally, he was allowed by one or two of the papers to run some errands—down to the newsstand in the lobby to buy some candy or magazines, to the deli across the street to buy a sandwich and some chips. Then, a promotion: the editor of the *Baltimore Herald* gave him some copy to rewrite for a few back-page stories of no particular importance. He did them well and quickly. As a result, he was assigned to cover back-page stories himself. It did not take long for him to work his way up to the front of the paper, by which time, quite self-satisfied, he was smoking cigars, not manufacturing them, as he had intended all along.

For most of his professional life, Mencken was a columnist and editor at Baltimore's leading paper, the *Sun*, and in addition coedited two of the most influential magazines of the era, the *Smart Set* and the *American Mercury*. The latter positions required frequent trips to New York that he would rather not have made. It was too far from Baltimore. Mencken was the most parochial of men in his personal habits, the most worldly in his thinking.

He wrote a number of successful books, some of which were collections of his journalism, but he also turned out a biography of the philosopher Friedrich Nietzsche, as well as three volumes of memoirs and several others of social criticism. His most famous work, *The American Language*, remains to this day a classic study of how and why we Americans speak as we do. It is a resource both for linguists in their studies and nonlinguists in their quest for enrichment and entertainment.

Mencken was a portly and pugnacious fellow, but also a dapper one, almost always dressed in a suit, a tie of solid color, and a pair of suspenders that served as hitches for his thumbs as well as support for his trousers. His hair was parted in the middle, and usually flopped across his forehead symmetrically. His eyes could twinkle, his lips often curled up; he could, when he so desired, look positively cherubic.

But he was probably the most controversial public figure of his time, and a hard man for us to understand today, when so many of our values as a society are so different from earlier in the century. For instance, Mencken wrote critically of blacks, at one point going so far as to say, "The vast majority of the people of their race are but one or two inches removed from the gorilla." There is no denying the meaning nor the scathing intent of the words.

But how, then, to reconcile them with the kindness of his deeds? Mencken went out of his way to praise numerous black writers, Richard Wright and Countee Cullen among them, and to publish their work in his magazines and recommend their longer works to his book publisher, Alfred A. Knopf. After the black poet James Weldon Johnson spent some time talking with Mencken, he departed feeling "buoyed up, exhilarated." At Mencken's recommendation, Knopf would later publish Johnson's memoirs. Never did Mencken refuse to see a promising black writer; never did he fail to find something in the man's work to encourage.

Black literature would have received much less attention, not only in the twenties and thirties but today as well, had it not been for the extent to which Mencken promoted it.

It was the same with Jews. Mencken would excoriate them in print: "I believe that [Jews] are the most imprudent, and in fact idiotic, people ever seen on earth." Again, what are we to make of this? Why would he write something so antithetical to his personal habits? Mencken delighted in the company of Jews, might even have called more of them friends than he did members of any other ethnic group. He worked with them, played music with them, and drank beer with them all through Prohibition. Mencken's coeditor of the *Smart Set* and the *American Mercury*, George Jean Nathan, was Jewish, and for many years was the closest of all of Mencken's friends. Had Mencken lived in France, he would without question have taken Dreyfus's side, and would have done so in language that would have left M. Drumont and the editors of *La Libre Parole* apoplectic.

The closest one can come to a conclusion about matters like this is that although Mencken was basically a learned man, there were times when he found himself needing to drink from the deep well of his era's prejudices for no other reason than that he enjoyed the coruscating effects such draughts produced in his prose, even though that prose did not represent his true feelings, even knowing it was more self-indulgent than truthful, and therefore he found himself oblivious to the reactions of others.

More than any other person, H. L. Mencken changed the reading habits of America, giving publishers the courage to bring out the kinds of work they never would have considered before. As a critic, he wrote favorably about a new wave of authors whose views were rooted in the financial crises of the late nineteenth century, the cosmic meaninglessness of World War I, and in a few cases, the disillusionment of the Great Depression.

These were men, and a few women, who did not believe in happy endings, who insisted that sex play as important a role in fiction as it did in real life, who saw the lack of heroism in most so-called heroes and the lack of humanity in the so-called robber barons; who understood the psychological motives that haunted so many of their fellow human beings, who understood the lengths to which those people would go to rid themselves of their demons. Theodore Dreiser, Sinclair Lewis, F. Scott Fitzgerald, Ernest Hemingway, James Branch Cabell, James T. Farrell, William Faulkner, Erskine Caldwell, Willa Cather—these were among the authors who pushed back the frontiers of American fiction, who felt ill at ease in a nation they found ever more restrictive and intellectually barren. They eschewed plots that were meticulously contrived and neatly packaged, and similarly turned against characters who could easily be categorized as good guys or bad. Mencken championed almost all of them.

And it was he who first proclaimed Mark Twain's *Adventures of Huckleberry Finn* the finest novel ever produced in the United States, in fact as the starting point of American literature, a view that would later come to be shared by many others, including Hemingway.

He knew that the books he favored were not to everyone's taste, probably not even to most people's taste. That was part of their attraction to him:

> The revival of literary controversy . . . is bound to be good, for the arts are always benefited by free discussion, riotously carried on. . . . Thus it has always been in periods of great literary fecundity. . . . I look confidently for the day when college boys will ride a professor on a rail for praising the wrong book. If that day ever comes, it will be easier to write books than it has been in the past, and better ones will be written.

Perhaps to Mencken's surprise, that day did come. Better books *were* written, and many of them by authors, black and white and Jewish, whom H. L. Mencken demanded be noticed. That the day has now passed is a subject for another volume.

* * *

Like Mark Twain, Mencken occasionally felt bogged down by the truth, felt its hands reaching up out of the mire, pulling him down into realms of the mundane. He tried to free himself from their grasp. Or, as he put it, "My own talent for faking fell into abeyance after I left the City Hall [where he was eventually assigned by the *Herald*], and especially after I became city editor. In that office, in fact, I spent a large part of my energy trying to stamp it out in other men. But after I was promoted to managing editor, it enjoyed a curious recrudescence."

As a result, he produced a classic piece of journalism, what he called a "synthetic war dispatch," which was published in the *Herald*, on May 30, 1905. Let us allow him to tell the story. It is a long one, but Mencken's version cannot be improved upon:

> The war that [the synthetic dispatch] had to do with was the gory bout between Japan and Russia, and its special theme was the Battle of Tsushimi or Korea Straits, fought on May 27 and 28. Every managing editor on earth knew for weeks in advance that a great naval battle was impending, and nearly all of them had a pretty accurate notion of where it would be fought. Moreover, they all began to get bulletins, on May 27, indicating that it was on, and these bulletins were followed by others on the day following. . . . Everyone knew that a battle was being fought, and everyone assumed that the Japanese would win, but no one had anything further to say on the subject. The Japs kept mum, and so did the Russians.
>
> Like any other managing editor of normal appetites I was thrown into a sweat by this uncertainty. With the able aid of George Worsham, who was then news editor of the *Herald*, I had assembled a great deal of cuts and follow stuff to adorn the story when it came, and though the *Herald* had changed to an evening paper by that time, he and I remained at our posts until late in the evenings of May 27 and 28, hoping against hope that the story would begin to flow at any minute, and give us a chance to get out a hot extra. But nothing came in, and neither did anything come in on May 29—that is, nothing save more of the brief and tantalizing bulletins from the China coast. On the evening of this

third day of waiting and lathering I retired to my cubby-hole of an office—and wrote the story in detail. The date-line I put on it was the plausible one of Seoul, and this is how it began:

From Chinese boatmen landing upon the Korean coast comes the first connected story of the great naval battle in the Straits of Korea on Saturday and Sunday.

After that I laid it on, as they used to say in those days, with a shovel. Worsham read copy on me, and contributed many illuminating details. Both of us, by hard poring over maps, had accumulated a knowledge of the terrain that was almost fit to be put beside that of a China coast pilot, and both of us had by heart the names of all the craft in both fleets, along with the names of their commanders. Worsham and I worked on the story until midnight, and the next morning we had it set in time for our noon edition. . . . It described in throbbing detail the arrival of the Russians, the onslaught of the Japs, the smoke and roar of the encounter, and then the gradual rolling up of the Jap victory. No one really knew, as yet, which side had won, but we took that chance. And to give verisimilitude to our otherwise bald and unconvincing narrative, we mentioned every ship by name, and described its fate, sending most of the Russians to the bottom and leaving the field to Admiral Count Heihachiro Togo. . . . Thus the *Evening Herald* scored a beat on the world, and, what is more, a beat that lasted for nearly two weeks, for it took that long for any authentic details of the battle to reach civilization.

As an example of journalistic ethics, the behavior of Mencken and Worsham is lacking. But they were not trying to tell a lie; their goal was to accelerate the truth, and they were so well informed that they succeeded remarkably in their prediction. They knew the strength of the adversaries, the biographies of those who led them, the terrain on which they fought, the politics and history of the struggle—they could have taught a postdoctoral course on the region and its background. Impatience might have gotten the better of them when they published the story, but the facts would in time catch up. "Years later," Mencken concludes his account of the synthetic war dispatch in his autobiographical

Newspaper Days, "reading an astonishing vivid first-hand account of the battle by an actual participant, Aleksei Silych Novikov, I was gratified to note that we were still right."

At the time it was written, however, the Mencken-Worsham report was fiction, and it was the longest and most serious foray into the field Mencken had ever made. It was not, however, his first. As he had previously admitted, he had a talent for fakery that seemed to desert him when he left Baltimore's city hall. But while there, it sometimes burst into full flower.

Mencken often found it difficult to come up with a story. Many of the elected officials he needed to interview refused to talk to him, unwilling to take him seriously either because the *Herald* was not Baltimore's leading paper or because Mencken himself was of tender years and aggressive manner. So he became more aggressive in his pursuit of those officials, which only made them more resistant to him. One judge complained that Mencken "pestered me with unanswerable questions," and he wanted nothing to do with him. It was not an uncommon reaction to the young journalist.

One week things got so bad that as Mencken's deadline approached for the *Herald*'s Sunday edition, he had nothing to write about. Afraid to tell his editor that he would not be filing a story, he instead made one up, a tale that had nothing whatsoever to do with city hall. For some unknown reason, he wrote instead of a wild man wandering through the woods on the edge of Baltimore, making loud, unintelligible sounds like a wounded animal and apparently bent on some kind of havoc. "For weeks afterward the children of the neighborhood were kept indoors," Mencken later boasted, "and the cops kept on dragging in suspects."

A few weeks later, when city council members refused to allow him to cover their meeting, Mencken, like Samuel Johnson almost two centuries earlier, covered it anyhow. He knew what the agenda was, so he would at least get the topics right. Unlike Johnson, though, who tried to make his accounts as realistic as possible, Mencken added an element of parody, poking fun at what he was certain was the banality and bloviation of the discourse.

Mencken wrote one or two more articles like this, informing his readers falsely but giving them many a chuckle, as they too suspected their representatives of being long-winded and parched of serious thought. But shortly after the first article was published, the council members complained and Mencken was called into the office of the publisher of the *Baltimore Herald*, Colonel A. B. Cunningham, where he expected a severe tongue-lashing, perhaps even dismissal from his post. That is not what happened. "The Colonel glared at me in silence while I told my halting tale," Mencken later wrote, "and remained silent for a full minute afterward. Then he suddenly ran both hands through his vast mop of black hair, threw back his head . . . and emitted a whoop that must have been audible in St. Paul Street, five stories below."

Colonel Cunningham fully supported his young reporter. The *Herald* might not have been as prestigious or as popular as the *Sun* or some of the other Baltimore papers, but it was just as good, thought the Colonel, and Mencken was the equal of any of the other reporters. If the members of the city council refused to allow the young man admission to their assemblies, they deserved whatever version of those meetings Mencken decided to write.

Before long, Mencken was given a seat in the press row of Baltimore's city council. His accounts of the proceedings were factual and objective and, as the Colonel believed they would be, as accurate and perceptive as anyone else's. Mencken had resorted to lies in his previous tales of the city's rulers not because he wanted to, but because he was unfairly denied access to the truth. He cannot be faulted for his methods, and certainly not for the quality of journalism he produced after gaining admittance to government chambers.

*   *   *

Finally in the annals of Mencken tomfoolery there is the report of the first president of the United States to take a bath in the White House. The piece was called "A Neglected Anniversary," and in Mencken's own words, it was "my masterpiece of all time." In it, the author claimed that America's first bathtub was installed in the president's dwelling in 1842, enabling Millard Fillmore to be its initial occupant. But nobody, Mencken complained, was paying any attention to the event:

> On December 20 there flitted past us, absolutely without public notice, one of the most important profane anniversaries in American history—to wit: the seventy-fifth anniversary of the introduction of the bathtub into these states. Not a plumber fired a salute or hung out a flag. Not a governor proclaimed a day of prayer. Not a newspaper called attention to the day.

And not a single reader or reporter from another paper questioned the story. It is still repeated and believed, at least by some, to this day.

Henry Louis Mencken was a serious man. But there was a jolly and capricious side to him, and when he indulged it he was capable of expressing almost any point of view about almost any topic. He was, in fact, capable of inventing the topic, as in the case of the wild man in the woods. "What ails the truth," he once said, recalling Mark Twain, "is that it is mainly uncomfortable, and often dull. The human mind seeks something more amusing, and more caressing."

PART TWO

Hiding the Truth

NEWSPAPERS HAD TO BE CAREFUL ABOUT AMUSING AND caressing. Too much of it meant too little space for reality, and as the years wore on, the twentieth century grinding toward the twenty-first, reality was becoming ever more painful and pertinent, demanding to be taken ever more seriously. As a result, Americans were taking their newspapers more seriously. We were finally becoming expansive, accepting the notion of the wider world's importance to us as individuals.

In the past, we had accepted it sporadically. We had depended on the press during the Revolutionary War, the first event in colonial history in which all colonists had an equal interest in, and passion for, the outcome. We continued to depend on the press in the war's aftermath, during the struggles to interpret the Constitution, which were so bitter and powerfully felt as to be a kind of war themselves.

Would the United States be a federalist nation, with a strong central government as its master, or would it be republican, with a weak central government and most powers invested in the states?

Our interest in journalism waned for a time after that, as the significance of events seemed to diminish, to become less personal. Manifest Destiny might have been a crucial matter for the country's future, but people in Connecticut did not rush for their papers every day or week to see whether Wisconsin had been added to the Union yet.

But how long would the Union last? As the tensions that would lead to the Civil War began to build, and as Fort Sumter was fired upon in 1861, we Americans turned to our newspapers again, desperate to know which side had won which battle, and how important that victory or defeat might be in the long run—the long run of course meaning whether or not we were to remain a Union and, if so, whether freedom would be granted to all men or just men of pale skin.

But we still had not developed an ongoing relationship with newspapers, a constant reliance on the events they reported and interpreted; we did not yet feel the need for such involvement in either our own country or the nations of Europe unless there was a crisis of some sort. When the Civil War ended, we once again drifted away from perusing our catalogs of daily occurrence.

Not, however, for long. The groundwork had been laid; habits were ready to be formed. Few Americans were as consumed by the press as young Henry Louis Mencken, but starting around the time of his birth, the newspaper took its final steps to becoming, for many of us, a constant requirement.

The momentous events of the forty-year period between 1880 and 1920 commanded the attention of readers, and we insisted on being told about them either honestly or in a manner that we believed to be properly biased, which is to say, one that satisfied our prejudices precisely as we wanted them to be satisfied. In virtually all cases, we could find a paper to do what we wanted.

Leading up to the four crucial decades there was the Panic of 1873, one of our country's early examples of capitalism run amok, mostly to the detriment of those who could afford it least. Then came the Panic of 1884 and the Panic of 1893, one taking us virtually to the doorstep of the next and making up probably the three most serious financial crises in the United States before the Great Depression.

There were the assassinations of Presidents Garfield and McKinley. There was the Haymarket Square riot in Chicago, which resulted in eight policemen being killed and eight anarchists jailed for the crime; and there were strikes in the steel mills, on the railroads, and in the coal mines, threats of labor overwhelming management, of these anarchists, inevitably foreign-bred, hatching plots not just in Chicago but all over the country, overwhelming democracy.

There was the Spanish-American War, during which the *New York Journal* and the *New York World* might have gained circulation but were not alone. Other papers in other cities, papers that covered the war more responsibly, if in less detail, also attracted new readers, although not as many as Hearst and Pulitzer did.

There was Prohibition, the law that everybody broke, that made many of us wonder what our legislators had been drinking on the day they voted, and that, most insidiously, caused great numbers of Americans to lose respect in, or at least question the priorities of, the country's entire legislative process.

And, of course, shortly before Prohibition began, Americans were faced with the pointless, spirit-crushing, and long-enduring horrors of World War I.

But even before the first shots were fired, we had gotten into the habit of looking across the Atlantic more often and more warily than ever before, wondering whether events in Europe could have repercussions on our side of the ocean. It was a worldliness we had not demonstrated in the past—comprised, perhaps, of equal parts fear and curiosity.

The Irish were demanding Home Rule from Britain at the same time that the British were going to war with the Boers in South Africa. The Russians and Japanese were also at war, with Mencken and Worsham so accurately predicting the results of the Battle of Tsushima, while China's Boxer Rebellion was war-fare against foreign influence of all kinds.

The French had their Dreyfus Affair, which stirred Jews in the United States, and in the Pacific, New Zealand granted women the right to vote, which stirred their already agitated American counterparts.

What it all meant was that the number of men and women for whom newspapers were a kind of sustenance was increasing. "We shall endeavor to record facts on every public and proper subject," publisher James Gordon Bennett had written in the first issue of the *New York Herald* many years earlier, "stripped of ver-biage and coloring."

In the 1930s, a reporter named Walter Duranty went to greater lengths. He stripped his articles of information, and in the pro-cess acted more as a saboteur than a journalist. Nothing like it had ever happened before in an American newspaper—at least not on a subject of such great importance, one whose repercus-sions would be felt in the body politic for many years afterward.

11

Their Man in Moscow

WALTER DURANTY, WE ARE RELIABLY TOLD, "FANCIED himself a Citizen of the World, a man of knowledge and influence, culture and wit, born, symbolically, on the Isle of Man, and this particular bit of fluff he obligingly spun out for anyone who cared to listen. It sounded good and enhanced his image. But it wasn't true."

The truth was that Walter Duranty was born in Liverpool, England, a place much more difficult to romanticize than the Isle of Man, on May 25, 1884. The most curious thing about his early years was the antipathy he developed for his family. We have no clue about the reasons. Duranty never said anything to indicate he had been mistreated by his kin or that his childhood was a travail to him in any other way. He was not poor, not abused, not bullied, not sent to his room every night after dinner and denied creature comforts.

Yet when his mother died in 1916, Duranty did not attend the funeral, nor, as far as anyone knows, did he admit to any sadness or communicate more than perfunctorily with his father and sister. The latter, who never married, died in 1930 at the age of forty-five; once again, Duranty was unmoved and unresponsive.

Nor did he express any grief, or even interest, when his father passed away three years later, although this is more understandable, as at some point in Duranty's childhood his father deserted his wife, son, and daughter, never to return. Duranty's "only acknowledgment of his family in all these years," according to biographer S. J. Taylor, "was a curt document notarized in Moscow, authorizing his father's solicitors to sell the house, take their fee, and send him the proceeds."

Much later there was another acknowledgment of his parents' death, of the most perverse sort. In 1943 Duranty published his autobiography, *Search for a Key*, the title of the book suggesting that Duranty himself was trying to unlock the bitterness of his feelings. Instead, he secreted them away more deeply, writing that he was an only child, "ten years old, a thin little wisp of a boy, when my parents were killed in a train wreck, killed quick in a shattering smash. Without any pain or fear, in a smash like the burst of a bomb." Now an orphan, he said, he was sent to live with his father's uncle, about whom he revealed virtually nothing.

Walter Duranty was an accomplished liar long before he was an accomplished journalist.

The motive behind his killing off his parents at so early an age is unknown, and virtually unfathomable. But it is not hard to discern where he got the idea to commit the deed via a train wreck. At the age of forty Duranty was himself the victim of an accident on the rails, which severely injured his left leg. He had to undergo surgery, but was not optimistic about the results, fearing not just that his injuries would not heal, but that he would die as a result of them. He later wrote, "One may think one believes in a life after death, but it is generally a vague sort of belief, rather a hope than a belief, and death is the End. If you come very near to death and get familiar so to speak with death, you begin to feel that you have reached ultimate issues and that you don't give a damn."

He did not die. But after the surgery his leg began to ache, and when he went back to his doctor he was told that gangrene had set in and the leg would have to be amputated.

Isn't there any other way? Duranty asked the doctors.

No, he was told, there was not.

The operation took place and was a success, Duranty always told people with a smirk, as he spent the rest of his life hobbling around to his various assignments on a series of wooden legs, a blow to his dignity no less than an awkward and sometimes painful means of locomotion.

Dignity was important to Walter Duranty. He was a prim and slender man, with a long nose, a receding hairline, and unflinching eyes. In any gathering of journalists, he was certain to be the best dressed: the most expensive clothes, the most precise tailoring, the fewest wrinkles in the fabric. If he could have been Richard Harding Davis, he would have; but he didn't have the panache, not to mention the ethics, and there was that damned wooden leg of his, the injustice of which he seems never to have gotten over. Richard Harding Davis did not have to limp here and there like some kind of lopsided beggar collecting coins for his next meal on the corners of city streets. Richard Harding Davis glided. Walter Duranty looked as if he might topple at any moment.

By the time of his accident, despite having no particular ties to the United States, Duranty was living in Moscow and working as the *New York Times*'s correspondent in the Soviet Union. His first few years on the job were uneventful. Most of the articles he wrote were short, and the subjects were not the kind that permitted the sort of political analysis he would have liked to interject.

But in 1931 he would become famous, and then infamous, for his reports on dictator Joseph Stalin's Five-Year Plan, a series of ideas both wildly impractical and barbarically inefficient, that aimed at making the Soviets, in many ways among the most backward of peoples of the time, an industrial power. And the benefits of that power, Stalin said over and over, would be shared by everyone.

In truth they were shared by the fewest of the few. The Five-Year Plan never had a chance. Yet Duranty reported it as if Moses had carried it down from Mount Sinai on a pair of stone tablets. "Stalin is giving the Russian people," Duranty wrote in the *Times*, "the Russian masses, not Westernized landlords, industrialists, bankers and intellectuals, but Russia's 350,000,000 peasants and workers—what they really want, namely, joint effort, communal effort."

Later, Duranty broadened his focus from the Five-Year Plan, and the citizenry's joyous and unanimous embrace of it, which did not exist, to the Soviet society as a whole. In part nine of an encyclopedic thirteen-part series on life under Stalin, he insisted that the Soviet military, which was beefing up at the price of a continually worsening economy, was no threat to either Soviet civilians or the populations of other countries. The headlines of the articles tell the tale:

RED ARMY IS HELD NO MENACE TO PEACE
Depicted as a Purely Protective Organization and Likely to Remain So.

EUROPE'S FEARS BELITTLED
Talk of Horde Sweeping Forward to Conquest of World Called Anti-Soviet Propaganda.

DEFENSE FORCE FORMIDABLE
Foreign Attachés Admit Equality with Other Armies in Discipline Training and Equipment.

In part ten of the series, Duranty praised Stalin for his personal touch, the way he was able to bring the multitude of Soviet ethnic groups together in acceptance of both one another and the Five-Year Plan—that "joint effort, communal effort," an extraordinary feat of diplomacy:

> Every nationality in the union was allowed full linguistic autonomy and what might have seemed a dangerously lavish degree of cultural and political autonomy. Thus the Jews, who had remained alien expatriates under Czardom, received a small autonomous area with the promise of an independent republic if and when the number of the population concentrated at any one point should justify the augmented status.

Stalin met the challenge of the Soviet version of the melting pot, Duranty wrote, "by a compromise, of which even British genius for making two ends meet need not have been ashamed."

There were times in later reports when Duranty criticized the Soviet Union, but not often, not harshly, and always with a caveat. More than once he admitted that implementing the Five-Year Plan required a certain amount of coercion and even violence; after all, in its actual workings, the plan involved the denial of resources to certain segments of the population so that other segments could prosper more quickly. It involved ignoring some Soviet republics so that others would be strong enough to support Stalin's industrial goals for the good of the nation as a whole.

But Duranty saw nothing wrong with this; in fact he believed it was inevitable, given that the Soviets had so far to go to attain industrial parity with the West. In several of his articles, he even resorted to the old saw about the need to break eggs to make an omelet. But his fundamental conclusion, expressed in a number of ways in a number of pieces, was almost word for word that of Stalin: the Five-Year Plan would ultimately be a blessing to everyone in the Soviet Union, no matter where he lived, no matter what his ethnic background. What was required was simply patience. And, of course, unwavering belief in the system, whose name was Stalin.

The dictator could not have been more pleased with Duranty's coverage. He allowed himself to be interviewed by Duranty more than by any other member of the Western press. During their final meeting, at Christmas of 1933, Stalin expressed his appreciation. According to Duranty, writing sometime later, the dictator said, "You have done a good job in your reporting the U.S.S.R., though you are not a Marxist, because you try to tell the truth about our country and to understand it and to explain it to your readers. I might say that you bet on our horse to win when others thought it had no chance and I am sure you have not lost by it."

But he *had* lost, and by this time Duranty already knew it. He was simply not aware of the extent to which his defeat was being publicized, primarily in Great Britain but in the United States as well.

The Ukrainian famine of the early 1930s was one of the greatest and least-known tragedies of the twentieth century. It is called Holodomor, which means "death by hunger" in the native tongue, and the number of victims staggers the imagination. Some accounts put the total at seven million, some at six. According to reports that seem more reasonable, however, and are more recent, somewhere between two and a half and three and a half million people perished. And they suffered so much before they died that they became creatures less than human, the life almost visibly seeping out of them, hour by hour, as they sat in front of their huts or the stores in their villages, too weak to move until they finally toppled over. Making matters worse, which hardly seems possible, there was a typhus epidemic at the height of the famine. Death became the only cure, and people longed for it as they used to long for life.

It did not have to happen. Although some historians believe that a lack of rain and poor planting and harvesting procedures led to the disaster, they are not taken seriously by their brethren, dismissed as propagandists. The truth is that the Five-Year Plan was responsible for the famine, with Stalin dismissing Ukraine as expendable, too primitive in its ways to contribute to the country's future might and prosperity, unworthy of attempts to modernize it. The Soviet Union was a huge land, after all, its population of 160 million people scattered over 8,144,228 square miles and some 20 republics. The Five-Year Plan could not possibly provide aid to so many people, even once it reached the ten- or twenty-year mark.

But not only did Stalin not provide aid to Ukraine, he also terminated essential services to the region, as well as ordered his soldiers to plunder its crops for consumption in more industrialized regions. In some villages, the troops "made sweeps through private homes, the kinder agents leaving a modicum of food behind for the family's use but the more ruthless ones taking everything." In the words of one reporter, "the famine was an organized one," and it was probably the only example of good planning in the Soviet Union in the entire decade.

The devastation seems to have been first reported by a Canadian agricultural expert named Andrew Cairns, who was traveling through some of the country's southern republics. He was expecting to gather information on crop yields, land usage, and storage methods. Instead he saw scenes so ghastly that he had a hard time writing them down. But write them down he did, and in June 1932, he notified the British embassy in Moscow. The British ambassador then informed the foreign secretary in London, who, in paraphrasing Cairns, stated that "the only creatures who have any life at all in the districts visited are boars, pigs and other swine. Men, women, and children, horses and other workers are left to die in order that the Five Year Plan shall at least succeed on paper." Cairns also noticed another "horrible sight," a man who seemed to have been driven insane by hunger, "as he was going through all the motions of eating and rubbing his stomach with apparent satisfaction." But not for long. Soon, Cairns wrote, the man stopped moving. He closed his eyes and quickly and with a whimper died.

Not long after Cairns visited Ukraine, he was followed by a young British writer named Arthur Koestler, a socialist at the time, who thought that he was not just crossing a border when he entered the Soviet Union but passing into a realm of time travel, journeying from the nineteenth to the twenty-first century. But Koestler was a realist as well as a socialist. He would eventually write the modern classic *Darkness at Noon*, an anti-Stalinist novel about a man who has devoted his entire life to the Communist cause. In his declining years, however, he begins to question the Soviet system, and as a result is imprisoned, tortured, and forced to confess to crimes he did not commit.

Like Cairns, Koestler was totally unprepared for the desolation that awaited him. The starving children, he said, looked like "embryos out of alcohol bottles." And staring out the window of his train as it chugged through the ruined farmland, past crumbling homes and villages, was "like running the gauntlet; the stations were lined with begging peasants with swollen hands and feet, the women holding up to the carriage-windows horrible infants with enormous wobbling heads, stick-like limbs, swollen, pointed bellies."

As S. J. Taylor tells us, it was shortly after this that the Soviet government issued an order to railway officials. From now on, shades were to be pulled down, and kept down, on all trains running through the Soviet Socialist Republic of Ukraine. It was the simple Stalinesque solution to the problem.

The British Foreign Office, despite its knowledge that Ukraine was wasting away, becoming as unlivable a place as an ice cap, did nothing, not even notifying other agencies or nations that might have applied pressure to the Soviets. The Foreign Office was as cowardly in reacting to Stalin's policies as future prime minister Neville Chamberlain would be a few years hence in reacting to the threat of Hitler. The British indifference to the plight of Ukraine is terrible to consider. But it is not inexplicable.

Socialist influence in Great Britain at the time was powerful, not necessarily *in* the government but *on* it. Imagine the socialists as a present-day lobbying group in the United States, a supergroup, a combination of the American Association of Retired People (AARP) and the National Rifle Association (NRA), and you have some idea of their hold on the British government.

The socialist leaders at the time of the famine were a married couple, Sidney and Beatrice Webb, who were close friends of the equally socialistic playwright George Bernard Shaw. As reports from Ukraine were coming in, the Webbs were working on a book called *Soviet Communism: A New Civilization.* It was a two-volume tome that would treat the Five-Year Plan as if it were the U.S. Constitution. The Webbs were among many at the time, both in Great Britain and the United States, who, reacting to the Great Depression and the societal inequalities that had preceded it, caused it, and continued to exist, believed the Soviet Union the only place on earth that cared about the evils of capitalism and thus the only place that would eradicate them once and for all; the only place, that is, where true brotherhood and sisterhood could possibly exist on Earth.

Actually, the Webbs would have rejected the comparison of Stalin's blueprint to that of James Madison and Gouverneur Morris. They would have found the Constitution wanting, a document for keeping the haves entrenched and the have-nots permanently on the outside. The Stalin brand of socialism, on the other hand, was to them the model for the future, not just of the Soviet Union, but eventually the world. The Webbs and Shaw and their accomplices took Stalin at his word, not at his deeds. Reports like Cairns's, had the British socialists known about them, would have been dismissed as anti-Soviet blather. The British socialists, with words as their weapons, would crush those who intruded on their optimism with truth. Only through optimism, after all, could one survive so bleak a period as the early thirties, and the British socialists were soulless in their optimism.

Enter Malcolm Muggeridge, he of comical name but the most serious of purposes. The Moscow correspondent for the *Manchester Guardian*, Muggeridge might have possessed "delicate, ascetic features," which gave him an appearance of indolence at times, but this was an illusion; his "quick and lucid mind" was never at rest. Muggeridge came to the Soviet Union not just to report, but to exercise his bias; his main purpose was to promote socialism, to make of it a lasting and beneficent edifice, and his leanings were so strong that he planned eventually to give up his British citizenship and become a resident of Stalin's Garden of Eden.

But Muggeridge, like Koestler before him, quickly grew disenchanted. There was, for one thing, the day he went to Lenin's tomb. He was surprised not so much by the number of people marching past it with their heads bowed, their gait little more than a shuffle, their lips moving silently—but by something he noticed in their eyes, a perverse kind of reverence, as if Lenin were a holy figure to those who attended him. It seemed to Muggeridge antithetical to the principles of socialism, according to which all people were even more equal than under democracy. "I didn't quite like it," he wrote about his visit to the tomb. "The whole thing was tawdry."

As were his accommodations. Because of a lack of lodging in Moscow, the Muggeridges, although they would later end up in a house of their own, started out in a small room, actually a portion of a room, separated from the families in other portions by a curtain. There was enough space to sleep and cook but nothing else. The situation was especially trying for the Muggeridges because Malcolm's wife, Kitty, was ill at the time, and such crowding was hardly conducive to recovery. Sanitary conditions were poor all over Moscow, medical care almost nonexistent. And even here, in the capital of the great socialist experiment, most of the people seemed to be hungry. Few of them, Muggeridge thought, were getting three meals a day. Certainly they were not getting three meals' worth of nutrition. He did not understand why. He was under the impression from reading the socialist press in Britain that the Five-Year Plan had gotten off to a soaring start. And then he went to Ukraine.

Muggeridge initially wrote a series of three articles for the *Guardian* concentrating on this part of the country. His conclusion: the citizens of the republic were starving. "I mean starving in its absolute sense," he explained, "not undernourished as, for instance most Oriental peasants . . . and some unemployed workers in Europe, but having had for weeks next to nothing to eat." He found an "all-pervading sight and smell of death," and, talking to some of the peasants, was told that government troops had been frequent raiders of Ukraine in the past, stealing their food and even some of their farm implements. They had not been seen recently, however; there was so little left to steal.

A few days later, a former British official named Gareth Jones, who also had toured a number of Ukrainian villages, published his own findings in the *Guardian*. "Russia today is in the grip of a famine which is proving as disastrous as the catastrophe of 1921, when millions died."

About two months after that, Muggeridge, no longer the naif he was when he arrived in the Soviet Union, went on in other articles to describe the same kind of wretched sights that had previously horrified Cairns and Koestler. But Muggeridge, unlike Jones, saw them on a wider scale. "The struggle for bread in Russia has now reached an acute stage. All other questions are superfluous."

Muggeridge would soon begin writing a book called *Winter in Moscow*, which contains the most horrifying anecdote of all about the famine. Although the book was a novel, the anecdote, Muggeridge insisted, about Russian soldiers raiding the houses of peasants to find sacks of grain they had hidden, was true. The house in this case belonged to a woman with three children:

> The children had fallen asleep. There was nothing to give them when they awoke. No food and no hope of getting food. The sack of flour that she had hoarded so carefully and used so sparingly had been taken away. She went into an outhouse and fetched an axe, a little rusty from disuse, but still in fairly good condition. Her fingers felt along the edge of the axe, testing it; then, with well-directed strokes, she killed her three children one after the other, doing the job so skillfully that none of them awoke or uttered a cry. She tied each of the children up in a sack, and carried the sacks and the axe upstairs, and hid them amongst the rafters.

Then she went to town and summoned a Stalin lapdog named Comrade Babel and some of his soldiers, telling them that she had more grain for them, grain she had kept from them before. Now, though, she was ready to hand it over. The men followed her back to her house, and she took Comrade Babel upstairs. As he saw the sacks on the floor and bent over, amazed that he and his men had missed three such bulging bags on their previous visit, she buried the axe in his head. "Unlike the children, a dry soft cry came from him as he fell forward."

Once again, the accounts of observers, whether in novels or news reports, had no effect on British foreign policy. After all, the Soviet Union was a faraway place and its problems were equally remote, if not even exaggerated. But those problems were now beginning to attract attention in the United States, especially in the newsroom of the *New York Times*.

Even before this, Walter Duranty knew he had to try to assuage American concerns. His first attempt showed a distinct lack of commitment. "The famine is mostly bunk," he wrote to a friend in the summer of 1933. Then a little later, in the *Times*, he declared that "any report of a famine in Russia today is an exaggeration or malignant propaganda." One searches his thirteen-part series in vain for news of Ukraine, finding only, in the final part, a lengthier-than-usual article that appeared in the paper's Sunday magazine, a fleeting reference to Ukraine's fertile acreage, filled, in Muggeridge's sarcastic words, with "apple-cheeked dairymaids and plump contented cows." His refusal to report the truth about Ukraine was, by the standards of journalism, virtually a criminal offense.

Eventually, Duranty admitted there was a problem of some degree or other. In one of his *Times* pieces that ran after the series he allowed that the Soviet Union was plagued by occasional "food shortages," though it was not clear how serious they were, nor how pervasive. He did not go into detail.

But it was not enough, and eventually Duranty realized it. Yet he could still not bring himself to face the reality of Ukraine and what it revealed about the entire Soviet system. In September 1933, unable to ignore either the magnitude of events or the massive coverage of them by his competitors from other papers around the world, he was forced to go to Ukraine himself. He had never been there before. He was one of the last Western reporters based in the Soviet Union at the time to visit the republic, and his unhappiness at having to do so was as apparent as his bias.

For the first time, he told of famine in the devastated area. But note that in the following paragraph, which does not lead his report but appears more than halfway through, he blames the Ukrainians for the starvation and death more than the Soviet authorities:

> The blunt truth is that early last year, under the pressure of the war danger in the Far East, the authorities took too much grain from the Ukraine. Meanwhile, a large number of peasants thought they could change the Communist party's collectivization policy by refusing to cooperate. Those two circumstances together—the flight of some peasants and the passive resistance of others—produced a very poor harvest last year, and even part of that was never reaped.

Even worse, the paragraphs that precede this almost belittle the famine because now, supposedly, only a year after the suffering was at its worst, "the harvest is so good that the grain elevators, depots and delivery points are overcrowded to bursting." The headlines of the article, which were not written by Duranty, nonetheless reflect his views accurately:

BIG SOVIET CROP FOLLOWS FAMINE
Grain Packs Storehouses after Hunger Decimated Peasants in the Ukraine.

KREMLIN WINS ITS BATTLE
Nearly a Third of the Populace of Kharkov Was Mobilized for Work in the Fields.

It is true that the harvest of 1933 was better than that of the previous two years. But the storehouses were not packed with grain. For one thing, there were not enough healthy peasants in Ukraine to pick their crops, much less haul them from their fields to a depot of some sort. For another, there were not enough crops to fill a few toolsheds, much less storehouses. The bounty was simply not all that bountiful. It certainly was not, as Duranty proudly wrote, "a triumph, one might say, of organized effort and Soviet mass enthusiasm."

Thus did the *New York Times*'s man in Moscow apologize for his initial conclusion that the Ukraine famine, one of the greatest man-made catastrophes of all time, was mostly bunk.

In the United States, opposition to Duranty among his fellow journalists, which had been festering for some time, reached a peak. On the next to last day of 1934, more than a year after the article just cited, syndicated Washington columnist Joseph Alsop, writing his final column before retirement, said that Duranty "covered up the horrors and deluded an entire generation by prettifying Soviet realities. . . . He lived comfortably in Moscow, too, by courtesy of the KGB." He was "a fashionable prostitute." Alsop went on to say that "lying was his stock in trade." It was as powerful an indictment as a responsible journalist, which Alsop certainly was, had ever made publicly against a fellow analyst of events.

Eugene Lyons, the United Press correspondent in the Soviet Union during the famine, agreed with Alsop about Duranty's KGB connection and went further, stating that the Soviets had provided him with an apartment, a car, and a mistress named Katya. The KGB charge may or may not be true; it does seem that Duranty, if not actually in the agency's employ, did communicate with them from time to time. About the car and apartment there are differing opinions. That Duranty had a mistress named Katya, who depended on him for nylons and makeup, who reported back to government officials about him, and who, according to Muggeridge, even had a child by him, there is no doubt.

Muggeridge kept up a drumbeat of criticism against Duranty once he returned to Great Britain, continuing to produce articles and speak out in public forums about his fellow Englishman's duplicitous reporting. Duranty was, he proclaimed, "the greatest liar of any journalist I have met in fifty years of journalism." Why? Muggeridge concluded that Duranty was less fascinated with socialism than he was with power, that he worshipped power, wanted nothing more than to kneel in its presence, to witness it in action. In one of his autobiographical volumes, Muggeridge, by this time a devout Christian with no socialistic inclinations whatsoever, wrote that Duranty "admired Stalin and his regime precisely because they were so strong and ruthless. 'I put my money on Stalin,' was one of his favourite sayings. It was the sheer power generated that appealed to him."

In fact, Muggeridge said, "I had the feeling . . . that in . . . justifying Soviet brutality and ruthlessness, Duranty was in some way getting back for being small, and losing a leg, and not having the aristocratic lineage and classical education he claimed to have. This is probably, in the end, the only real basis of the appeal of such regimes as Stalin's, and later Hitler's; they compensate for weakness and inadequacy."

There is no way of knowing what course history would have taken if Walter Duranty had reported on the Ukrainian famine quickly and honestly. The course it *did* take, as far as the role of American journalism is concerned, was not his fault alone. Once Duranty acknowledged Ukraine's starving millions, which could have been the first step in acknowledging that Stalin's Five-Year Plan was the vision of a madman, U.S. newspapers other than the *Times* remained slow to report the story, slower still to send reporters to the Soviet Union to investigate for themselves. And before long, with the Soviets becoming America's allies in World War II, such an investigation was out of the question.

What can be said with certainty is this: by sanitizing his reports as he did, Duranty encouraged support for Stalin in the United

States. As a result, those who believed in him most had more time to organize, increase their numbers, and build a foundation of chimerical socialist fantasies before the truth of Soviet barbarity was known. But what was built upon that foundation?

The uncertainty creeps in already. In the long run, did Duranty's delays, and the minimal reporting of other Americans after him, embolden Stalin to believe that he could behave even more savagely toward his own people than he had already done, not having to fear censure from abroad? Did they lead Americans to more disenchantment with capitalism than was warranted? Did they lead to more hostility between Americans who believed in the Soviet experiment and those who did not? Did they lead to greater enemy infiltration of the American power structure than would have otherwise occurred? In the longest run, did they allow enough infiltration so that when Joe McCarthy *occasionally* got it right, or close to right, in his anti-Communist rantings of the fifties, the reason can be traced all the way back to the *New York Times*'s man in Moscow in the thirties?

There can be no answers here, only speculation.

By 1949, Walter Duranty was sixty-five and living in desolate retirement in the United States. He had long since been dismissed by the *Times* and was becoming frantic about his legacy in the world of journalism. Whether he admitted to himself that his reporting in the Soviet Union was dishonest no one can know; he was certain, however, that this was the opinion of the majority of others in his field, and he knew he had to make amends.

His attempt to do so was a book called *Stalin & Co.: The Politburo, the Men Who Run Russia.* "Whatever Stalin's apologists may say," he wrote—and he was of course among the leaders of those apologists—"1932 was a year of famine in Russia." He described "the mass migration of destitute peasants from the countryside to towns and cities, epidemics of typhus and other diseases of malnutrition; great influx of beggars into Moscow and Leningrad." He continued to insist that the citizens of Ukraine were at least partly to blame for their woes, but now placed the blame primarily with Soviet officials.

It was too little, too late. Duranty died in Florida eight years later, and to this day his reputation is, as it deserves to be, one of the most tarnished in the history of print journalism in the United States.

In 1932, Walter Duranty was awarded the Pulitzer Prize in the category of "correspondence" for his thirteen-part series on the Soviet Union. Despite its pro-Stalin slant, the pieces contain much information never known before in the West, and they demonstrate the results of solid research and thoughtful, if tilted, commentary.

Yet ever since, journalists and foreign policy specialists have demanded that the Pulitzer committee revoke its decision. In the past seventy-seven years, hundreds of different people have sat on the committee. Some of them have agreed that the prize should be taken back. Others have disagreed. But in all that time, the committee as a whole has refused to change its mind. Walter Duranty was honored for what he revealed, not what he secreted away from public view for so long, refusing even to believe it himself. For that, the various committees have always concluded, he deserves to be a winner of the prize that Joseph Pulitzer had endowed for journalistic excellence.

In 2008, the government of Ukraine, as well as those of several other nations, officially recognized the Holodomor as an act of genocide.

12

Sins of Omission

XCEPT FOR THOSE TIMES WHEN HE WAS DENYING THE Ukrainian famine, ridiculing it as bunk, what Walter Duranty demonstrated is that it is possible for a journalist to lie without actually misstating the facts, that the same results can be achieved by simply turning one's back on the truth. Actually, the latter is an easier way to lie than misstating the facts; it does not require any energy or special storytelling skills, nor does it require that one remember the details of the falsehood so that he can recall them later. One can be passive, not active. For this reason, ignoring the truth has been an attractive alternative to many dishonest journalists over the years for many different reasons, from ideological bias to financial gain to sheer indolence. In New Orleans, in 1927, the motive was, of all things, civic pride.

Late in the winter of that year, a man named John Klorer, a local government official who had formerly been an engineer, was asked to inspect the city's levees. There had been reports of severe flooding on the Mississippi north of New Orleans, and city officials wanted to make sure that they were prepared when the high waters made their way past them into the Gulf of Mexico. Thinking he had no time to waste, Klorer went promptly to his task.

He found some sections of the levees in good shape, but others weakened to such an extent that, in his opinion, they needed to be shored up immediately. That was what he reported to the city council, where he received a respectful but not enthusiastic hearing. It would cost money to shore up the levees. It would make the city look bad to admit it had let them deteriorate. It would frighten the townsfolk to know the levees were not ready for the churning river.

Some members of the council wanted to follow Klorer's recommendation. Some did not. Those who did were overruled by three men who held no positions in local government, men who knew nothing whatsoever about the condition of either the levees or the raging waters heading toward them. They were Jim Thomson, Robert Ewing, and Esmond Phelps, and it was because of them that the levees would remain as they were. After all, there had been a flood in 1922, hadn't there? The levees had held back then, hadn't they? They would be just as likely to hold now, wouldn't they?

The Red Cross did not believe the city council's decision. Nor did it care about the flood of 1922. It sprang into action immediately, setting up relief stations throughout the city, preparing for the worst as the disaster upriver surged toward them. It had no faith in the levees, no faith in the three men who had ignored Klorer's warning.

The residents of New Orleans were confused. Why was the Red Cross preparing for the worst when the city's elected officials, having heard the latest reports, had decided there was no reason to act? Another question: everyone knew about the damage that the river was causing elsewhere in the state, and in other states; why were the local newspapers not keeping them better informed? "No word of this activity appeared in any New Orleans paper," says historian John Barry. "As the Mississippi grew more threatening, New Orleans papers gave it less space. This lack of news attention was no accident."

Barry exaggerates and in fact contradicts himself. If no word of this activity appeared in any New Orleans paper, how could a paper give it less space as the threat grew greater? There is nothing less than zero. In truth, the papers did cover the flooding to the north; there was just not enough coverage and not enough detail to warn a reader sufficiently. There was not, in other words, enough of a connection between what was happening within a hundred miles or so of New Orleans and what was likely to happen in the city several days hence.

Barry is correct, however, when he says this inadequate reporting was not an accident. The city's newspapers had a history of aversion to bad news. Three years earlier, a ship from Greece had docked in New Orleans with a sailor on board suffering from bubonic plague. He was taken immediately to a hospital and isolated from other patients. His condition was grave.

When the New Orleans Association of Commerce found out about the man, it pleaded with the papers not to run the story. It would frighten away tourists. It would even frighten away natives, who might be afraid to leave their homes and would therefore not spend money in shops and restaurants.

The Association of Commerce did not have to plead hard. The four major dailies in New Orleans either ignored the story altogether or claimed, in a paragraph or two buried in the back pages, that the sailor had an ailment other than the plague. He would be fine. He had been quarantined merely as a precaution. That his symptoms resembled those of bubonic plague was merely a coincidence. His actual ailment had not yet been identified. The papers blathered on.

But the people who worked at the hospital knew the truth, and despite warnings from their superiors to keep silent, they began to tell friends and family. Word circulated through the city, one person informing another in tones that were whispered headlines. As a result, the following year, 1925, "the papers helped the

Association of Commerce circulate seventy-two different articles boosting New Orleans, including a piece claiming that it was one of the healthiest cities in America."

The four newspapers in question were run by Thomson, Ewing, and Phelps. So was much of the rest of New Orleans. There was nothing special about any of the men. Every city has its power brokers. These three just happened to be New Orleans's in the mid-twenties. In another decade, they would be replaced by three other men who would be equally forgotten after another ten years had passed.

Thomson, who, as seems to be the case with so many pompous men, liked to be called "the Colonel" despite a lack of military background, oversaw two papers, the *New Orleans Morning Tribune* and the *New Orleans Item*. Yet he had always shown more of an interest in politics than in journalism. He "had worked in several presidential campaigns and, using family like a medieval potentate cementing alliances, became the son-in-law of the Speaker of the House and the brother-in-law of a senator, with his niece married to a senator." The *Morning Tribune* and the *Item*, then, were meant to promote his political interests more than the public good. He paid just enough attention to them to make sure they did not stray from either the Democratic party line or the service of his personal interests. When they did, he saw that they strayed back the following day and that those responsible were punished.

Ewing, the head man of the *New Orleans States*, was also a politician at heart, once serving as a Democratic national committeeman and afterward keeping his contacts alive as much as he could, often by seeing to it that the *States* published stories that read more like Democratic press releases than investigative journalism. Ewing also served as a thorn in the side of several New Orleans mayors, as he was constantly demanding, and usually receiving, favors for his friends—sometimes jobs, sometimes higher pay for those already employed. One of those mayors described him as "the most insatiable patronage grabber" in the city. Like Boss Tweed, although on a smaller scale, Ewing dispensed favors as well as demanded them. He considered each of the former an IOU made out specifically to him, and he did not hesitate to call them in.

Phelps too had a political background, but despite lacking any journalistic training, he was the most interested of the three in his paper, the *New Orleans Times-Picayune*. Although he was only a member of the paper's board, not even its chairman, he took an extraordinarily active role in the *Times-Picayune*'s daily operations. He called the newsroom several times a day and paid a personal visit once or twice a week. He loved to give advice to reporters and editors—or, as the reporters and editors would have put it, loved to distort the news, and sometimes turn his back on it, for his own gain and that of his cronies. His stature in the city was such that he always got his way. The *Times-Picayune* was a reflection of the city not so much as it was but as Esmond Phelps intended it to be.

The three men were not close friends. In fact, they were often at odds, engaged in power struggles that resulted in bitterness and resentment, sometimes using their papers to carry out attacks against one another. But in the early spring of 1927, as the floodwaters continued to roar toward New Orleans, they put aside their animosities and organized themselves and their associates into a kind of information-withholding monopoly.

First they assured the general public that they would *not* withhold information; they would publish news of the Mississippi's behavior quickly and honestly so that the citizens would be ready for whatever happened. They did not. Then they assured the city's business interests that they would stifle the news if it looked bad for them. This was the promise they kept.

On April 9, 1927, the *New Orleans Morning Tribune* printed an article about damage caused upriver by the flooding. Then, right next to it, under a larger headline, it printed another article about what would *not* happen when those waters made their way farther south. With the weather bureau predicting a possible river stage three inches higher than in 1922, previously the highest ever recorded, Guy L. Deano, president of the Orleans levee board, said that New Orleans was amply protected by her reinforced levees. "We were able to take care of the flood stage of 1922 and since then a survey of all levees has been made," he said. "Whatever low gaps there were have been built up. The levees in Orleans parish are in much better condition than they were in 1922. We do not expect any trouble."

Peter Muntz, secretary of the board, concurred with President Deano's opinion that New Orleans had nothing to fear. But the city was not amply protected. The levees had not been reinforced. They were not in better condition than they had been in 1922. The whole story was, quite simply, a fairy tale.

It is hard to imagine what Thomson, Ewing, and Phelps were thinking, impossible to believe they did not realize what harm they were likely to cause with their monkey act of see no evil, hear no evil, speak no evil toward the approaching floodwaters. They did not want to alarm anyone, but for the most selfish of reasons. When alarming circumstances exist, only an alarmed—or at least an informed—citizenry can react to them properly.

But Thomson, Ewing, and Phelps would not allow such news to roll off the presses. There had been reams of information about the 1922 flood, and what had happened? New Orleans had been made to appear an uncivilized outpost at the whim of nature. And the damage, once all was said and done, hadn't been that bad. Not really. To the city's reputation, yes. To the city itself, no.

Well, nothing like that was going to happen again. Maybe the waters would not be so high this time. Maybe there would be no reason for angst, for bad press, for financial loss. Why not look at the bright side of flooding so bad that a man upriver could not see the tops of the waves as they thundered toward what was left of his town? Why not whistle a happy tune and hope to be on key?

So it was that the three monkeys made a kind of Faustian bargain, only dumber: for the sake of a few days of good press in New Orleans, good press that a lot of people had already begun to doubt, the city's ruling triad was laying the groundwork for something much more likely—years of bad press around the nation and a depressed economy at home for a similar period.

In the end, however, it did not matter. For perhaps the first time in his canny and timeless career, the all-knowing Faust got caught unaware. Through the most fortuitous and unforeseen of circumstances, the city of New Orleans would be saved.

The great Mississippi flood of 1927 was the worst in the history of the United States. At one point, the river was seventy miles wide, and more than twenty thousand square miles of land, mostly farmland, were underwater in Illinois, Arkansas, Missouri, Mississippi, and Louisiana. Seven hundred thousand people were driven from their homes. More than 1.3 million acres of corn were not planted, and the same was true for almost half a million acres of hay, not to mention more than two million acres of other crops, including cotton, soybeans, and sorghum. Twenty-five thousand horses lost their lives, as did twice as many head of cattle.

In New Orleans, fifteen inches of rain fell in slightly more than eighteen hours. But, as it turned out, the city did not suffer nearly as much damage as it might have. At the last minute, state engineers surprised everyone by deciding to plant thirty tons of dynamite on the levee in the nearby village of Caernarvon. When they set it off, a huge section of the levee collapsed, causing the floodwaters to take a mighty detour into the village, submerging it for a time and causing major destruction in two counties, or, as Louisiana calls them, parishes.

So as the Mississippi continued to make its way south, it was calmed somewhat, the pressure eased, and it became even calmer as levees in other small towns gave way without the aid of dynamite, rerouting even more of the surging river. By the time the waters reached New Orleans they were still surging, but not nearly as much. The city, even with its inadequate levees, a few of which gave way just as Klorer had predicted, and the enormous rainfall it was still receiving, managed to survive. The cleanup lasted only a few days, and business and social activity were back to normal after only a week or so.

Thomson, Ewing, and Phelps were lucky. But their behavior is not to be excused. When they published their articles of reassurance, and when they refused to emphasize articles telling the truth about the deadly, overflowing Mississippi heading toward New Orleans and the towns that had been overrun in its path, they had no idea what would eventually happen at Caernarvon. In retrospect, they must be judged on their actions, not the unexpected intervention of state engineers, of which they had been totally ignorant. Had it not been for that intervention, Thomson, Ewing, and Phelps would have been remembered as three of the greatest villains ever known to journalism. Instead, they are not remembered at all. For a time, in fact, they were hailed as civic benefactors, calming influences in a literal time of storm. Then history, as is its way, forgot them.

Fifty years later, on March 27, 1977, Pan American World Airways Flight 1736 took off from Los Angeles International Airport, bound for Las Palmas on Gran Canaria, an island off the northwest coast of Africa. It would make an intermediate stop at New York's JFK. On the same day, KLM Flight 4805 set out from Amsterdam's Schiphol Airport, also bound for Las Palmas. Both planes were Boeing 747s. Both planes had more empty seats than usual. Both planes would fail to arrive at their destination. They would crash into each other that afternoon at Los Rodeos Airport in the Spanish Canary Islands, killing 583 people. Not counting casualties on the ground, it was the deadliest aviation accident of all time.

"Neither of the planes had been scheduled to stop at the airport where they collided," the next day's *New York Times* reported. They had been diverted after a bomb went off in a florist's shop at the Las Palmas airport and a phone call had been received threatening a second bomb, to be placed somewhere else at Las Palmas, that would cause far more damage. The call came from a group calling itself the Movement for the Independence and Autonomy of the Canaries Archipelago. Authorities had never heard of the group, but they took the call seriously. They shut down Las Palmas and diverted air traffic to several nearby airports. The Pan Am and KLM flights were among five 747s rerouted to Los Rodeos, which is known today as Tenerife North, and which, in 1977, had but one runway, and it had not been built to support jumbo jets.

While there the planes refueled and the passengers on one or two of them were given a few minutes in the terminal to buy snacks, use the restrooms, and stretch their legs. Then they were herded back into their seats to grumble about the delay and wait for clearance to take off. When it finally came a few hours later, Las Palmas officials now certain that there would be no second bomb, the planes at Los Rodeos were notified to start their engines.

For Captain Jacob Van Zanten of KLM, the signal came not a moment too soon. In fact, it might even have come a few moments too late. According to Dutch law, pilots were required to take rest periods a certain number of hours after their flights initially took off. "Flying after the start of his mandated rest period was out of the question [for Van Zanten]—it wasn't just against policy; it was a crime punishable by imprisonment." Van Zanten checked his watch. His hand twitched on the throttle.

Adding to his anxiety was the layer of fog that had suddenly begun to envelop the airport. It was crucial, Van Zanten believed, that he take off immediately. Within seconds, apparently, he could; for some reason, he seems to have believed that the control tower had given him permission to begin taxiing. Unfortunately, and no more explicably, the Pan Am crew believed that it had been given permission as well.

The two airplanes, facing each other at opposite ends of the runway, began to inch toward each other, slowly at first and then more quickly. It is not known whether the fog prevented the pilots from seeing each other's craft, but in retrospect, what was happening now looked like a game of chicken that neither pilot wanted, but neither thought was his responsibility to avoid.

The KLM flight was going 165 miles an hour, full takeoff speed, at the moment of impact. The sound of the crash, as described by people standing nearby, was like thunder in their eardrums, and it continued to echo long after the planes had come together. The crash was followed by a burst of flame so intense that it caused the onlookers to back up; it was the heat of a blast furnace, of incineration, of skin feeling as if it were peeling off the body. After a few moments other sounds could be heard—of screams, of people starting to run for cover, of sirens in the distance.

A later investigation by officials from the United States, Spain, and the Netherlands would assign a number of causes to the disaster. Among them:

- The KLM plane had begun taxiing without proper clearance from the control tower.

- Radio messages between the two planes and the tower were indecipherable because everyone was talking at the same time.

- The Los Rodeos Airport was not equipped to handle the air traffic that had been diverted to it that day.

- The air traffic controllers were also overwhelmed.

- It was charged, although never proven, that the controllers were listening to a soccer game on the radio when the KLM and Pan Am planes began rolling toward each other.

None of the questions has ever been answered to anyone's satisfaction. Neither has the most obvious. Why did the pilots keep on their collision course rather than stop or veer off in different directions out of simple self-preservation? Was the fog *that* thick? Why would anyone play chicken when the stakes were so horribly high?

A few days after the accident, newspapers reported that Lee Fried, a student at Duke University in Durham, North Carolina, had predicted the disaster a week before it happened. He had written his prediction on a sheet of notepaper, sealed it in an envelope, and then placed it in the safe of Duke's president, where it could not be tampered with.

When the envelope was opened and the sheet of paper read aloud before a number of witnesses, including the president and other school officials, it was found to contain the following message: "Five Hundred Eighty-three Die in Collision of 747s in Worst Disaster in Aviation History." Almost as one, the witnesses, stunned beyond comprehension, drew in a collective breath. They looked at one another through suddenly widened eyes. What was going on here? How could Fried have known? What kind of powers did this Lee Fried possess?

The answer was that he possessed the powers of a trickster, not those of a prophet.

James Randi, a magician known as the Amazing Randi but who has devoted more of his professional life to debunking rather than performing, does not believe that human beings possess extrasensory abilities. He does not believe we can communicate with the dead or communicate with the living telepathically. He does not believe we can bend spoons by force of will or cite the details of an airline crash that has not yet happened. He does not, in short, believe in magic except as a display of gimmickry. And he has written scores of articles and conducted scores of demonstrations proving his point, providing practical explanations for what seem to be otherworldly phenomena. There remain, however, doubters, which is to say, those who insist on powers beyond the quotidian and are bitter about Randi's constant efforts to spoil their various parties.

About three months after Fried's envelope was opened, Randi spoiled this one. In an article in a magazine called the *Humanist*, he said,

> I have in my possession seventeen newspaper clippings dealing with that prediction. Some are from England, one from Canada, one from France, and the rest are from the United States. In that

collection is ample proof that the media are editing news items to slant them toward promoting belief in the paranormal; for in *all but one* [italics in original] of these articles, an important section is cut out. That section reveals that Fried, unlike other claimed "psychics," is quite clearly admitting that he is a conjuror and makes no claim to divine inspiration or to supernatural abilities.

The *New York Daily News* was the only paper to include the otherwise omitted section, and it makes all the difference.

Fried, eighteen, an electrical engineering student from New Orleans who described himself as an amateur magician, said in an interview, "I don't claim to have any supernormal abilities, ESP or anything else like that. I don't claim to have any of these things. I've been a performing magician for some time."

Another claim Fried did not make was that he had good judgment. To use an airplane crash that killed almost six hundred men and women as the basis for a magic trick only a matter of days after the crash occurred is, to say the least, insensitive to both the magnitude of the disaster and the pain of the victims' families.

But the larger point is not Fried's timing; it is the actions of the sixteen papers that wrote about his prediction without including the disclaimer. There are many who disagree with Randi's explanation, many who do not believe that the disclaimer was omitted to promote a belief in the paranormal. Surely that was the effect among some people, a number of Americans suddenly given reason to accept the presence of a seer in their midst, perhaps the prophet of a new faith. But the newspapers intended nothing so otherworldly.

Instead, for financial reasons, the press ignored Fried's stated lack of supernatural abilities. Publishers had known, since the days of William Randolph Hearst, if not before, that the more sensational their stories, the more product they would sell. And now, the age of broadcast having arrived, such stories would attract more viewers for television and listeners for radio.

In this case, the newspapers and broadcast outlets had three choices. The first, and most responsible, was not to run the story, as it had no news value whatsoever and in fact served to trivialize the importance of the crash, making it secondary to Fried's showmanship. The second was to do what the *Daily News* did, run the story with the caveat. The problem with this option is that when you acknowledge Fried was a prestidigitator rather than a psychic, you emphasize the pointlessness of his deed. Magic tricks are not news. Why treat this one as if it were? The third was to do what the other sixteen newspapers did, make it seem as though Fried was a man of inexplicable gifts and, at least by implication, raise the possibility that he might be able to use those gifts not just to predict catastrophes in the future but to prevent them. Lee Fried, Superman of the mind.

But, ultimately, Fried was a young man who probably ended up wishing he had not done what he did. Writes Randi about the eighteen-year-old in the weeks after the story, "Fried says that he has received requests for assistance in locating missing persons, medical advice, and other boons that 'psychics' claim to be able to grant. And the believers are ready to pay." Just as the newspapers would be ready to print.

Some years earlier, the *Wall Street Journal* had demonstrated that it was possible to tell a lie not by omitting the truth, but by hiding it away in the interior pages of the paper. In other words, a publication does not have to ignore reality to provide a disservice to its customers; it needs only to report it in a context that makes it seem less significant than it really is.

Burying the lead, this is called in the news business, and it is usually not a nefarious practice. It is, rather, a mistake by the reporter or the result of an honest difference of opinion between the reporter and those who supervise or read his story. What follows, however, is an account of lead-burying that reflected a sameness of opinion between reporter and readers, and was *so* nefarious, not to mention so obvious, that it is in its own unintended way laughable.

The *Wall Street Journal* was founded as a telegraphic news service in 1907, but it took on its present form as a conventionally formatted newspaper in 1941. That year, under the leadership of managing editor Bernard Kilgore, who would later go on to be the paper's CEO, its circulation was 33,000. By the time Kilgore passed away in 1967, the circulation was 1.1 million and growing, and the *Journal*, despite being named after a single street in a single American city, had become the country's first great national newspaper.

The *Wall Street Journal* was always a business publication, always a conservative publication—the two, of course, going hand in hand. It supported tax breaks for investors, less government interference for corporations, and Republicans for president. It was especially hopeful of the latter in 1940, when the Democrat, Franklin Delano Roosevelt, seeking an unprecedented third term, seemed especially vulnerable.

One of the reasons had to do with the very fact of precedent. As the first incumbent in American history to seek a third term, Roosevelt seemed to some voters megalomaniacal. Two terms had been good enough for Washington, Jefferson, and Lincoln— why shouldn't they be good enough for Roosevelt? Even some of those who supported him were puzzled. There was a war on the horizon, and Americans did not like to change chief executives at so critical a time; they would like to have defended Roosevelt on the grounds that he was merely doing his duty, putting his concern for country above his desire to leave the White House behind and retire to Hyde Park. But Roosevelt, like Wilson before him, had insisted that the United States would not enter the war. Thus there was no reason for him to stay on. What was a person to make of all this?

And what was he to make of surveys revealing that the majority of Americans still respected Roosevelt and believed he had done a good job, at the same time that fewer said they would vote to reelect him a second time? Perhaps they simply thought that the president, capable though he had been, had overstayed his welcome. It was nice to have had him around for all these years but it was time for him to go now, if for no other reason than that this was the time when all of his predecessors had gone.

Republicans certainly wanted him to go. Although willing to give him a chance in the woeful early days of the Great Depression, they had since come to despise him. They thought him not just the wrong man for the wrong job at the wrong time but, worse, a traitor to his people. To a degree, it was true.

Roosevelt's father, although not as wealthy as the so-called robber barons, had amassed at least a small fortune in coal, while his mother had inherited a million dollars from her own father, who had made it selling opium to the Chinese during America's Civil War. As for Roosevelt himself, his pedigree could hardly be improved upon; he had gone to Groton, Harvard, Columbia Law, and even clerked on Wall Street for a time. He should have been more sympathetic to the desires of the moneyed classes. He should have been less concerned with people who did not have the Ivy League in their backgrounds. He should have been a subscriber to the *Wall Street Journal*.

But even though Roosevelt's answer to the Depression, a basketful of programs called the New Deal, began by trying to strike a balance between the needs of big business and the needs of the laboring man, Roosevelt had in time concluded that the latter's needs were greater, and the New Deal began to tilt leftward. It provided jobs for the unemployed or underemployed, allowed people on the payrolls of private business to join unions, and perhaps most controversial of all, at least as far as some Republicans were concerned, insisted that working men and women invest a portion of their paychecks with the government so that they would have money to live on when they retired. The government had no business, Republicans believed, coddling people like this.

And Roosevelt would have gone even further had the Supreme Court not struck down even more of his coddle-the-working-man measures. The president, it was charged by those on the extreme right, was "killing free enterprise; he was destroying the instinct for competition; he was regimenting and cheapening the whole American society; he was ending the power of management to manage and the willingness of the worker to work; he was sapping the vital strength of capitalism, and so on, and so on."

Roosevelt also seemed vulnerable in 1940 because his opponent, Wendell Willkie, a corporate lawyer who had never before held public office, had a certain "rough-hewn, benignly ursine Midwestern integrity." He also had a large, full-cheeked smile that came to him naturally, rather than as an effort, something he called upon as a campaign device. His hair was rumpled, his clothes rumpled; he did not have the look of a corporate lawyer, but rather of the fellow next door, someone you could trust not to pervert democracy to get you back on your feet, but who would help you stand again by giving you sound advice and timely exhortations that would, in the long run, be much better not only for you but for the nation as a whole.

Even the Republican's foe was impressed, Roosevelt admitting to a friend at one point during the campaign that he could not help but admire Willkie, albeit grudgingly. He had not felt that way about Herbert Hoover in 1932 or Alf Landon in 1936.

By the summer of 1940, Willkie was trailing Roosevelt in various public opinion polls by between five and ten points. But as election day grew closer, the margin narrowed. The Republican arguments against Roosevelt seemed to be taking hold, as did a new one, which was whispered more than shouted from the stump. Agree with him or not, even a Republican had to admit that the president was a hardworking man. Maybe *too* hardworking. Didn't he seem worn out sometimes? Weren't his cheeks sagging a bit, his eyelids drooping? Wasn't his facial tone more gray than rosy? What were the chances he would survive a third term in the world's most demanding job? After all, as a Yale man named George Frederick Gundelfinger wrote in a pamphlet he distributed anonymously, Roosevelt was "a crippled imbecile, paralyzed in body and mind." Didn't he deserve to retire?

The voters did not want him to. On November 5, 1940, almost fifty million Americans marked their ballots, with 27,313,945 of them deciding to give Franklin Delano Roosevelt a third term as president, and 22,347,744 choosing to give Willkie a first term.

The *Wall Street Journal* covered the story on November 7, 1940, with its eyes closed and its teeth gritted. It was the most embarrassing display of reporting on a presidential election that the country has ever witnessed from a major newspaper.

On page 1 there was but a single article related to the voting, and it did not even mention the name of the winner.

WASHINGTON—A reshuffling of the personnel and policies of the National Defense Advisory Commission tops the list of important defense and diplomatic events which will follow in the wake of the Presidential election.

Emergence of a new official, probably to be known as defense coordinator, is the most important pending change in the NDAC organization. On the policy side, the pressure of rearmament will force an abatement of the NDAC policy of superimposing defense on normal business without interfering with the latter.

Next to the article were others with these headlines:

SHARP DROP INDICATED IN FREIGHT LOADINGS FOR LAST WEEK

and

STANDARD POWER & LIGHT FILES INTEGRATION PROPOSAL WITH SEC

There was no story on page 2.

The most prominently placed election-related piece on page 3 discussed the makeup of the new Congress:

WASHINGTON—So far as national legislation is concerned, particularly legislation related to domestic economic policy, a significant fact about Tuesday's elections is that the political complexion of Congress did not change very much.

At the top of the same page, a relatively brief story focused on the loser in the presidential race, with the headline reading:

MILITANT WILLKIE MINORITY LOOKED LIKE MAJORITY SAYS KILGORE OF VOTE WHICH UPSET PREDICTIONS

Under that account, which had been written in an apologetic, even puzzled tone, was the small headline "Election Results," with the *Wall Street Journal* finally getting around to giving its first clear indication that Roosevelt had won a third term:

Tuesday's election lined up like this on the basis of the latest returns Wednesday night. President Roosevelt had apparently won 449 electoral votes and Wendell Willkie 63, with Michigan's 19 votes still in some doubt. President Roosevelt's popular majority, on basis of the latest tabulation, was something over 4,000,000 votes.

Nothing on page 4. Nothing on page 5. On page 6 was a laudatory article about Willkie, praising him as "a real leader of his party, a real 'Leader of the Opposition.'"

And on page 7, an editorial pointed out that opposition to the current administration was more important than ever because "ten million people started regularly receiving [Social Security] checks from the United States treasury," and this was something that could not be allowed to pass unnoticed. The editorial went on to say that "for the opposition to cease opposition . . . for it to slink away, crushed and cowed—that is not in the national interest and no such obligation rests upon it. . . . On the contrary, to cease opposing now is distinctly against the national interests. Quite clearly opposition is more vital now than ever before."

Perhaps. But so were several stories on page 1 about Roosevelt's history-shattering third term. The National Defense Advisory

Commission—now *there* was a story that could have waited for page 8. Even November 8!

The lead, of course, would not stay buried. Leads never do. If the most important facts in a story have been interred accidentally by a reporter, an editor will usually spot the infraction and have the story rewritten. If one has been interred deliberately, by editorial policy, the attentive reader will spot it with no less difficulty.

Even readers of that day's *Wall Street Journal*, no matter how much they might have disliked the man and his politics, knew that Roosevelt's election to a third term in the White House was the most important story in the country and would affect the nation dramatically for the next four years.

The *Journal* had made its position on the president clear—in fact, it had done so many times in the past. All that it accomplished with its election coverage, at least for the time being, was to bury its own reputation for presenting news that did not agree with its collective editorial conscience.

13

The Same Team

S INS OF OMISSION ARE OFTEN CALCULATED. THEY MEAN TO deceive people about the chances of their city's flooding or the odds that a man can predict when two airplanes will crash into each other or the importance of a president's re-election.

Other omissions, however, are more innocent by nature. They have the same effect—giving readers a false view of the world's workings by withholding information from them, but they do so as a kind of by-product. It is not a case of a newspaper publisher or one of his reporters being cunning, but rather being timid.

Yes, timid. It seems a strange word to use to describe the behavior of journalists, especially these days, when it is almost impossible to watch a presidential press conference or a debate among candidates or even an interview between a reporter and a politician with a controversial position and see the press being anything less than aggressive—sometimes properly so, sometimes obnoxiously. But in the first half of the twentieth century, most denizens of the newsroom were just as awed to be in the company of celebrities, political or otherwise, as the rest of us would have been. They did what they were told to do to be granted a place in that exalted company. They did what they were told to do to remain in that company. At some level of consciousness, they had determined that once a figure elevated himself to that stage of life known as eminence, he was entitled to certain privileges. One of them was to be able to manage the news that was reported about him.

There was, however, the occasional exception. For instance, there was the unidentified member of the press corps who was so eager to take a picture of Charles Lindbergh and his new bride, Anne Morrow, on their honeymoon cruise off the coast of Massachusetts that he rented a small boat and kept circling his victims' cabin cruiser, "hoping the chop of his boat would make the Lindberghs seasick enough to come topside," into the range of his lens. It did not. Eventually Lindbergh tired of the photographer's antics, hit the gas, and outdistanced him.

And then there were the two American cameramen sent abroad in 1956 to take pictures of Grace Kelly, the actress from Philadelphia, as she married Monaco's Prince Rainier and became royalty herself. After the ceremony, the photographers demanded that a Monagasque policeman allow them to drive up the hill from the security gate to the prince's palace. The policeman explained to them as courteously as he could that there were no parking places at the palace, but to accommodate the press the royal family had arranged for a shuttle bus to provide transportation. The photographers should simply dispose of their car elsewhere and return to the gate, and the bus would be along shortly.

The two men would not hear of it. They had a job to do, a deadline to meet. So, "furious, [they] simply backed their car off—and when, still polite, the policeman tried to stop them, they literally ran him down; he was taken to the hospital." He survived, although with serious injuries. The cameramen, who did not bother to check on the officer's condition, roared up the hill and snapped away at the bride and groom until their fingers were sore.

But these and a few other examples were not only exceptions; they were rarities. In the period that we now consider, beginning with the declining days of Richard Harding Davis and ending with the mid- to late sixties, timidity was a much more common trait of journalists than was belligerence, or even perseverance. During this time, when a prominent newsmaker said omit, the press's most common reaction was to sin.

Power silences. Absolute power silences absolutely.

Andrew Mellon looked like a prominent newsmaker. More than that, he looked like a senior member of a private club of prominent newsmakers, which was also how he thought of himself. His personality, however, always threatened to betray him. He was, according to his son's description, a "thin-voiced, thin-bodied, shy and uncommunicative man." But he dressed superbly, tended his mustache so that not a single hair strayed from its assigned position, and kept his fingernails manicured to such perfection that he always showed his hands when he sat for a portrait.

His most thorough biographer, David Cannadine, says that to some people Mellon's blue eyes looked "dreamy and distant," and to others resembled "sharp blue daggers." The latter is a far better description. There was a coldness about the man, in both demeanor and appearance, that was probably his most salient feature. It might have been due in part to shyness, an oddly incongruous part of his makeup, but no less was it a reflection of a ruling elite's haughty demeanor. When Mellon allowed his face to droop, which it almost always did, he managed to convey, if not a disdain for those with whom he associated, at least a reluctance to linger in their presence. His daggers glared right through them. He talked as little as he could to coworkers, and although polite to customers at the banks he owned, he "rarely looked them in the eye, and he seldom spoke, and then only haltingly."

It is a wonder that a man like this ever accomplished anything. Yet accomplish he did. As a banker, Mellon was more responsible than any other man, with the exception of Andrew Carnegie, for the western Pennsylvania steel boom of the early twentieth century, which was itself responsible for building booms all over the country: skyscrapers in New York and Chicago; coal barges on the Great Lakes; warehouses in Buffalo and Cleveland; rail lines crossing the Midwest. He knew how to finance them so that both he and the owners would profit. Like Carnegie, he gave away much of his proceeds. Like Carnegie's associate and in later years his bitter enemy, Henry Clay Frick, he spent profusely on art.

And he was the most influential and controversial secretary of the Treasury in American history since Alexander Hamilton, as well as the only one to serve under three presidents: Harding, Coolidge, and Hoover. (As such, of course, it might be said that he was responsible more than anyone else for the ragingly pro-business policies that helped lay the groundwork for the Great Depression.) The only modern-day comparison to be made is with former chairman of the Federal Reserve Alan Greenspan. But Mellon had more control over the economy than Greenspan did, and he exercised it more selfishly. The three presidents who kept Mellon in office did so because of his brilliance, not because of his civic-mindedness. Unlike Franklin Delano Roosevelt, it could not be said of Mellon that he was a traitor to his class.

Since Carnegie had gone back to his ancestral home in Scotland at a relatively early age, returning to Pittsburgh only when there was a strike at one of his mills or some other kind of emergency, Mellon became the crown prince of the Steel City. When, late in 1900, he decided to marry—and a commoner at that—it seemed as if the nineteenth century was ending in the grandest way possible, by ensuring the future happiness of its leading citizen, a man who would surely blaze a continuing trail of wealth and progress into the twentieth century.

Andrew Mellon was forty-five years old. Nora McMullen, an attractive Englishwoman, demure even for her years, was nineteen. Despite her youth, she apparently had a remarkable skill. "In her presence," it has been written, "the famous Mellon reserve vanished like a cloud before an April breeze. To establish talkative relations with Andrew was at best a difficult, long drawn out process, but this girl evidently possessed the gift, known to few, of immediately putting him at his ease." People who saw the couple together saw an Andrew Mellon they were pleased to say they did not easily recognize.

It did not last. Before long, the new husband was reverting to form, finding his ease, if that's what it truly was, in his banking and other businesses, his philanthropy and art collecting, and his solitude, which he was unwilling to allow other human beings, including his own wife, to penetrate except on rare occasions. He seemed to find fault with Nora more and more, to find fewer and fewer things to talk to her about. She was, after all, twenty-six years his junior; she was not of his generation, not of his world. She did not comprehend banking and economics, steel and coal; he did not comprehend her lack of comprehension, and her increasing lack of interest in his passions. She grew ever more distant from him, and ever more sad and frustrated at the life she had chosen for herself.

In 1907, Mellon and Nora and their two children, one just a few months old, spent the summer in London and Paris—until, that is, a financial crisis back in the United States demanded Mellon's presence. He left his family hurriedly and, to all appearances, with a certain relief. It was for Nora the final straw. She begged him not to go. He told her he had to. Her tears left him unmoved as he explained to her in cold hard numbers the details of the economic problems that waited him. She listened to a few of them and told him she did not want to hear any more.

A week or two later he wrote her a short note from Pittsburgh, ending by telling her he missed her. Her response was a cri de coeur that still resounds over the years:

> I never can understand how you can possibly miss me or want me when I am away from you, for you never seem to want me when we are together. . . . Why must that loathsome *business* take all the strength and vitality which you ought to give to me? Why should

you only give me your tired evenings? Why should I give you all my strength and health and youth and be content with nothing in return? For I am not content and never shall be as long as I have to be second—always second. I am feeling so desperately lonely I could almost kill myself, but I would rather be lonely here than in Pittsburgh.

Nora would not be second much longer. In the heart of Alfred George Curphrey, whom Cannadine believes to have been "a cad and a confidence man who seduced the wives of unsuspecting husbands, a predator of unhappy women of means," she was about to be first. Or so he claimed. So she believed. The two of them, who apparently met on a ship traveling from England to the United States, would soon begin an affair.

Mellon suspected it almost at once. Hiring a private detective to follow his wife, he found his fears confirmed. Should he talk to her about this man, reason with her, threaten her? Threaten him? Surely he could buy the scamp off. Perhaps that is what Curphrey had in mind in the first place. But he did not, did not even make an offer. Since expense was not an issue, all we can conclude is that Mellon did not want Nora enough to go through the trouble. Ultimately, what he decided on was a divorce.

What a difficult choice it was. Divorces were not common in those days, and in Mellon's social circles they were not only less common, they were scandalous. One did not break a wedding vow any more than he did any other kind of contract. Of course, Mellon had not broken it. His wife was the one at fault, and everyone who knew Mellon would realize that. Still, people would wonder. Nora was such a sweet young thing, surely not the type to have an affair, especially with a roué like Curphrey, not unless there had been some kind of extreme provocation. What could it have been? What secret lurked in the inner chambers of what had outwardly seemed a marriage so typical of its type? The taint of the union's failure, Mellon realized, would be a cloud over both parties for the rest of their days. Thus did a gloomy man become gloomier than ever.

*   *   *

There were seven daily newspapers in Pittsburgh at the time. Not one of them published so much as a single word about the Mellon divorce. Everyone in the city was aware of it; no one in the city could read about it.

When George Seldes of the *Pittsburgh Leader* took a seat in the courtroom for one of the early days of the proceedings, he was surprised to find himself the only journalist there. Then again, as he later mused, "Why waste a reporter's time when there was no intention to have him write anything?" He decided to stay anyway. Surely he would find an outlet for his observations sometime, somewhere.

Perhaps in some city other than Pittsburgh. The Mellon divorce was a big story all along the eastern seaboard, and details were more easily accessible elsewhere, as the bride's family and friends, many of whom had sailed to the United States to support her, were more than willing to talk to the press. As Seldes points out, however, only one newspaper, Philadelphia's *North American*, was enterprising enough to ship copies of its publication into Pittsburgh to break the local news embargo. It seemed like a good idea. "But the moment the Mellon forces heard about it, they created another sensational news item: they sent the Pittsburgh police into the streets by the dozens, the papers were grabbed, the newsboys clubbed, their property destroyed. The next day's bundles were bought up at the railroad station."

The journalists in Pittsburgh might have been timid. The police, acting on behalf of Mellon, at the urging of Mellon's associates, were not.

And as Seldes goes on to reveal, there were other illegal activities performed in the service of Andrew Mellon. When the *North American* could not get its papers into Pittsburgh, it sent a reporter instead. Shortly after the man arrived, Seldes said,

> I gave him my notes and he wrote a thousand-word story, which he sent press-rate collect, as usual. It was suppressed by Western Union. He tried the rival company, Postal Telegraph, and again he could not get through. Both great national services

deliberately violated the law at Mellon insistence. But even the Mellon hundred-million-dollar fortune could not stop telephonic communication, and this is how the *North American* got through.

Pennsylvania lawmakers, who had once established such a reputation for corrupt practices that John D. Rockefeller and his Standard Oil trust were said to have "done everything with the Pennsylvania legislature except refine it," were equally willing to serve the Mellon interests now. The legislature did not violate the law at Mellon insistence; it created a new law. On the spur of the moment, and by a vote of 168–0, it put an end to jury trials in divorce cases in the state. They now became a secret from both the public and the press. The latter never even thought about protesting the decision. In fact, the state's major newspapers did not even report on the vote.

The entire state seemed to be bowing down before the lord of western Pennsylvania banking. It was a show of obeisance virtually medieval in its magnitude.

To Seldes, a young and idealistic reporter at the time, it was astonishing, a subversion of democracy such as he had never imagined possible. And there was more to come. Many years later, he would write about something he noticed when the case had been concluded and Mellon had won his divorce. "Surely it was not a mere coincidence," he said, "that the *Dispatch*, the most respectable of the morning journals [in Pittsburgh], shortly afterwards blossomed with page advertisements for not only the Mellon bank but other Mellon enterprises." It was Andrew Mellon's equivalent of a thank-you note for services not rendered to the community.

Sometimes, not rendering services to the community was a matter of good taste rather than a lack of courage. After covering William McKinley's inauguration as president, Richard Harding Davis wrote a letter to his brother Charles telling him that he chose to portray the event as "a sort of family gathering" rather than a tedious political formality. For instance, he said, he found much to like about McKinley's elderly mother, ebullient despite her years, and he devoted an unusual amount of space to her in his article. About the new president's wife, however, he was reticent. "Mrs. McKinley has epileptic fits and can only walk with the help of someone. She is also weak minded like a little girl of ten but her sufferings have given her a really beautiful face. She dressed the part exquisitely in blue velvet but it was a pathetic spectacle."

Davis included nothing about Mrs. McKinley in the article he published about the inauguration. As he told his brother, he was "not saying anything to hurt anybody's feelings but praising whenever I can." Since William McKinley was the story, not Ida, Davis could praise without compromising the integrity of his journalism, and that is precisely what he chose to do.

More often, though, the information that a reporter chose not to include in his article was information from which the reader would have benefited.

When McKinley was assassinated a year into his term, Vice President Theodore Roosevelt took up residence in the White House and proved himself to be the first modern master of withholding news from compliant journalists. As *Washington Post* media reporter Howard Kurtz points out, "For much of this century, the press and the president really were on the same team." And during the Roosevelt presidency, more than any other, there was no doubt who the captain was. In 1908, Roosevelt's last full year in office, Kurtz relates, a reporter for the *New York Times* named William Bayard Hale interviewed Germany's Kaiser Wilhelm II. The kaiser told Hale that he fully expected his country to be at war with the British in the not too distant future. It was a startling admission, and Hale, relatively inexperienced, was not sure how to handle it.

Neither were his editors, with whom he immediately discussed the matter. Did the kaiser mean what he said? Did he make the comment for some political purpose known only to himself, and was he hoping to use the *Times* to further that purpose? Or was he just having sport with Hale, demonstrating not a political purpose but a perverse sense of humor?

The editors suggested that Hale take his notes to Roosevelt and talk over the matter with him, something newspaper executives would not even consider today, viewing it as a surrender of their First Amendment freedoms. Back then it was different. The editors reasoned that since Roosevelt knew the kaiser, knew how his mind worked, he was the best source of advice available. They would turn to the expert.

So Hale made an appointment with the president, handed over his notebook, and waited for Roosevelt to read and react. It did not take long. The president told him not to publish. The notes would only create hard feelings—or harder feelings—between the two countries involved. No possible good could come out of making the information public, Roosevelt insisted. He returned the notebook to Hale with an imperious glare and dismissed him. Hale relayed the message to his superiors, who followed the president's counsel, apparently without a dissenting voice—something else that would never happen today.

Six years later, Germany would take up arms against the British Empire in World War I. It was doubtful that the *Times* felt any remorse about the story it did not publish in 1898. It was simply the way things were done back then, especially when the prominent newsmaker was the most prominent of them all, and a bullmoose of a personality like Teddy Roosevelt.

Roosevelt was used to telling reporters what to publish and what not to publish. And he was used to their obeying him, whether the subject was comments made by someone else or comments of his own. The latter was the more common case. Roosevelt knew he had a tendency to speak in a highly unpresidential manner from time to time, using inappropriately belligerent language, sometimes telling what amounted to state secrets, and he expected reporters to edit him even if he forgot to remind them. They invariably did.

On the few occasions when a reporter published something that displeased Roosevelt, the president would not only call the reporter a liar but exile him to the informally organized but nonetheless dreaded Ananias Club, named after the biblical figure who attempted to deceive the Holy Spirit. Members of the club had to repent to and have their repentance judged as sincere by a number of administration officials before the president would speak to them again.

Usually, though, Roosevelt would not have to resort to such a step. Usually it was enough for him to say to journalists, "Mind, this is private," and the information would remain just that.

But there were times when Roosevelt wanted his comments, even some of the most incendiary of them, to be published—times when he wanted to deliver the insult, create the controversy, state his position in the clearest, least politic terms. Here, too, he proved that his skills at handling journalists were without equal. Mark Sullivan, in his six-volume history of the first twenty-five years of the twentieth century, writes about Roosevelt as follows:

> He was the earliest American public man to grasp the syllogism that on Sunday all normal business and most other activities are suspended; that Sunday is followed by Monday; and that, therefore, the columns of the Monday papers present the minimum of competition for public attention—whence many of the public statements, epithets and maledictions with which Roosevelt conducted his fights were timed to explode in the pages of the Monday morning newspapers.

It did not take long for journalists to realize that Roosevelt was manipulating them. They were delighted. Finally, those Monday morning papers that used to be so dull, that sold so few copies and stimulated so little conversation had some juice in them, some spice, some *news!*

Calvin Coolidge's personality, to the extent that he had one, was the opposite of Roosevelt's. As taciturn a man as ever occupied the White House, Coolidge smiled so seldom that his lips might have been sutured into a frown, and he spoke in such short sentences that he might have been hoarding his words, believing he had been apportioned only so many for mortal use and wanted to take no chances on running over. His nickname, "Silent Cal," could not have been more appropriate.

One evening, according to his wife, as the two of them made their entrance to a dinner party, the hostess walked confidently up to the president and said, "I made a bet today that I could get more than two words out of you." She looked at him with a self-satisfied grin on her face. The president erased it with his reply. "You lose," he said.

He was not, then, humorless. But he was better at inspiring humor in others than issuing bons mots of his own. He "could be silent in five languages," one person said of him. Said another, he appeared "much like a wooden Indian except more tired-looking." And when told of Coolidge's death, the noted Algonquin Round Table wit Dorothy Parker is supposed to have replied, "How could they tell?"

Coolidge did, however, have something in common with Roosevelt. He insisted on being in control of his relationship with reporters. His first step was to place them in his debt, which he did by allowing them to come to a number of White House social events, something most of his predecessors had not done; taking them for cruises on his yacht, the *Mayflower*; and occasionally even inviting them to accompany him on vacation, although making sure they kept their distance from family activities. Granted, he had little to say to the press at these or any other events; still, they were pleased enough just to be in such favored company.

The quid pro quo was obedience. Coolidge insisted that the journalists submit questions for him in writing and in advance, something that even Roosevelt did not require. Coolidge would look through the questions and decide for himself which ones were worthy of a response. Those that he rejected once were not to be presented a second time.

And when Coolidge did answer a question, he was not to be quoted directly. In fact, the president of the United States was never quoted directly by reporters until the Hoover administration. Instead, his answers were to be attributed to a White House spokesman. It was a practice that fooled very few readers and was ridiculed so much that Coolidge finally found it necessary to offer a defense. "The words of the President have an enormous weight," he said, "and ought not to be used indiscriminately. It would be exceedingly easy to set the country all by the ears and foment hatreds and jealousies, which, by destroying faith and confidence, would help nobody and harm everybody." It is impossible to know whether Coolidge actually believed this twaddle or was earnestly trying to answer his critics, and using up a significant quantity of his allotted earthly verbiage to do it.

During another meeting with journalists, discussing the fact that they were under orders to quote the White House "spokesman" word for word, interjecting no analysis or commentary or even punctuation marks of their own, Coolidge told them that he was surprised "at the constant correctness of my views as you report them." Whether his listeners got the joke is also impossible to know.

Whereas Teddy Roosevelt and Coolidge were primarily concerned about restricting the use that journalists made of their words, Franklin Delano Roosevelt and Harry Truman were more interested in the censorship of their pictures.

Of some thirty-five thousand photographs taken of FDR during his years in the White House, only two included his wheelchair, and he does not seem to have been in the device at the time, but seated elsewhere, next to an adviser or a fellow statesman with whom he was engaged in conversation; the wheelchair was out of the frame, off to the side. One would have expected the chair to show up more than twice in twelve years just by accident—the cameraman's hand slipping as he pressed the button, his foot giving way on a patch of wet lawn so that he lost his balance and the camera swung to the right or left. Considered all together, 34,998 "properly framed" pictures out of 35,000 add up to a remarkable display of omission.

And neither Roosevelt nor his aides even had to insist on it; photographers knew without being told not to shoot him looking "unpresidential." They were not trying to fool anyone by failing to snap Roosevelt in his wheelchair or struggling to get out of it and into his crutches; they had agreed, either on an individual basis or as a matter of company policy, for what they believed to be the good of the nation, not to reinforce the image of a chief executive who had been stricken by polio. Since the handicap did not seem to affect the way the president did his job, since in fact he seemed a more energetic presence in the White House than several of the men who had preceded him, the cameramen felt that by ignoring his disability they were giving a truer picture of the man than if they had shown him looking compromised.

Nor would they compromise British prime minister Winston Churchill in less serious circumstances. In January 1943, Roosevelt made a seventeen-thousand-mile trip to Casablanca to meet with Churchill about the course of World War II and efforts between their two countries to bring it to a close. After ten days of secret meetings, the president was scheduled to return to the United States one morning at seven-thirty. As Doris Kearns Goodwin writes:

> Churchill had intended to see Roosevelt off, but after a long evening of food, drink, speeches, and songs, he had trouble getting out of bed. At the last minute, still clad in his red-dragon dressing gown and black velvet slippers, he raced outside to catch the president's car. At the airfield, the photographers begged for a shot. "You simply cannot do this to me," he laughingly remarked, and they obliged, lowering their cameras.

Today's picture takers would not have obliged. They would have been clicking away so loudly and insistently, hoping for a shot they could sell to a tabloid, that they would not even have heard Churchill's plea.

As for Truman, he was the subject of a reminiscence by Henry Brandon, who for many years was the Washington correspondent for the *Times* of London. Hedrick Smith, who would go on to report for the *New York Times*, tells us in his book *Power Game* that Brandon

> recalled traveling with a small White House press corps to Key West [Florida], where President Truman relaxed. Truman, who normally wore a corset to tuck in his tummy, would hold bare-chested press conferences in swimming trunks. Even though this exposed a pear-shaped profile, Truman did not flinch at this informal snapshot taking. On such trips, the U.S. Navy not only provided billets for reporters but arranged deep-sea fishing excursions for their amusement. Brandon, thinking of the angry confrontation between press and government since Vietnam and Watergate and everyone's sensitivity to buying influence with favors, chuckled quietly, and asked, "Can you imagine either side putting up with that kind of arrangement these days?"

The photographs of Truman uncorseted never made their way to publication.

The two kinds of stories that reporters reported the least during the first half of the preceding century—which is to say, in most cases not at all—involved politicians who had overindulged on women and politicians who had overindulged on liquor. Foremost among the latter was Russell Long, who was born in Louisiana about a decade before the flood that did not destroy New Orleans. Russell was the son of Huey Long, as controversial a politician as this country has ever known and, in his way, as spellbinding an orator. Long père was a former senator from Louisiana and governor of the state, whose "Share Our Wealth" program was supposed to make "Every Man a King," and who was assassinated in 1935 by someone even more fanatical than he. At the time, Long was planning to run for president, disgusted that the incumbent, Franklin Delano Roosevelt, was not doing enough to dismember the nation's power structure for the good of the poor and otherwise unfortunate.

So his son Russell was born with politics on the brain. He was also born with a shot glass at his lips. The two made for a volatile combination.

Russell Long was elected to the United States Senate as a Democrat in 1948, twenty-nine years old when the voting took place, but the mandatory thirty when his term began. He would immediately become a strong supporter of President Truman's cold war policies and, later, a major obstacle to President Lyndon Johnson's civil rights program.

By this time, the mid-sixties, Long had risen through the Senate ranks to attain the chairmanship of the nearly omnipotent Senate Finance Committee. He was also, as he had been since the first U.S. troops landed in Southeast Asia, a powerful voice for the war in Vietnam. He could not understand why so many Americans were so ignorant as to oppose it, and was pleased to run roughshod over their opposition to provide the necessary funding.

And he was, by this time, reacting to the pressures of his office and its controversial duties by drinking too much, more than he had ever poured down his gullet before. He would drink with his pal Johnson when Johnson tried to persuade him that if the Democrats didn't become the party of civil rights, the Republicans would, and all those black votes, which counted just as much as the white ones, would go to the GOP—just enough, perhaps, to put the Republicans in the White House. Russell would drink with his pals from the Senate in the Capitol's nooks and crannies when the topics were not so monumental, and with other friends at parties and with strangers in hotel bars and at home all by himself late at night, his wife asleep upstairs, his marriage of some twenty-five years crumbling around him because he could not stay sober long enough to hold it together.

In 1969, Long, as assistant majority leader of the Senate, and his wife, the former Katherine Mae Hattic, divorced. Predictably, Long's drinking reached a peak. Sometimes he did not show up on the Senate floor; sometimes he showed up late and so heavily under the influence that he weaved down the aisle to his seat, his voice slurred, his eyes still red, and head throbbing from last night's binge. He was no longer the "youthful energetic" legislator he had once been, no longer "one of the keenest" young men in all of Washington. He felt like an old man, aging by the glassful, and his remarriage to a former Senate staffer did little to reinvigorate him and nothing to change his drinking habits.

Soon Mike Mansfield, the Democratic majority leader, would replace Long as his top aide with Massachusetts senator Edward Kennedy, fearing that Long's boozing had reached a point at which he could no longer be trusted to perform his duties. Kennedy, a drinker himself but better able to control his behavior even when he consumed enough alcohol to approach Long's standards, was nicknamed Teddy. Long's nickname was Jack Daniels.

And journalists knew it. They had known it for a long time. In the mid-sixties, before Mansfield had demoted him, Long was so drunk on the Senate floor one afternoon that he held up passage of a bill very important to his Democratic colleagues. It was a tense session of the senior legislative body, with Long thwarting the will of his own party and perhaps not even being aware of it and the afternoon dragging on into evening. *New York Times* reporter Eileen Page, afraid she was going to miss her deadline, called her editor and told him why. She also told him she wanted to write the story, to let readers know what effect Long's inebriation was having on the pending measure. Her editor told her she could not. Page argued with him, and with others at the *Times*, but to no avail; Russell Long's drinking, and its possible effects on the nation's governance, would remain a secret from the general public until much later, when the history books, rather than the daily press, got around to revealing it.

Earlier in the century, in fact in its first decade, the *Times* had developed a new kind of ink to use for its paper, one that did not so easily rub off on the reader's hands, as most newspaper ink did at the time. As a result, it came up with a new slogan. The *New York Times* was now the newspaper that would not soil your breakfast linen. It still seemed to have that kind of prissy attitude decades later; it would not allow news of a United States senator's addiction to the bottle to soil the readers' belief in the high-toned behavior of their elected representatives.

The *Times* was not the only paper or news organization to shield the public from knowledge of their seventy- or eighty-proof representatives. Larry Sabato, director of the Center for Politics at the University of Virginia, has collected several examples in his book *Feeding Frenzy*, the first from Ben Bradlee of the *Washington Post*. "I remember as a kid reporter going up to the Senate to watch a filibuster," Bradlee says, "and seeing Thruston Morton [R-KY] almost fall down as he was talking, and I was just stunned [because] nobody ever reported it." Bradlee thought the *Post* should be the paper to report it. The editors disagreed. Poor taste, they thought. Poor government, thought Bradlee.

George Herman, of CBS News, says, "When I first came to Washington there were a lot of senators who were well-known as terrible drunks, including one Senator Herman Welker of Idaho, who burst out of the Senate Republican Cloak Room just in time to hear a unanimous consent motion on something like declaring National Pickle Week, shouted, 'I object,' and fell over in a dead faint on the floor, half drunk, and was carried away." CBS did not cover Welker's collapse, nor did any of the television stations or newspapers in Welker's home state.

Jack Germond, of Gannett News, relates, "In 1962 Senator Pete Williams [D-NJ] was running for reelection and he had a drinking problem. We decided we were going to do the story about this guy [even though] that was almost never done." Nor would it be done in this case, Germond's resolve notwithstanding. The leading paper in New Jersey, owned by Gannett, refused to run the exposé. Other Gannett papers followed its lead. Pete Williams was reelected handily, and celebrated, one presumes, by elbow-bending with staff, family, friends, and reporters.

All of this was lead-burying of a sort—some of it imposed by politicians, some by publications. It would be years, and in a few instances decades, before the facts were finally exhumed. And surely a few of those facts, because of reportorial subservience to Teddy Roosevelt and Coolidge, among others, still lie interred.

Sex was not just a topic that journalists did their best to ignore in those days; it was a source of discomfort to the entire mass culture, no matter who was having it or under what conditions. Hugh Hefner had not even been born. There were no miniskirts on the market, no bra ads in magazines, no glorification of starlets getting pregnant out of wedlock and vowing to have their children rather than terminate the pregnancy. There were no wardrobe malfunctions at halftime of the year's biggest sporting event. There were no sex scenes in movies and fewer of them in books, and those that were published were very circumspectly worded. Even fewer trysts were reported in newspapers, and those usually because a more heinous deed was associated with the copulation; that is, a murder had been committed by one of the members of a romantic triangle. "Newspapers are read at the breakfast and dinner tables," wrote W. R. Nelson, publisher of the *Kansas City Star*. "God's great gift to man is appetite. Put nothing in the paper that will destroy it." Unless, Nelson might have added, absolutely necessary.

Warren G. Harding's affairs were judged not to be. Harding had developed a reputation for carrying flirtation to its extreme long before his most famous, yet not unequivocally proven, episode: uniting with a young woman named Nan Britton while both remained upright, locked in an embrace resembling a wrestling grasp as they banged against the walls and door of a White House closet, scaring the hell out of those nearby, who thought wild animals had found their way into a corner of the nation's most famous residence. Either then or on some other occasion, claims Britton, Harding sired her daughter, Elizabeth Ann.

Another tale of Harding's amours is provided by the wife of a reporter covering the 1920 presidential campaign, most of which Harding spent in his hometown of Marion, Ohio. "Three newsmen invited to dine at the home of one of Harding's widow neighbors were, during the evening, taken upstairs by an innocent eight-year-old member of the widow's family, and proudly shown Harding's toothbrush. Said the child, 'He always stays here when Mrs. Harding goes away.'"

Not long after this, William Estabrook Chancellor, a professor at Wooster College in Ohio, published a scathing pamphlet about Harding. Chancellor was more of a crank than a true academic, the kind of man who might be seen today in the midst of an urban center proclaiming the imminent end of the world, although in surprisingly literate language. In the pamphlet, published at his own expense, Chancellor gave credence to rumors about the president that had been circulating around Marion for many years that Harding was something less than a purebred American. Without citing any evidence, he claimed that Harding's great-grandmother was a Negro and his great grandfather had at least a soupçon of Negro blood. And, of course, "like all Negroes," Chancellor went on, Harding had an eye, not to mention other body parts, for the ladies.

No major newspaper carried the story. Democratic president Woodrow Wilson, on his deathbed, urged his party to disregard it. James Cox, the Democrat who would succeed Wilson and run against Harding in 1920, never referred to it.

The irony of Harding's being the victim of Chancellor's pamphlet, which included some unsavory jokes along with the racial allegations, was that prior to seeking the presidency, Harding had been a newspaper publisher in Marion, and was regarded as one of the most fair-minded journalists in the state. In fact, after he defeated Cox and moved to Washington, some of Harding's associates jotted down the rules that he had spoken to them as he wandered through the newsroom. They made copies of them, and circulated them not only in Ohio but all over the country. They were talked about and posted in newspaper offices for a decade. Among them:

> If it can be avoided, never bring ignominy on an innocent man or child, in telling of the misdeeds or misfortunes of a relative.

Don't wait to be asked, but do it without the asking. . . . Never needlessly hurt the feelings of anybody. Be decent; be fair; be generous. I want this paper to be so conducted that it can go into any home without destroying the innocence of any child.

If only Harding had conducted his personal life with an equal concern for propriety.

In 1940, both presidential candidates were guilty of extramarital dalliances, although Roosevelt's behavior might have been unknown to most journalists. After all, he was severely restricted in his movements and could not easily go gallivanting around town with Lucy Mercer on his arm. And Mercer was an employee of the White House—Eleanor Roosevelt's personal secretary, of all things. The president often sent his wife on trips, both domestically and abroad, asking her to serve as a kind of unofficial ambassador and report back to him. For some reason, she seldom took Mercer with her, often traveling with a friend, and perhaps lover, named Lorena Hickok.

Thus the president and Mercer spent many hours together in the White House, some of them alone, without any danger of the First Lady's intruding. It might well have appeared to a journalist who dropped into the president's office that Mercer was simply briefing the president on her boss's activities. Until, that is, the couple repaired to Roosevelt's private quarters, where they appeared to no one.

But Wendell Willkie's affair was common knowledge, not only in journalistic circles but in New York social circles as well. The lady in question was Irita Van Doren, who "was not pretty," according to famed journalist William L. Shirer, "but she was beautiful." She had acquired her last name by marrying Carl Van Doren, a future Pulitzer Prize winner for his biography of Benjamin Franklin. Their union lasted for twenty-three years, from 1912 to 1935, before the pair went their separate ways. Thus she was single, and Willkie was not, when the latter sought the

White House. It did not matter to either of them. Willkie was in love with Van Doren and she with him, and they would remain so for the rest of their lives. Van Doren would, in fact, be more of a wife to Willkie than Edith Wilk, the woman to whom, in order to avoid the stain of a divorce, which was in effect in all ways but legally, he continued to stay married.

Irita Van Doren was the literary editor of the *New York Herald Tribune* at the time, a position she held for thirty-seven years. She served not only as Willkie's mistress, but as the occasional editor of his speeches. So well known was their relationship, we are informed, that "reporters sometimes called Willkie at Van Doren's apartment at night if they needed a quote for the next day's paper." Willkie would answer the phone without embarrassment.

Once, during his campaign against Roosevelt, he went even further. He told the advisers accompanying him that he had decided to hold a press conference at Van Doren's apartment the next day. The two men dropped their jaws in unison. You can't do that, they scolded. You want to make headlines, but not like that!

Willkie disagreed. "Everybody knows about us—all the newspapermen in New York. If somebody should come along to threaten or embarrass me about Irita, I would say, 'Go right ahead. There is not a reporter in New York who doesn't know about her.'"

Willkie exaggerated. And despite what we have come to believe since, there were reporters in Washington two decades later who did not know about President John F. Kennedy and his various mistresses. "I never even heard the rumors," says Sander Vanocur, an NBC correspondent who was not assigned to the White House beat but was one of the best of the time covering politics. So perhaps reports of a widespread, if informal, press conspiracy to protect Kennedy's reputation over the years have been exaggerated—but not by much.

Most journalists had at least heard the rumors. Many of them knew the rumors to be true. They knew about Kennedy and Marilyn Monroe; about Marlene Dietrich, the aging movie queen who had slept with the president's father as well and supposedly told Kennedy that his old man was a better bedder; and about Judith Campbell Exner, who was also making her services available to mob boss Sam Giancana. They knew about hastily arranged rendezvous with White House secretaries, White House interns, campaign workers, schoolteachers, real estate agents, stewardesses, waitresses, college students, strippers, prostitutes who had decided to work pro bono for a change—so many women in so many places that Kennedy could not keep track of their names, having sex with them and then calling them "kiddo" or "sweetie" as he sent them on their way afterward with a pat on the fanny and a memory for the ages.

"Let's sack with Jack," one newsman suggested as a campaign slogan for the Wisconsin primary in 1960, and the line got a chuckle from his mates. But it did not lead to coverage of a president's extracurricular sex life. And it seems certain that no president in our nation's history ever had a busier one than John Kennedy.

It is also likely that no president in our nation's history has ever been a more genuinely charming human being than Kennedy—and the relationship between his adulterous frenzies and his personality is an important one. Simply put, if it were not for the latter, the former would almost certainly have been front-page news from coast to coast. The reporters who knew about Kennedy's love life agonized over it more than their predecessors did over Roosevelt's or Harding's, not just because the times were changing and sex was inching its way into the various forms of mass media, but because Kennedy could be so blatant about his trouser-dropping. Not only did he do it often, but, if he was not otherwise engaged by matters of state, he talked about it often between engagements, never seeming to worry about where he was or who might overhear:

Bobby Baker, Senator Lyndon Johnson's aide, once ran into Jack in the congressional dining room where he was sitting with a friend named Bill Thompson and a stunning woman. Thompson waved Baker over, obviously put up to it by Jack, and said, "Bobby, look at this fine chick. She gives the best head in the United States." Baker glanced nervously at the woman, who was smiling obliviously while Kennedy was convulsed with laughter. "Relax, Bobby," Jack finally said. "She's German and she doesn't understand a word of English. But what Bill's saying is absolutely right."

Kennedy was seen once or twice by members of his staff hugging and kissing a woman in public after a roll in the hay. Might there have been someone else who saw, a passerby or two across the street, strolling through a park, just a John or Jane Doe who would gulp in wonder and then tell all of his friends? Might Kennedy's political opponents have been spying on him and used the information against him, as a means of "persuading" him to alter some of his positions? Might the agents of foreign powers have known about Kennedy's philandering and threatened him with exposure unless he altered or softened other positions? Historian David Kaiser, in his meticulously researched book *The Road to Dallas: The Assassination of John F. Kennedy*, writes, "News of the President's indiscretions, indeed, had traveled through mob circles around the country." In this case, Kaiser insists, there is no "might" about it.

There are some who go so far as to believe that Soviet premier Nikita Khrushchev was emboldened to place missiles in Cuba because, aware of Kennedy's often lascivious behavior, he thought the American president a man of little substance, a foe who would not rise to the challenge. It is true that Khrushchev had little respect for Kennedy; there is no evidence, however, that Kennedy's extramarital behavior had anything to do with it.

Regardless, the president seemed oblivious to any such possibility or its consequences.

To arrange his liaisons, Kennedy enlisted his top aides, who, although often reluctant, felt compelled to accept their assignments and sometimes performed them with a zany choreographic brilliance that the Marx Brothers could not have improved upon, as one woman would be pushed out the back door of a hotel suite as the next was stumbling through the front.

And sometimes Kennedy's liaisons were arranged without the slapstick. In fact, according to evidence compiled by Kaiser, they were sometimes arranged in a way that could have contributed to Kennedy's death, although this latter circumstance was not common knowledge among journalists. It is possible, perhaps even likely, that most of them did not know about it at all until later.

Kaiser concedes that Lee Harvey Oswald fired the fatal shots at the president. But he convincingly demonstrates that Oswald was encouraged to do so, perhaps even paid to do so, by a number of prominent underworld figures. "Where did these men find the audacity to kill a president of the United States? [Government investigator] G. Robert Blakey and [former journalist] Richard Billings speculated convincingly in the 1970s that John Kennedy, because he accepted women as favors through [mob-connected] Frank Sinatra (and perhaps in other contexts as well), had lost the immunity from retaliation that truly incorruptible public officials generally enjoyed."

Behavior like this from the chief executive of the United States was news—or should have been. But Kennedy's manner captivated the press. They had never encountered a politician of such grace and style, and to be treated kindly, even intimately, by such a man was not just flattery; it was an honor, especially since most reporters identified themselves as liberals who reveled in Kennedy's politics no less than his personality.

In addition, Kennedy surrounded himself not with the ward heeler types who had been the advisers of so many chief executives in the past, but with academics, intellectuals, authors, historians, artists. When Kennedy and his associates gathered in the White House it was a salon as much as a strategy session, and when the members of the salon treated the press as warmly as did the president himself, the journalists were even more flattered.

Not only were they on the same team as Kennedy and his men; it was an all-star team.

But therein lay the conundrum; their pleasure in the circumstances was matched by their awareness that as soon as one of them wrote a story about JFK in the bedroom or wherever else he chose to indulge in a quickie, the golden days were over; the team would become the Black Sox.

And so the reporters were constantly ill at ease, questioning one another and themselves, wondering whether they were doing their jobs, whether the voices whispering in their ears belonged to demons or their better angels. They talked to one another in bars late at night, the last dregs of their drinks in front of them. "The reason we didn't follow up [on the womanizing stories]," according to the *Washington Post*'s David Broder, who followed Kennedy around on the 1960 campaign trail, "is clearly because of that 'gentleman's understanding' that boys will be boys—and it was all boys. Nobody wanted to spoil the fun for anybody else, and besides, the attitude back then was, what the hell difference does it make? . . . The hypocrisy was evident, was acknowledged, and indeed was institutionalized. But I would argue that it was as much self-protective of the press corps as it was protective of the candidate. What people said was, 'Well, shit, if you're going to whistle on this guy . . . are we going to go back and start telling about each other? Is that the next step?'"

As late as 2008, Vanocur said, "Even if I did know about Kennedy, what would I have done about it back then? Tell me."

John F. Kennedy was the last president to receive such treatment from American journalists.

As far as the press was concerned, there were practical reasons for not writing about Kennedy. Or Long or Morton or Welker or any of the rest of them. They were afraid that if a politician's drinking or skirt-plundering were revealed, his colleagues, especially those who themselves drank and plundered, would be so upset at this breach of decorum that they would clam up, refuse to make themselves available anymore to journalists, as politicians in Baltimore had once snubbed the *Herald*'s young Henry Louis Mencken. Theodore Roosevelt, after all, would not talk to members of the Ananias Club until their mea culpas were judged to be humiliating enough. News organizations could not report the news if those who made it would not grant them interviews. The press would rather have access to those who had the scoop on international affairs than get the scoop themselves on matters of less global import like extramarital affairs.

Another reason for not writing about lawmakers under the influence of either alcohol or lust is that news organizations did not want to disillusion the public for what they persisted in believing was insufficient reason. A man's appetites were a personal matter between him and either his bottle or his libido—weren't they? To make public what a government official did in private was to break a sacred trust, not just between journalists and those officials, but between journalists and the men and women who read their stories. Besides, was there any way of knowing, *really* knowing, whether a legislator's peccadilloes affected the way he did his job? Russell Long showed up for most of the Senate votes and voted in line with the views he always professed. John Kennedy gave every sign of growing more and more competent and knowledgeable during his tragically short presidency.

Yet another reason for journalistically imposed silence, and perhaps the most compelling, is that journalists at the time still had faith in government officials, disagreeing with some of them on this issue and some of them on that, but on the whole trusting them to follow their consciences for the good of the country. If they needed to fortify themselves with a little extra time in the bed or the bar, who was the reporter to pass judgment? What mattered were the results.

The mid-sixties, however, was the beginning of the end of that trust.

*   *   *

During the Vietnam War, reporters like the New York Times's David Halberstam, United Press's Neil Sheehan, and CBS's Morley Safer caught political and military figures in a number of lies—about the goals of the war and its progress, about the number of fatalities so far, and the number of years that lay ahead for an American troop presence in Southeast Asia. Never before had this happened, at least not to such a degree.

Of course a president or a general would bend the truth from time to time about his position on a certain issue, or about whether or not he was going to run for higher office, about the precise strength of his troops in a certain part of the war zone. But this was something different, this was lying on so widespread a basis, misleading the American people on so many different, albeit related, subjects that it amounted to a matter of policy. Before long, the sorrow and eventually bitterness that journalists felt over Kennedy's assassination turned into a raging distrust of his successor. Kennedy would never have deceived them, of this they felt certain; Johnson and his military advisers did nothing but. Camelot had become cornpone, and suddenly, at this most critical of times, journalists began to feel they were slumming it, no longer attending salons.

And then in 1972 the strained relationship between public officials and the press became something more, virtually a war of its own. This was the year when a band of bumbling burglars, under orders from the White House, broke into the headquarters of the Democratic National Committee in the Watergate hotel complex in Washington, D.C. To this day, what they were looking for is uncertain. What they turned up was a constitutional crisis.

Most members of the press disliked President Richard Nixon even more than they did Johnson. When Nixon and his top aides began lying to them about the break-in, when the lies began to pile on top of one another, lies being told today to try to control the damage from yesterday's lies, it was more than reporters would bear. Their fangs came out as well as their pens, and their disdain for Nixon and his inner circle metastasized into a wariness about virtually all politicians, at all levels, with the governmental figures in many cases feeling the same way about those who covered them, hostility feeding hostility.

And with the success of Bob Woodward and Carl Bernstein, who broke the Watergaze story, came a new dynamic in the journalist-subject relationship. They rose from mere general assignment reporters to superstars in a matter of months, their names on everyone's lips, faces on all of the magazine covers, book advances in the millions and lecture fees in the tens of thousands, Robert Redford and Dustin Hoffman playing them on the big screen. When all of this happened, the lesson many young reporters took from it was the wrong one. They did not assume that the means of success in journalism was ceaseless and meticulous investigating, as Woodward and Bernstein had done; they assumed it was simply bringing down the mighty. Find a crook in public life and ride the coattails of his degradation to fame of one's own. The hostility, at least in some cases, became positively venomous.

No more would journalists believe it was in their interests to drop a cloak of secrecy over the misdeeds of politicians. No more were they on the same team. The team had broken up. The politicians and the press would never wear the same colors again.

14

Rejecting the Faith

THEODORE H. WHITE, KNOWN FAMILIARLY, LIKE THE FIRST Roosevelt and the younger Kennedy, as Teddy, was not a team player, not really. He was too independent, too intelligent, too self-reliant. And, probably most important, too geographically removed. The team was headquartered in Washington, D.C. White got his start as a journalist in the late thirties in China.

He is best known for a series of four books he published later: *The Making of the President 1960; The Making of the President 1964; The Making of the President 1968;* and *The Making of the President 1972.* They were the ultimate insider's accounts of life on the campaign trail before such books became commonplace.

But at the very beginning of his career, before it really took root, White feared his own unmaking. As a twenty-three-year-old graduate of Harvard, elfin and bespectacled, White set off for the Far East, whose language and culture he had studied at Harvard. He wondered if it could possibly fascinate him as much once he was actually there as it did from thousands of miles away in Massachusetts. Could it engage his mind in its exotically non-Western ways? Could it stimulate his senses? Could it give him an entirely different grasp of the spiritual?

It could, and he knew it immediately. He arrived in Chung-king (now usually called Chongqing), China, in 1939 and wrote about it many years later as if he were a young man catching a first glimpse of the woman he knew would one day be his wife. What especially captivated him was that the flowers,

> it seemed, forgot to blossom by the season. Paper-white narcissi (shui-hsien) came in midwinter; plum blossoms spotted the hills and decorated the markets in March; azaleas bloomed all year round, and the stalls offered little pots of flowering shrubs, which lit the dingy, shadow dark alleys around the calendar. Then, fruits: tiny orange cherries, sticky sweet, in baskets, as early as May; followed by peaches in June . . . ; then the apricots and lichee nuts of mid-summer, followed by the watermelons of August and September; followed again by pears; by the red and rosy persimmons of late fall; to be overwhelmed finally by the magnificent citrus fruits of winter— pink pomelos, oranges and, at their glorious best, the tangerines of December. In a few years, I, like most Chinese in Chungking, learned to mark the rhythm of the seasons by the fruits.

White was determined to stay in Chungking. He found a position as the supervisor of news-feature stories for the China Information Committee.

One of his duties, he admitted in his autobiography, although it was never explicitly said to him at the time, was to "manipulate American public opinion" in favor of the Chinese against their Japanese aggressors. In order to accomplish this, he had to learn a highly specialized vocabulary.

The Japanese, for instance were to be referred to in articles not as Japanese, but as "dwarf bandits." The Japanese army never attacked; it "sneaked about." When the Japanese won a military victory against the Chinese, they did not conquer their foe; instead, "traces of the enemy appeared in Hankow." And the Chinese military did not retreat; it performed "a major strategic outflanking movement." Despite his fondness for the Chinese, White was not the kind of young man who was happy with this kind of Orwellian prose. He might have taken solace, however, in the knowledge that journalists abroad could easily see through it and rewrite it less pointedly.

A greater problem for him than duplicitous language, however, was demands on his time. The United Press International correspondent assigned to China was expected to file a five-hundred-word story every day. The Reuters appetite consisted of two thousand words daily. It was up to White to provide the fodder for these and other members of the press corps, and on some days there was simply not that much happening, forcing White either to admit he could not do his job or to skim the Chinese papers frantically for items that lent themselves to embellishment. He chose the latter. He would not let his clients down no matter what the state of China on a particular day. He would always be someone to depend on.

Once he saw a story, no more than a paragraph, about a Chinese woman in a remote Japanese-occupied province who sneaked into a movie theater and threw a grenade down the aisle, killing an unknown number of the foe. Then she ran back out into the street and to safety in a secret hiding place. The woman's name was Tsai Huang-Hua, which White literally translated to Miss "Golden Flowers" Tsai. Ironic, he thought: so attracted had he initially been to China's flowers.

According to the story he wrote about the woman, based on nothing but her name and the grenade and the theater, she was "the guerrilla chieftain, the Amazon leader of a band of Chinese resistants." White says the foreign press loved the story and demanded more—more information and this time some pictures of the woman.

Pictures? Of someone who would be virtually impossible to find if he had the time to look for her? Of someone who would not let him approach her even if he *did* find her, because she would suspect him of working for the Japanese? Of someone who lived in a province so far away he had never heard of it? What was he going to do?

When White shared his dilemma with coworkers at the Chinese Information Committee, they smiled and told him not to worry. One of the young women in the service, and a pretty one at that, would be happy to pose for some shots. Who would know the difference? Besides, the real Miss Golden Flowers would be pleased to have her identity confused.

White was dubious, but the woman in question was not. She layered on some lipstick, eye shadow, and rouge, slipped as seductively as she could into some army togs, posed with a pistol in each hand, and snarled into the camera at the Japanese soldiers who were both the imaginary and genuine targets of her wrath. The Information Committee photographed her from several different angles. The pictures were sent around the world. This woman, whatever her real identity, was now "Pistol-Packing Miss Golden Flowers," and her increasing popularity meant that White had to provide more and more information about her.

He does not tell us what he wrote, and his stories no longer exist, but let us take a moment to fantasize about White doing his own fantasizing. He sits at his typewriter, rolls in a sheet of paper, and out comes a series of overheated tales of a sweet young thing raised on a farm in rural China, performing her daily chores of milking and feeding and planting, until one day, without warning, her entire family is slaughtered by a horde of rampaging dwarf bandits from whom the girl herself just barely manages to escape by hiding—where? In a pile of hay, that's it, a pile of hay. It is all she can do not to sneeze. Or cry.

After the dwarf bandits flee, the future Miss Golden Flowers runs into the woods, and over the course of the next few years assembles a small army of other girls just like herself, all of them once innocent, all of them now vowing revenge most vicious against those who have massacred their closest kin. They live on tree bark, mushrooms, other forms of wild vegetation, and water from the streams. They spend their teenage years growing beautiful and pulchritudinous, and at the same time training themselves into a military cadre more brutal and efficient than any the Chinese people have ever known before. Superheroes, they become; comic-book queens of violence, practicing their deadly arts on small contingents of Japanese civilians who make the mistake of crossing their path. When Miss Golden Flowers thinks they are ready to attack Japanese soldiers, attack they do. Single-handedly, they blast the tiny but menacing invaders back to the Middle Ages, and their own exploits become legends that will live on in the glorious history of their nation.

Or at least long enough to embarrass Teddy White. "Three years later," he wrote, "long after I had left the service of the Chinese government, the now defunct *American Weekly* [magazine] gave [Miss Golden Flowers] a full front-page spread. By then I was temporarily Far Eastern editor of *Time* magazine in New York and when it was suggested that *Time* pick up the story I had to demur and confess my role as father of a fraud."

But a fraud of a much more insidious nature was taking place at *Time* by then, and in this case White was a victim. So were the magazine's many thousands of readers. The perpetrator was Henry Luce, one of the weekly's two founders, born in China in 1898, the son of a Presbyterian missionary. The other founder, Britton Hadden, died in 1929, when *Time* was but six years old, and from that point on the magazine, often to its detriment, was Luce's personal fiefdom.

Luce was even more enchanted by China than White was, and more determined to play a role in its future, which is to say, more determined that China become a Christian country and not be ruled by the godless Communist Mao Tse-tung. White, a Jew, was more strongly anti-Communist than pro-Christian.

He and Luce, and in fact much of the Western world, were united in their support of Generalissimo Chiang Kai-shek, Mao's sworn enemy for control of China. Luce went so far as to name Chiang and his wife *Time*'s "Man and Wife of the Year" in 1937, the magazine proclaiming—prematurely and, as it turned out, erroneously—that "Chiang Conquers All." But White was already beginning to have his doubts about Chiang's leadership abilities, and as the years passed they would grow into certainty. He would eventually come to see Chiang as "a pathetic man" who "did not know how to be a good ruler."

Chiang fumbled and bumbled at his tasks; he had achieved greatness in the twenties by clearing the Yangtze basin of old warlords and setting up the Nationalist government there; he had reached heroic stature in the first two years of the war against Japan, organizing the coalition of resistance, drenching his cities in blood rather than yield them to the Japanese; after that, the fronts stabilized and the war froze him. Then, sometime after America entered the war, or possibly *because* America entered the war, his Mandate of Heaven ran out. By Chinese tradition, dynasties rule only so long as they keep the Mandate; when it is mysteriously withdrawn, the dynasty crumbles. Chiang was mystified when slowly he began to realize not only Heaven no longer supported him, but that he was powerless outside his palace. And as his bitterness grew, so did his resentment toward America, which he held duty bound to save him from both the Japanese and the forces of communism. The Americans would do neither.

As White's misgivings about Chiang were building, he could not help but clash with Luce, who refused to entertain such doubts and would not tolerate their appearing, or even being hinted at, in his magazine. Actually, White's articles could have been much worse. He could have written about the barbarous manner in which Chiang treated his troops. He could have written about widespread corruption throughout Chiang's army, especially the misappropriation of funds from the United States, some of which went to support Chiang's lavish lifestyle rather than to sustain his beleaguered soldiers. He could have written about cowardice under fire that sometimes extended to the point of Chiang's troops deserting a battlefield and leaving weapons behind that Mao's soldiers confiscated to use against Chiang in future conflicts.

Nonetheless, what he did write troubled Luce, who at one point responded in a telling manner:

> In Chungking you are, of course, daily confronted with all the things that are not being done as well as they should be. But just think, Teddy—the great fact is that Chungking is still there! That's the fact that you have to be concerned about explaining. . . . You have always had immense faith in China and the Generalissimo. . . . Perhaps you felt that you had communicated too much faith. I simply write you to say you need have no such fears. It is still the faith—and not the defects of the faith—which it is most of all important to communicate.

It was a remarkable thing for one journalist to say to another, a remarkable twisting of everything that journalism is supposed to be. When the facts do not suit our preconceptions, Luce was telling White in effect, write fiction, think of it as faith, and trust that the facts will one day transform themselves accordingly. It was also a remarkable statement in that it reveals Luce's true motives in his coverage of China. "Faith" is a religious term; the Chinese were not flesh-and-blood human beings to him so much as potential vessels for his own religion, and as such were to be treated as the Almighty's most precious assets, something more valuable to a zealot than a flesh-and-blood human being.

White could not accept such advice. He went on writing the truth of China, and of Chiang, as he believed it to be and as it in fact turned out. But to little avail. More and more, he found that his copy was being rewritten in New York, primarily by Whittaker Chambers, who would later carve out his own place in history as the primary witness against Alger Hiss in his trial as a Communist, the trial that would first bring Richard Nixon to center stage in American public life.

Finally, White and another *Time* correspondent in China, Annalee Jacoby, whose copy was also being completely camouflaged in New York, decided to bypass the censorship of Luce and Chambers and write a book called *Thunder Out of China*. Even before it was published, Luce realized that as much as he liked White as a person, and as much as he admired his energy and commitment as a journalist and fellow Sinophile, he would have to reassign him. He had not read the early drafts of *Thunder*, but could imagine the claps. There would be harsh analysis of Chiang for a number of reasons, a grudging acceptance of support for Mao attributed to a majority of China's peasants—a direct contradiction of *Time*'s editorial policy. He knew, in other words, that the book would be blasphemy. He would not stand for it.

Luce told the chief of correspondents for *Time*, a man named C. C. Wertenbaker, to find somewhere else in the world for White to ply his trade. He wanted him out of the Far East. Wertenbaker suggested Moscow, and White was enthusiastic. Luce, however, was not. "I'm not sure you're the man for Moscow," he told White. "It seems to me that you and [your fellow correspondent and author John] Hersey have been using Time for your own personal advancement." With that, White concluded that his relationship with Luce was over. Perhaps he had known it for some time. There would be no reassignment; instead, White handed in his resignation.

As a result, readers of *Time* remained ignorant of Chiang Kai-shek's graft and military ineptitude for years to come, just as readers of the *New York Times* had been for so long ignorant of Joseph Stalin's monstrous cruelty to the residents of Ukraine.

Time readers, as well as a lot of other Americans brought up on a diet of Luce-inspired journalism, also remained ignorant of the growth of communism in the world's most populous land. Which meant that when we finally did find out about it, when Chairman Mao's godlike status was finally acknowledged in the West, it seemed all the more menacing than if we had acquired our knowledge more gradually. One of the results was that right-wing demagogues like Senator Joe McCarthy were able to turn the situation to their advantage. They bedeviled the State Department by asking, "Who lost China? Who lost China?" It was a question that resonated in some circles like the exhortation from a previous time to "Remember the *Maine*."

The answer, of course, was that no one had lost China—no one in the State Department, no one in any other position in our government. The Chinese were people, not objects that had been misplaced by inept or treasonous U.S. diplomats. The Chinese followed the leader they wanted to follow, and there was nothing Americans could have done about it. Henry Luce and other journalists of conservative bent simply refused to publish the truth until so late that it came as a shock, which thus made it all the more potent a weapon for those who preached that communism was becoming an equally powerful force in the United States.

15

Janet's World

WHEN TEDDY WHITE CONFESSED THAT MISS GOLDEN
Flowers was, in large part, a figment of his imagination,
no one seemed to think there was anything scandalous
about it. He was just a newsman doing what newsmen sometimes
did, especially on a day when not much was happening, and his
saga of the young woman's adventures was reminiscent of the cliff-
hangers that would soon be so popular at American movie theaters.
It brought him no derision, did not affect his career. He went on to
publish a number of critically acclaimed books, including his four
volumes about the presidency, and starting in the sixties began to
appear on NBC News as the network's resident election analyst.

When the editors of the *Washington Post* found out that "Jimmy,"
the adolescent drug addict from one of the District of Columbia's seedier neighborhoods, was entirely a figment of reporter

Janet Cooke's imagination, the reaction could not have been more different. She became an untouchable in the world of journalism and an object of scorn to almost all who knew about her. She has not worked in the business since. She will not work in it again.

What was the difference between White's hoax and Cooke's? It was not that White was white and Cooke black, nor that White was male and Cooke female, nor White Jewish and Cooke Christian. The most salient answer is: time. Almost four decades had passed between Miss Golden Flowers and Jimmy, *the* four decades during which reporters outgrew their timidity and turned not only on officials of the government and the military, but also, if circumstances called for it, on their fellow reporters. A journalist who lied in print, after all, was a blot not just on her own reputation but on the entire field.

And as such, Cooke's hoax became a turning point in the public perception of journalism in the twentieth century, one that has not turned back since. She did not single-handedly undo all the good that Halberstam, Sheehan, Safer, Woodward, Bernstein, and others had done for the public perception of journalism, not by any means. She did not, however, contribute to it. In truth, the public has never perceived journalists as especially admirable figures. After all, the best work that reporters do is often controversial in nature, and that means it cannot help but make enemies among those who are accused of acting in an improper manner. Controversial stories often result in a backlash. There were, for instance, those who thought reporters had hounded President Nixon out of office, and in the process had gone further than they were entitled to go.

Cooke, however, raised suspicions not about journalistic bias or overzealousness, but about the even more important issue of veracity. For the rest of the century and into the next one, suspicions about the motives of the press would not only grow, but become too often justified.

It was certainly not what Janet Cooke had intended.

Cooke came to the *Post* from the *Toledo Blade*, a twenty-six-year-old woman of color who listed all the right credentials and, however subtly, gave off all the wrong vibes. According to her résumé, she had been a Phi Beta Kappa graduate of Vassar in 1976. She claimed various other academic honors as well, such as the ability to speak several languages, including Portuguese and Italian. Her manner was such that when she interviewed with the *Post* about six months before she got the job, no one with whom she spoke had any reason to doubt her résumé. They were impressed with her writing ability, her attire, her ambition. Perhaps too much ambition, a few people thought, but better too much than too little. And she was a minority, a so-called double minority—no wonder she was ambitious! And no wonder the *Post* wanted her so much, especially Ben Bradlee, who was no longer a cub reporter but the paper's head man, its executive editor.

Another possible problem in addition to her ambition was her smarts. They were more of the classroom variety, some of the *Post* staffers thought, than the street variety. But that did not bother anyone more than her ambition did; she would get her street smarts where others got them, on the streets.

Finally, half a year after her first trip to Washington, a time during which Cooke was much on the mind of the *Post*'s editors, there was an opening at the paper that seemed just right for her, and she was hired. Everyone expected big things from Cooke, she most of all, and her initial stories gave every indication that she would realize her potential. They were written with a flair that was more literary than journalistic, and with a speed that seemed to indicate she had been on the job a long time.

Still, there was the occasional troubling sign, not apparent to everyone, but certainly to those closest to her. Cooke's first roommate when she moved to Washington was fellow *Post* reporter Elsa Walsh, and although Walsh was looking forward to the arrangement, it did not work out as she had hoped. For one thing, Cooke's rent checks kept bouncing. Perhaps it was because she seemed to do nothing with her money but buy clothes—not to impress men; there was no man in her life. She bought them to impress herself. The first day on the job, she "sashayed" into the *Post* newsroom "wearing a red wool suit over a white silk shirt, the neck opened casually to the second button, exposing a thin gold chain, a teasing glimpse of lingerie, the slight swell of a milk-chocolate breast. Her long acrylic nails gleaming in the hard fluorescent light, she made her way down a long aisle between the desk pods."

For another thing, says Walsh, Cooke "was very hard to live with, very high-strung. . . . She had no sense of the past or even the present, except for its consequences for the future. She always looked to the future, and she didn't care about the people she left behind." It was too much ambition, all right, ambition to the point of ruthlessness. And, eventually, truthlessness.

Then came the early autumn of 1980 and "Jimmy's World." Cooke had been working on the story for a week or two, shown early drafts to her superiors. All were encouraging. Finally she got permission to publish. It was to be Janet Cooke's big break, a story of her own that appeared right where she thought her name was always meant to appear, on the front page of the *Washington Post*. Street smarts? This was street smarts on parade:

Jimmy is 8 years old and a third-generation heroin addict, a precocious little boy with sandy hair, velvety brown eyes and needle marks freckling the baby-smooth skin of his thin brown arms. He nestles in a large, beige reclining chair in the living room of his comfortably furnished home in Southeast Washington. There is an almost cherubic expression on his small, round face as he talks about life—clothes, money, the Baltimore Orioles and heroin. He has been an addict since the age of 5. His hands are clasped behind his head, fancy running shoes adorn his feet, and a striped Izod T-shirt hangs over his thin feet. "Bad, ain't it," he boasts to a reporter visiting recently. "I got me six of these."

Jimmy's is a world of hard drugs, fast money, and the good life he believes both can bring. Every day, junkies casually buy heroin from Ron, his mother's live-in-lover, in the dining room of Jimmy's home. They "cook" it in the kitchen and "fire up" in the bedrooms. And every day, Ron or someone else fires up Jimmy, plunging a needle into his bony arm, sending the fourth grader into a hypnotic nod.

The story ends with Ron doing just that, and Jimmy's "head dipping and snapping upright again, in what addicts call 'the nod.'"

"'Pretty soon, man,' Ron says, 'you got to learn how to do this for yourself.'"

The story leaves no doubt that Jimmy will, and that it will be a proud moment for him when he does.

Just as Miss Golden Flowers had been a sensation in Chungking and beyond, so was Jimmy in Washington. There was a demand for more information, not just from people in suburbs like Chevy Chase who had no idea children like Jimmy existed in the inner city, but from District officials who began searching for the boy, wanting to help him. Cooke said she could not cooperate, in part because her life would be imperiled by drug dealers if she did. There was also a demand for pictures of Jimmy, even television appearances. Cooke said no. She had promised to protect the privacy of Jimmy, his mother, Ron, and those who had led her to them; there was nothing more she could say or do for public consumption. She had given her word, and a journalist's word to a source was gold.

One of Cooke's supervisors was Bob Woodward, *the* Bob Woodward, now the *Post*'s Metro editor. "Janet had written a great piece," he said. "In a way, both she and the story were almost too good to be true. I had seen her go out on a complicated story and an hour later turn in a beautifully written piece. This story was so well-written and tied together so well that my alarm bells simply didn't go off. My skepticism left me. I was personally negligent."

Others, however, were not. A veteran black reporter named Courtland Milloy was assigned to work with Cooke on a follow-up story. "We were supposed to be finding another kid," Milloy said. "But I'll tell you the truth, I wanted to find Jimmy. Hell, that kid needed help. So as we drove around I circled through Condon Terrace, the general area where Janet said he lived."

Milloy became immediately suspicious. As reported by his *Washington Post* colleague David Maraniss, Milloy said, "It didn't take long to see that she didn't know the area." Both Milloy and his co-workers were starting to believe that Cooke did not have sources to protect so much as secrets to hide. But Cooke dismissed the doubters. "They're just jealous," she told Walsh. "They are not going to get where I'm going."

Thanks primarily to Woodward, Cooke went all the way to a nomination for a Pulitzer Prize. But by the time she won the award for best feature report, those in the *Post* newsroom did not consider her work a prizewinner so much as an ever-growing source of controversy. Eventually Cooke was summoned to the office of Ben Bradlee. Much later, she would discuss what happened with journalist Mike Sager, a friend and onetime lover. In Sager's version:

> "Say two words in Portuguese," challenged Ben Bradlee.
> Janet shrugged.
> "Do you have any Italian?"
> "No."
> "If you had to speak French to me right now to save your job," said Bradlee, sighing heavily, "what would you say?"
> Janet could speak French. All those nights as a girl, lying in bed, conjugating verbs, dreaming of Paris. But as she stood before Bradlee, seated in his big chair, something just came over Janet, and she dug in her heels. Four French words echoed in her mind. They translated, "Go fuck yourself."
> In the end, it was the résumé that got her. Supernigger fell to earth.

Two days after Cooke won the Pulitzer, Woodward returned it, and Cooke resigned from the *Washington Post*, her career in journalism at an end.

*   *   *

In 1982, Cooke made her first and only appearance on national television, answering Phil Donahue's questions about her actions. She explained to him that ever since the *Washington Post* had broken the Watergate story, making journalism a more glamorous profession and the *Post* its pedestal the pressure to succeed alongside the Woodwards and Bernsteins was unbearable; in dreaming up Jimmy and his tribulations, she had done nothing more than succumb to that pressure. She gave the impression that, at least in her opinion, most other people would have done the same.

What she did not say was that, however much pressure existed in the *Post* newsroom, and there was surely a great deal and had been even before Watergate, Cooke brought a suitcase full of her own pressures, for her own reasons, and that they, ultimately, were the reason for her cheating.

Another fourteen years would pass before Janet Cooke went public again, so to speak. In 1996, she asked Mike Sager to write a profile of her for *Gentlemen's Quarterly* magazine. Seven years later, Sager published a collection of his interviews in a book called *Scary Monsters and Super Freaks: Stories of Sex, Drugs, Rock 'n' Roll and Murder*. Nothing in the title, except a fondness for Steely Dan and the Rolling Stones, has anything to do with Cooke.

Since ending her employment with the *Post*, Sager tells us, Cooke had "spent her life on the run: first as the wife of an American diplomat in Paris, more recently as a divorced, nearly part-time retail clerk in Toledo; Ann Arbor, Michigan; and Kalamazoo." Her Kalamazoo position was in the Liz Clairborne women's boutique in a shopping mall department store. Her pay: six dollars an hour.

"I want my life back," Cooke said to Sager the day they met, knowing it would never happen. "What I did was horrible, believe me, I think that. But I don't think that in this particular case the punishment has fit the crime. I've lost my voice. I've lost half of my life. I'm in a situation where cereal has become a viable dinner choice. It is my fault that I've never spoken up. But I'm a 41-year-old woman now, and I'm starting to understand some things about life, about my life. If people only understood why this really happened, maybe they'd have a different take on things. Maybe they'd think I wasn't so evil."

And maybe she wasn't. Maybe Sager, who was in a position to know, realized that Cooke was so tyrannized in her childhood by a father demanding perfection in everything from academic performance to piano lessons that only by lying about her accomplishments could she survive his scrutiny. Maybe Sager knew Stratman Cooke's scrutiny was so great that his daughter had never learned how to relate to other people, that she never had any friends in school because the family lived in a run-down black neighborhood and Daddy believed none of the kids in a place like that were good enough for his daughter. Maybe it was Stratman Cooke who packed Janet's suitcase for her.

This does not excuse her behavior as a journalist, but maybe it does provide an explanation, and in doing so will also provide a means for her to find the other half of her life, outside a newsroom, out of the shadow of her father's insistent specter.

16

What a Picture Is Worth

U P TO THE TWENTIETH CENTURY, JOURNALISTS HAD, FOR THE most part, only two recourses for distorting reality: make up people who did not exist or write about occurrences that did not occur. It had begun to seem limiting, like shooting craps with only one die. Surely, if they put their minds to it, the press could expand the bounds of duplicitous reporting.

The development of technology cooperated. Advances in both still and moving photography and, later in the century, the development of videotape would provide a third means of fictionalizing the news—producing pictures of events that had occurred without a camera or a photographer being present and thus were being re-created for an audience, or that would not happen under any circumstance whether journalists were present or not.

The *New York Graphic* seems to have led the way in this dubious practice as it had done in so many other dubious journalistic practices. According to one of the paper's readers, for whom it was the guiltiest of pleasures, "The only value ever claimed for [the *Graphic*] was that it educated readers up to a point where they were able to understand the other tabloids."

It was sometime during the twenties that the paper got truly innovative with its introduction of the "composograph," a rather elegant term that meant nothing more than photographically attaching one person's head onto another person's body. It sounds simple enough now, but it had never been done before. The first composograph, Neal Gabler tells us, illustrated "the Kip Rhinelander trial at which the wealthy playboy Rhinelander was seeking an annulment of his marriage to Alice Jones on the ground that Jones hadn't told him she was a Negress. Jones had been ordered to bare herself in court to show her skin color. The *Graphic* found a model to reenact the scene, and the composograph was born." That day's *Graphic*, with Alice Jones's head magically appended to who-knows-who's body, sold a hundred thousand copies more than usual.

A later *Graphic* composograph may well represent, as author Ben Yagoda has said of the paper in general, "one of the low points in the history of American journalism." In this particular tableau were a fifty-one-year-old millionaire named Edward W. "Daddy" Browning, who had divorced his first wife because he suddenly decided that, at twenty-one, she was too old for him; a teenage girl named Frances "Peaches" Heenan, whom Browning had married after winning her heart at a high school dance that he had sponsored for the specific purpose of finding his next bride; and an African honking gander, or male goose, which, apparently at the *Graphic*'s urging, became a frequent companion of Browning's.

As for the composograph, it was published shortly after Peaches, claiming to have had a nervous breakdown, deserted her husband and ran home to Mama, although not before accepting a thousand dollars from the *Graphic* to write about "Daddy's" strange sexual behavior—the implication, of course, being that the gander was part of it. The three principals in the story—man, woman, and fowl—were "photographed" in the Browning bedroom. The caption for the picture was "Honk Honk. It's the Bonk." One was free to interpret as he or she chose.

Less ludicrously, as virtually anything would have to be, Charles Lindbergh's mother came east to watch him make some final test flights before his attempt to cross the Atlantic in the *Spirit of St. Louis*. Afterward, the two of them posed for photographers, one of whom asked her to kiss her son goodbye. Mrs. Lindbergh refused. "I wouldn't mind if we were used to that," she replied, "but we come of an undemonstrative Nordic race."

Then mother and son walked away from the cameramen and had lunch in a restaurant close to the airfield. When they finished, they strolled to a nearby train station, the press still hovering, clicking off a few final rolls of film. Mrs. Lindbergh patted her son on the shoulder, whispered a few final words of encouragement, and boarded her train home. They waved to each other as the train chugged slowly into the distance, the two of them not to see each other again until he was the most famous man in the world.

The next day Lindbergh picked up a New York paper—we do not know which one—and found a picture of himself on the front page kissing his mother on the lips. He had never heard of such a thing as a composograph. Still, he was not surprised that a newspaper had found a means of obtaining a photograph of people doing something they had never done in real life. He threw the paper away and went out to the airfield for the day's preparations.

The novelist Upton Sinclair was the son of a liquor salesman who spent too much time sampling his wares, and as a result kept his family in constant financial straits and fear of his irrational behavior. It was probably this more than anything that led Sinclair to grow up wanting the world to be a better place and to take an active role in the process. His heroes, he often said, were Jesus Christ, whose moral teachings were perfect, and Percy Bysshe Shelley, whose poetry was very nearly perfect.

Sinclair's writing was not perfect, a bit rough at the edges, but he cared more about moral instruction than fluent prose. He is best known for his book *The Jungle*, an exposé of the meatpacking industry in Chicago: its dreadfully unsanitary conditions, the corruption of the men who ran it, the hopelessness of those who toiled in it. The novel was more a work of muckraking journalism than a conventional work of fiction; Sinclair wanted to reform the society in which he lived more than titillate it with stories.

And, in fact, he did. The book led not only to the passage of legislation to improve conditions in the meatpacking industry, but to the creation of the Food and Drug Administration. It might not have been moral instruction, but *The Jungle* was a work of legislative instruction at its best-selling best.

Unfortunately for him, Sinclair allowed himself to be too encouraged by the book's success. He used some of his profits to indulge his socialist proclivities and start a utopian community. Like all such American experiments, it proved costly, short-lived, and disillusioning. Sinclair's profits from *The Jungle* might just as well have vanished into a jungle.

More books followed, the author taking on the coal and oil industries, financial wheeling and dealing in many of its forms, the military, public education, the treatment of men and women in prisons—Sinclair taking on much of America. But America proved much more resistant to his later books than it had been to *The Jungle*. So in 1934, he decided he would try to influence the course of society as a politician rather than as a wordsmith and announced his candidacy for governor of California. It was not his first bid for elective office, but it seemed his most promising; he surprised many in the state, perhaps even himself, by winning the Democratic nomination.

Even President Franklin Roosevelt was among those who, as late as a month before the election, thought Sinclair had a chance to defeat his Republican foe, Frank Merriam. But Roosevelt, like Sinclair, underestimated the lengths to which the opposition, especially the movie industry, would go to thwart him. Sinclair's most recent book had urged federal regulation of motion pictures, and in his campaign speeches Sinclair proposed higher taxes on the studios, the money from which would go to relieve the burdens of poor people. "End Poverty in California," or EPIC, was his slogan. "Empty Promises in California" was the taunt of his opponents.

As Sinclair's campaign began to gain momentum, the major newspapers in Los Angeles reported on it less and less, finally ignoring it altogether. It might have been the Mellon divorce a few decades earlier in Pittsburgh. As for the movie industry, it levied a tax of its own to support Merriam. Writes historian and biographer Ian Hamilton, "MGM employees were invited to donate a day's pay to the Republican and the clear hint was that anyone who didn't would be looked on with disfavor. The employees were actually given checks made out to Louis Mayer." The higher the amount they filled in, the greater the gratitude from Mr. Mayer. And of course, the greater the job security.

At Columbia Pictures, studio head Harry Cohn threatened those who did not contribute to Merriam with blacklisting. When one writer refused, Cohn pleaded with him to donate a dollar, only a dollar, just to show that his heart was in the right place. Still the writer refused. Cohn skipped the blacklist and just fired the man.

It is believed that the studios raised close to half a million dollars this way, most of which they used for "leaflets, radio broadcasts, and billboards proclaiming the Democrat's intention—and that of his 'maggot-like horde'—to Sovietize California. The Bolshevik Beast, they said, would dynamite churches and nationalize children." Dynamite churches? Nationalize children?

There was more. In the greatest act of underhandedness in their history, the movie studios produced fake newsreels and flooded California theaters with them. Sometimes they ran once a night, before the feature, sometimes twice, before and after. The newsreels showed hobos and whores and hoodlums leaping out of trains, throwing off their hats and ripping off their coats, joyfully invading Southern California because Sinclair was going to be the new governor and he had promised to throw money at them. What the moviegoers did not know was that the lowlifes were in fact not lowlifes at all but movie industry extras, forced to donate their services for the cause.

Another of the newsreels featured more admirable folk, "sturdy, decent workmen and women who looked like Whistler's mother." One of them, an "elderly bit actress, dressed as a kindly grandmother, declared that she could never vote for Sinclair because he believed in free love, while elderly male actors appeared with fake beards and stage accents shouting aggressively that they were supporting the author ('Vell, his system vorked vell in Russia, vy can't it vork here?')"

When California voters went to the polls that November, the results were predictable. Frank Merriam won by 259,000 votes. The election is regarded as a landmark in U.S. political history— not, as it should be, because of the dynamic new form of dishonesty it introduced to the political process, dishonesty to which we are much more accustomed today, but because it was the first use of the motion picture as a campaign tool.

Sinclair's next book was yet another exposé. He called it *I, Candidate for Governor: And How I Got Licked.*

Fourteen years later, it was television's turn to rig up something that looked like reality. The occasion was the 1948 Democratic National Convention, and the truth of the gathering was rancorous enough not to need any rigging.

At issue was the party's position on the treatment of black Americans, who had fought so nobly for the United States in World War II and returned home to be treated so ignobly. The Axis powers might have been vanquished abroad, but Jim Crow and his "Whites Only" dicta remained as powerful in the southern United States as they had been before Pearl Harbor.

When Hubert Humphrey, then the mayor of Minneapolis, stood at the podium at Philadelphia's Convention Hall and urged those before him to "get out of the shadow of states' rights and walk forthrightly into the bright sunshine of human rights," some of the delegates stood and erupted with cheers and applause. Others, primarily from the South, simply erupted. They stormed out of their party's meeting place and turned their backs on their fellow Democrats, instead nominating for president the governor of South Carolina, Strom Thurmond, on a party they created just for the occasion, the States' Rights Party, known more familiarly as the Dixiecrats.

Thurmond's position on race could not have been more different from Humphrey's. Or more clear. "And all the laws of Washington and all the bayonets of the army," Thurmond said, as he accepted the Dixiecrat nomination, "cannot force the Negro into our homes, our schools, our churches, and our places of recreation and amusement."

It was not the first time that delegates had left the Convention hall in anger during a debate about civil rights. A day or so earlier, a smaller group than those who would form the Dixiecrats decided to depart rather than listen to more blather about equality of the races. As they approached the exit they tore off their badges. They tossed the tiny pieces of cardboard onto a small table. Then they went outside for some fresh air, a smoke, and a series of curses aimed at their more liberal-minded brethren.

As it happened, NBC had set up a camera at precisely the place where the delegates removed their badges. It had set up another camera at the table, close enough to get a tight shot of the badges piling up. It was great television—it should have been. The whole protest had been set up with the tube in mind, arranged with the delegates by an NBC director who had not only given instructions to the delegates but worked out the staging.

When the network was done filming the walkout, one of its floor managers signaled the delegates that the sequence was over and they could now reenter, stage left. They picked up their badges, put them on again, and returned to their seats. It was the new medium at its most gripping, and at its most phony.

The emotions the delegates had displayed were real. They had shown a national audience their true feelings about the notion of equal rights for blacks. But this particular demonstration was pure theatrics, the first time, as far as anyone knows, that TV journalism had engaged in such a practice.

Unfortunately for NBC, the Dixiecrat exodus was more spontaneous. Its cameras were not in position to cover the full magnitude of the furor.

In 1992, the network was at it again, this time with special effects. *Dateline NBC*, the network news division's magazine program, reported on the tendency of certain models of older General Motors pickup trucks to explode when hit from the side because that was where the gas tanks had been installed. In the first fourteen minutes of the report, *Dateline* made a fairly, if not entirely, convincing case. It was almost surely exaggerating when it suggested that half of the trucks would explode in such a collision; still, it sounded alarms worth sounding, and illustrated its claim at the end of the story by showing a truck being struck on the side, then bursting into flames that soared skyward for fifty-seven seconds. The point was clear. No one inside the truck could have survived.

For General Motors, the timing of the *Dateline* piece could not have been worse. The preceding week, a jury had ordered the automaker to pay more than $105 million to an Atlanta couple whose son had been killed in just that kind of crash. He had been driving an old GM pickup, had been hit on the side, and had been consumed in flames. NBC News seemed to have confirmed the justice of the verdict; so-called sidesaddle gas tanks were every bit as dangerous as the court decision had made them out to be.

Of course, General Motors would appeal and would eventually end up paying less than $105 million; it was always the way in such cases. Still, in the court of public opinion, it was the guilty verdict that mattered, not the amount of the fine.

But there was something about *Dateline's* verdict that did not seem right to GM, again a matter of timing—the way the vehicle slammed into their truck just as the camera was rolling, the way the truck exploded right on cue, not a wasted moment. And fifty-seven seconds! It did not seem to GM engineers that the fire could have burned for almost a minute. Had the flames been edited to extend the length? Had other tricks been employed as well?

Then came some good timing: an anonymous phone call to General Motors corporate headquarters to confirm their suspicions; something had not been kosher with NBC's taping, although the caller did not reveal any details or how he might have known them. GM didn't care. Although it probably would have done so anyhow, it responded to the *Dateline* report by hiring a team of detectives, and they were quick to discover the truth.

The men scoured more than twenty junkyards in the Detroit area for less than a day, "and found evidence to debunk almost every aspect of the crash sequence. Last week, in a devastating press conference, GM showed that the conflagration was rigged, its causes misattributed, its severity overstated and other facts distorted. Two crucial errors: NBC said the truck's gas tank had ruptured, yet an X-ray showed it hadn't; NBC consultants set off explosive miniature rockets beneath the truck split seconds before the crash—yet no one told viewers."

Nothing like it had ever happened before. In the words of former network news president Reuven Frank, "This is the worst black eye NBC News has suffered in my experience, which goes back to 1950." Making matters worse was that the network's initial reaction was to deny GM's charge, and then the very next day do an about-face and issue an apology that NBC had written. It had then been shown to General Motors for final approval before it was read on the air.

That task fell to the two coanchors of *Dateline NBC*, Jane Pauley and Stone Phillips. An excerpt from Pauley's section:

First, and most importantly, we want to emphasize that what we characterized in the November "Dateline" segment as an unscientific demonstration was inappropriate and does not support the position that G.M.'s C.K. trucks are defective. Specifically, NBC's contractor did put incendiary devices under the trucks to insure [*sic*] there would be a fire if gasoline were released from the truck's gas tank. NBC personnel knew this before we heard the program but the public was not informed because consultants at the scene told us the devices did not start the fire. We agree with G.M. that we should have told our viewers about these devices. We acknowledge the placing of the incendiary devices under the truck was a bad idea from start to finish.

Pauley mentioned a contractor. She mentioned consultants. Not journalists, these people, but outsiders one and all—and this was a controversy of its own. It was the reason that old-school NBC News correspondents (including the author, one of the younger old-schoolers, serving as a correspondent from 1976 to 1983), were almost as unhappy with the mea culpa as we were with the incident that made it necessary.

In my days at NBC, and long before that, we did our own work, and if we could not do it we would have concluded that it did not fit under the heading of journalistic enterprise and therefore should not be done at all. Of course, we reported all the time on events that happened because of the enterprise of others; that is the very essence of news. But we did not report on events that happened because we were paying people to make them happen.

One could only conclude that the network had malice—or at least high drama—on its mind and therefore decided to farm out some employment to people who were better at pyrotechnics than ethics. How could it happen? How did the network where I still knew so many people, and knew the standards to be high and the employees to be fair and thoughtful, ever find itself in such a position?

For one thing, the *network* did not. A very few employees at the network did—three producers—and they should not be seen as representatives of the standards of the entire company. All three were promptly fired, as they should have been. To analyze the motives of these three people after all this time is a highly speculative enterprise, but one possibility is that they might have thought they had done nothing wrong. After all, it is true that *some* GM trucks caught fire when struck from the side. That the producers were unable to duplicate this result with their own experiments did not make the result fallacious. What they were doing, according to this scenario, was creating an occasional reality that, for whatever reason, they could not create on this particular occasion with their particular set of efforts.

Or the producers, like Janet Cooke before them, were yielding to pressure, in this case the pressure from *60 Minutes*, the magazine program at CBS News, a television landmark with which *Dateline* tried so hard, so long, and so unsuccessfully to compete.

Or, since television news had by this time become perceived as such a glamorous occupation, paying high salaries, offering jet-set lifestyles and, to those on the air, varying amounts of fame, the three-man NBC bomb squad might have been operating, at a level just beneath that of conscious plotting, under the influence of mammon's sultry lure. If the piece had worked out the way they wanted, they might have become stars of a sort. But it didn't. So under scenario number three we imagine that they could not bear to come so close to the pot of gold and, when all was said and done and broadcast, still be the same old anonymous producers they had always been.

The three producers would later regret the lengths to which they had gone, and might have done so even had they not gotten caught, but in the meantime they had shamed themselves, their company, and the entire field of broadcast journalism. Nothing like it has happened since. Special effects have remained in superhero movies, where they belong, not in TV news programs.

The fundamental irony here is that the *Dateline* story was in its broadest assertions true, and General Motors knew it. By telling the story in such an unscrupulous manner, NBC might have blackened its own eye, but called more attention to the possible perils of the trucks in question than responsible reporting would have done.

But it was all too late, which brings us to another irony. Beginning in 1988, four years before the *Dateline* report, GM had begun to move the gas tanks on its pickup trucks to a safer location—this, as the *New York Times* later reported, after "critics contend that at least 300 people have died in crashes related to the location of dual fuel tanks on the outside of the trucks' protective metal frames."

Thus the National Broadcasting Company had tarnished its reputation not because of a potential headline-making scoop, but over a four-year-old story that General Motors had for that entire period been in the process of rectifying. The real news was that GM had not issued a recall on the older vehicles, the ones with the sidesaddle tanks. This, perhaps the most damning of charges against the automaker, NBC never mentioned at all.

17

The Most Hated Man in American Newsrooms

MOST OF THE OFFENSES IN THE PRECEDING PAGES, WHETHER pranks, misdemeanors, or felonies; whether motivated by squeamishness or egotism or fear of failure; whether they led to major repercussions or minor turbulence, were perpetrated by an individual reporter or a single news organization. There are few examples of journalists conspiring to tell a lie, and according to the verdict of a jury in Flemington, New Jersey, they did not do so in the case that will now be presented.

But that the press had made up its mind about the truth of this case before the truth was officially known is certain. That the press had ganged up on a poor German carpenter in the most unscrupulous of ways because it believed he was a liar is certain. That the press had no right to make a decision about whether the man was lying is certain. That the press acted unethically and even illegally in promoting the man's guilt is even more certain.

His guilt was in fact established by a jury of his peers, and he was put to death for his crime. Recent forensic evidence indicates that the jury was correct. But although it is not the place of this volume to go into detail, there is also reason for doubt. Two respectable authors, British journalist Ludovic Kennedy and American author Noel Behn, both cited in the bibliography, published books in 1985 and 1994 that raise intelligent and nagging questions about the verdict. Other questions come from other sources and are equally perplexing.

Regardless, there is no doubt about the behavior of reporters. On this the gavel sounds conclusively. And if by some chance the recent forensic evidence had been either tainted or misinterpreted; if by some chance the jury was wrong—and among the evidence they considered in arriving at their decision was evidence that had been fabricated by journalists—then those same journalists are, in the court of empyreal justice, guilty of being accessories to state-sanctioned murder.

Again, Charles Lindbergh. This time, though, reporters and photographic tricks were not his problem. This time his problem was something worse, something much worse.

On March 1, 1932, Lindbergh's twenty-month-old son, Charles Augustus Jr., was put to bed at the usual time, eight p.m., by his mother and his nanny, a very carefully vetted Scotswoman named Betty Gow. Half an hour later, Mrs. Lindbergh and her husband had dinner, then sat before the fire for a few minutes in their Hopewell, New Jersey, home, talking idly about a subject that neither of them later remembered. Afterward, they took turns bathing, Lindbergh first, Anne following him.

At about ten p.m., Gow, who was finishing up some chores in the kitchen, decided to go upstairs and have a look at the child. He was not there. She told Mrs. Lindbergh, who was still in the tub, but quickly got out and began to dry herself.

"Are you sure?" she said.

"Yes, ma'am."

Anne Lindbergh initially suspected her husband of having hidden the child; it was the kind of perverse practical joke he sometimes liked to play.

Gow went downstairs and asked Lindbergh about the baby. He assured her he hadn't played a joke, and it was obvious by the shocked expression on his face that he was telling the truth. He ran upstairs, Gow trailing after, and into the baby's room. The first thing he noticed was an empty crib. Next to the crib, the curtains fluttering toward it, was an open window; an envelope, which Lindbergh immediately assumed was a ransom note, had been placed on the sill.

His wife dashed into the nursery in her robe. He turned to her. "Anne," he said, "they have stolen our baby."

He cautioned the two women not to touch the envelope. It is not clear whether he called the police or told the butler to do it. But moments later he ran outside and slowly circled the house. Beneath the baby's room, he found a crude homemade ladder, just tall enough to reach the window.

Lindbergh was right. It was a ransom note, demanding fifty thousand dollars for the return of his son. Using the services of a man named Dr. Jafsie Condon as an intermediary, the money was paid to the kidnappers, but the deadline for the baby's return passed and he was not handed over to his parents. Nor did it happen the next day or the next. Nor the next week or the week following. The Lindberghs waited anxiously, frantically, but their baby did not come back to them, and they heard nothing from the abductors.

Finally, two and a half months after Charles Augustus Lindbergh Jr. was snatched from his crib, his mutilated body was found in a wooded area about four miles from their home, his skull protruding from the ground. The cause of death: a severe blow to the head.

It was not first event to be named "the Crime of the Century" by the press, and there would be many afterward, but until the Kennedy assassination it wore the label as well as any. Bruno Richard Hauptmann, a German carpenter, was arrested for the child's murder in September 1934 when he tried to spend some of the ransom money.

There was other evidence against him. He was identified as the man to whom the ransom had been paid, although it had been paid at night and the recipient was not clearly visible, nor did he speak in such a way as to easily identify himself. And Hauptmann had been absent from work the day of the kidnapping. This was the core of the prosecution's case—strong, but not conclusive.

There were also cases, although they would not be made until much later, by Kennedy and Behn, and they, too, were inconclusive, against Gow and one of Mrs. Lindbergh's sisters. Other scenarios have it that a gang of organized criminals was behind the kidnapping, although if so their methods seem exceedingly amateurish, and that Hauptmann was somehow involved in the deed, but was joined by other culprits, including at least one person with strong connections to the Lindbergh household. None of these suppositions can be dismissed with certainty.

Regardless, Hauptmann's trial was "the Trial of the Century." He was "the Most Hated Man in the World." The latter designation, like the others created by American journalists, was an indication that they had found Hauptmann guilty well before the Flemington jury had heard the first word of testimony in the case. Consider: Hauptmann was a German, and the Germans had been our foe in World War I. His features were coarse, his speech guttural. He had entered the United States illegally. He had a criminal background, having resorted to burglary for a time when he could not find work as a carpenter. There was, as far as anyone knew, more evidence against him than against anyone else. He was as perfectly cast for the role of villain as Lindbergh was for the role of hero.

And so, just as the police had decided to make the jury's job as easy as possible by refusing to investigate anyone other than

Hauptmann, the press decided to make things even easier. Tom Cassidy, a reporter for the *New York Daily News*, a paper that was rumored to keep cops on its payroll for just such occasions as this, was allowed to enter Hauptmann's apartment when police first searched it. He was also allowed to slip away from the police to a corner of one of the rooms where he could not be observed and write Condon's name, address, and phone number in pencil on one of the walls. When he finished, he smeared the information to make it appear that Hauptmann had tried to erase it. This "evidence" was entered into the case, even though Cassidy was overheard in a tavern one night bragging to several of his friends that he was the person responsible for it.

"The worst offender," though, according to Ludovic Kennedy, was not the *Daily News*, but William Randolph Hearst's *Journal*,

> which claimed falsely that maps found in the Hauptmann apartment included those of the roads around Hopewell, that the chisel found on the lawn at Hopewell was the only one missing from a similar set in Hauptmann's tool-chest, that a "canoeing" shoe of Hauptmann buried in his garage matched the footprint found beneath the nursery window at Hopewell, that the caliber of Hauptmann's pistol fitted a hole in the baby's head. But the *New York Times* was not far behind, with equally false stories that writing paper found in the Hauptmann apartment was the same as that used in the ransom notes, that ladder rungs found there were the same as those in the kidnap ladder . . . that Hauptmann had written to a man in a prison in Ohio saying he intended to kidnap the Lindbergh baby, that several people living near Hopewell had seen him there before.

It is a roster of reportorial malfeasances that should have taken a dozen news organizations a century to compile. That the *Daily News*, the *Journal*, and the *Times* were able to demolish so many rules of their profession so quickly demonstrates not only the depth of their bias but their disregard for the workings of the judicial system.

Reporters did not stop there, however. They not only played God with Hauptmann's fate, they played prosecutor. The *New York*

Journal, which cannot help but assume a major role in a book like this no matter what the year, no matter what the event, was one of twenty-four Hearst papers that had declared Hauptmann guilty before the judge made his first appearance behind the bench. The *Journal*'s star columnist, a woman named Adela Rogers St. Johns, was also the daughter of one of the nation's foremost attorneys, and she took advantage of her dual role to pass notes to both prosecutor David Wilentz and defense lawyer Edward J. "Death House" Reilly during the trial. Reilly's nickname was well earned. Before Hauptmann, he had represented some fifteen hundred people accused of homicide. One thousand four hundred ninety-four of them had been executed by the state.

Another member of the press who had declared Hauptmann guilty prior to the trial's opening, and persisted in so declaring in article after article, was Walter Winchell, the most famous gossip columnist of the time. When Jafsie Condon finished testifying that he had handed the ransom money to Hauptmann, Winchell leaped from his chair and ran forward to shake his hand. When the verdict was announced, Winchell leaped again, shouting to the entire courtroom, "I said that in October. I predicted he'd be guilty. Oh, that's another big one for me! Come on, fellas, put it in your stories. I was the first one to call it." To which the United Press's Robert Musel responded, "How do they let a fucking child like this in the room?"

But there were other children about, children behaving even more outrageously. Earlier in the trial, less famous journalists shouted at the defense counsel, shouted at Hauptmann, sometimes even shouted questions at him and berated him for not answering. They called him a liar and worse when he gave answers to questions that the attorneys had asked.

Sometimes Hauptmann hollered back at the reporters. Sometimes he shook his fist. Once or twice, bracing himself on the arms of his chair on the witness stand, he looked as if he might do some leaping of his own, flying at the press to do battle. The judge, who did not so much preside over the trial as enjoy his front row seat at the mayhem, was as likely to tell Hauptmann to behave as he was the journalists.

In 1962, NBC News presented an edition of its documentary series *David Brinkley's Journal* that focused on the Lindbergh kidnapping. It was called "Trial of the Century: Press Coverage of the Hauptmann Trial . . . 'It Was a Sickness.'"

To the surprise of no one who had followed the case, Hauptmann was found guilty. Newspapers all across the country gloated over the verdict. But when it was announced, and the final stories filed, the party was over for the press. Reporters packed their bags and notebooks, settled their tabs at Nellie's tap room at Flemington's Union Hotel, and headed back to their newsrooms. They had been brought together for an occasion that today would have resulted in the arrest of many of them, but which was for all a heart-thumpingly good time. It was hard to say good-bye to friends newly made in such a historic occasion, one in which they had found themselves, more than ever before, in the middle of an epic struggle between good and evil. In all likelihood, they landed on the side of truth. But they could not have done so in a more corrupt and disgraceful fashion.

As for Bruno Richard Hauptmann, he swore his innocence until his dying day, April 3, 1936, when he was put to death for the murder of Charles Augustus Lindbergh Jr. His body was cremated, and it is believed that his wife returned to Germany with the ashes. She never visited the United States again.

18

What Haste Makes

A T THE OTHER END OF THE SPECTRUM OF JOURNALISTIC wrongdoing, there is the mistake: the simple, ordinary, innocent mistake—unintended, but over the course of time equally unavoidable. It may be caused by impatience or misunderstanding or perhaps even typographical error. It is not caused by greed, bias, arrogance, or self-promotion. The mistake may have the same effect on the reader as deliberate deception, but it does not mean to, and for that reason it is usually corrected as soon as possible—in the next day's paper, on the next day's broadcast.

Thomas Alva Edison was misled by circumstances and made a mistake. Roy W. Howard was misled by even more elaborate circumstances and made an even greater mistake, one that brought joy to millions for several hours and then a hangover to those same people for several days. But how was he to have known? How was Edison to have known? Everyone makes mistakes.

I have made several in the preceding pages, although it should go without saying that I have not made them deliberately. As a result, I do not know what they are and will not know until someone calls them to my attention. At which point I will scold myself for my negligence and hope that few people have noticed.

A lot of people noticed what Edison did. An itinerant telegraph operator, he was living in Louisville, Kentucky, a few years after the Civil War, and developed a reputation as the fastest operator in town. He took pride in getting out the news as quickly as he could. On one occasion, though, he was too eager. He explained as follows:

> Down in Virginia the Legislature was trying to elect a United States senator. John M. Botts was the leading candidate. But he never received quite enough votes to elect him. Day after day, the sessions dragged along. One day news came that the opposition to Botts was going to pieces and that he would undoubtedly be elected the next day. The next day, just as a dispatch from Richmond began to come, the wire "broke" just as I had received the name "John M. Botts." I took a chance and wrote out a dispatch to the effect that Botts had been elected. The Louisville papers printed it. The following day, they printed a correction. Botts hadn't been elected. The Legislature, as usual, had only adjourned for the day.

Shortly after that, despite Edison's promptness at transcribing and a past relatively free from errors, his boss fired him. Yet, as biographer Ronald W. Clark suggests, the young man might have learned a valuable lesson from the experience. As an inventor, Edison seldom jumped to conclusions, even when a conclusion seemed obvious. He experimented, experimented again, made certain his results were accurate before proceeding. The memory of the Virginia legislative election may have stayed with him longer than his dexterity with a telegraph key.

One of the most famous journalistic mistakes involves the most deadly of wars to be fought to that time. It was also the most innovative. World War I was the first in which tanks played a role; the first in which grenades, trench mortars, and heavy artillery were employed; the first to befoul the air with mustard gas and other poisonous fumes; and the first to make significant military use of submarines, airplanes, and zeppelins. The last two, however, were better at surveillance than bombing; it would not be possible to hit a target consistently from the air until World War II.

World War I began in 1914 with the assassination of Archduke Franz Ferdinand in Sarajevo. Because of a complicated series of alliances, which historians still have a hard time figuring out, twenty-eight countries were eventually drawn into the fighting, with more than twenty of them aligning themselves against Kaiser Wilhelm's Germany, as Teddy Roosevelt had long since predicted, and the other so-called Central Powers. Virtually all of Europe was a battlefield, as well as Mesopotamia, Palestine, Africa. There was even fighting on some remote islands in the Pacific.

Because the United States did not enter the war until three years after the fighting began, we suffered the relatively modest total of 116,500 deaths and 204,000 injuries, but the numbers for those engaged from the outset were much greater. More than 5,100,500 Allied soldiers, not counting Americans, were killed and another 12,600,300, again excluding Americans, were injured. The corresponding totals for the Central Powers were 3,386,200 and 8,388,480.

The cost of the fighting varies according to who is making the estimate, but most estimates place the total between three hundred and four hundred billion dollars. These, however, are partial figures. They do not include the interest that would have to be paid on war debts, the pensions owed to veterans, or the costs of rebuilding the economies not only of defeated nations but many of the victors as well. And, of course, they are reckoned in early-twentieth-century dollars. In today's terms, the amounts would be exponentially greater.

For the disillusionment that the war caused, the nightmares that did not confine themselves to the hours of darkness, that would destroy the very notion of a hopeful dream and would last for generations and exact costs of a very different nature, no one could attach a price tag.

As far as Americans were concerned, there has probably never been a war that combined brutality and pointlessness to such an extent. We were heartsick about it, not certain that we should have gotten involved in the first place, wanting to do nothing more, as the autumn of 1918 drew to its midpoint, than bring our troops home. They had, after all, never been abroad before, not in such numbers, not with so little, if anything at all, to gain.

On November 7, it seemed that we were about to get our wish. All reports indicated that the fighting appeared to be over, that nothing remained except the formality of signing a peace treaty. In fact, to a reporter from United Press International, one of the world's largest wire services, it looked as if even that might have been accomplished. From a vantage point in the Bois de l'Aigle, the Wood of the Eagle, Roy W. Howard saw French soldiers standing with their guns at their sides as a party of German soldiers passed by, heading for a railroad car pulled onto a nearby siding.

He did not see the car. Nor did he see what the Germans were carrying in a leather pouch: a proposal for a peace treaty that the Allies had not yet seen either. The French were simply assuring the messengers a safe passage to the car, where the Allied commander, Marshal Ferdinand Foch, would review the proposal. Howard, as eager as the rest of his countrymen for the war's end, and as eager as other journalists to be the first to break the news, mistook the procession for something more definite. "Urgent," he cabled to his New York office in the peculiarly abbreviated language of the telegram. "Armistice Allies Germany signed morning. Hostilities ceased two afternoon."

The UPI executives in New York trusted their man. And why wouldn't they? Howard was the president of UPI! Like him, they knew that journalism was a competitive sport; the first one into print wins. So they did not try to check Howard's information with government officials, which they normally would have done, and they did not wait for further confirmation from Howard. Instead, UPI's New York contingent released the story to the papers they serviced all over the country. The news that all Americans were waiting for was on its way.

Unfortunately, so was another cable from Howard. This one arrived at UPI headquarters a few hours after the first one, with Howard admitting that, try though he had, he could not confirm the contents of the previous message. In fact the contents of the initial message were untrue, but by that time it was too late to undo the damage. It had been published in scores of newspapers in the United States, and the celebrations, wild and frenzied, merry and unfounded, had begun.

On November 8, once the truth was known, the *New York Times* reported that

> all the joyful enthusiasm pent up by New Yorkers through the long ordeal of the business of war and the waiting for peace and victory was wasted on a fake. When the sirens, whistles and bells rose in a resounding clamor, about 1 o'clock in the afternoon, carrying the news of the supposed signing of the armistice and the cessation of hostilities, men and women of all ages, all stations, in every part of the city, with an unspoken accord, suddenly stopped their business and poured into the streets to join through the afternoon in a delirious carnival of joy which was beyond comparison with anything ever seen in the history of New York.

But it was not just New York that had been fooled. Chicago burst into a "carnival of noise and ribaldry," the shouting just as loud, the enthusiasm just as unrestrained, the belief in the UPI report just as great. In Washington, D.C., people flooded into the streets, and President Woodrow Wilson's daughter "was deliciously caught up in a whirlpool of men and women dancing, singing, shouting and celebrating that Thursday's premature report of an armistice ending world war." Wilson himself, although he knew the peace treaty had not yet been signed, "understood that America now was roaring in repetition of the same kind of high spirits and fulminations loosed when the news came of the Rebel surrender in Virginia. The catcalls for the Kaiser recalled the readiness with the noose and the sour apple tree for Jeff Davis. There were fewer cowbells now and more auto horns."

When later editions of papers in New York, Chicago, Washington, and other cities printed denials of a peace treaty from State Department officials, many Americans could not make themselves believe them. They bought the papers just to tear them up and throw the pieces over their heads, allowing them to fall into the streets like confetti. They were good, surely, for nothing else.

By the night of the seventh, however, most Americans knew the truth. When the *Times* published its report on the eighth, everyone knew. It was, the *Times* went on to say, "the most colossal news fake ever perpetrated upon the American people." The *New York Tribune* was more wistful. In an editorial the next day titled "The Thief of Joy," it said, "When the real news of peace arrives shall we have another celebration as good and joyous as those first hours? Hardly, we think. The edge has been taken off."

The real news arrived on November 11, a mere four days after the mistaken report. Fortunately, it seemed, the *Tribune* was wrong. Most Americans did *not* seem to have their edge taken off and to all appearances were just as hearty and grateful as before in their revelries.

Roy W. Howard had not been responsible for a colossal news fake. He had simply misinterpreted what was happening before him. His heart, certainly, was in the right place, the same place where all American hearts resided at the time. He went on from his premature report to a long and distinguished career in journalism, cofounding the Scripps-Howard newspaper empire and providing the materials for the prestigious Roy W. Howard Archive at the School of Journalism at Indiana University in Bloomington.

None of the episodes detailed in this book have been given a place of honor there.

Epilogue

A Few Final Mistakes

Late in the nineteenth century, the St. Louis *Globe-Democrat* hired a reporter who did not really want to be a reporter. After a while, he was assigned additional duties as a theater critic, although he did not want to review plays either. He thought he was wasting his time. And also his skill, unpolished though it was. He wanted to go someplace bigger than St. Louis, do something more important than write for a newspaper. There was something of Upton Sinclair in him— Sinclair the novelist, that is, not Sinclair the aspiring politician. Like Sinclair, he wanted to write books that made people think, made a difference in how they acted, made the world a better place for those born into it without advantages.

But he did not confront his editor, Joseph McCullagh, with his dissatisfaction. McCullagh was a highly respected man in

St. Louis. The reporter was lucky that a man like McCullagh would hire him. He was lucky that anyone would hire him. But he did not feel lucky. Instead, he felt "private rages and despairs" that were sometimes not so private. People in the *Globe-Democrat* newsroom had begun to whisper about him, finding his behavior erratic at times. He had to be more careful. If he lost this job he was afraid he would end up a beggar.

Then one day he found himself with more to rage and despair than usual. Three plays were scheduled to open in St. Louis on the same night, an April Sunday. *Three* plays, *one* night. What was he supposed to do? He could ask some of his fellow reporters to help him, but wasn't sure they would, or that he could trust their judgment. He could ask McCullagh to let him review one play on each of the next three nights, but was afraid that would make him seem lazy. Besides, the other papers in town would scoop the *Globe-Democrat* on two of the plays, and he was certain McCullagh would not take kindly to that.

Instead, what he decided to do was this: he would write his "reviews" of the plays on Sunday afternoon, before any of them opened, based on materials provided by the press agents, which included real reviews by critics in other cities where the plays had run. Then he would leave his pieces at the copy desk with orders not to print them until he personally gave permission. That night he would drop into each play for half an hour or so and dash back to the office to rewrite the articles, adding or altering his opinions based on what he had seen, making his reviews as legitimate as possible given the circumstances. When he had done so, he would send the pieces down to the composing room for typesetting.

Unfortunately for the reporter, just as he was getting ready to depart from the newsroom for the first of the theaters, one of the paper's associate editors called to him. It seems there had been a streetcar holdup earlier in the day in one of the city's distant suburbs, but the paper did not have enough information for its story. The reporter was told to head out to the suburb and fill in the holes.

He was about to protest, but decided against it. It would do no good, and besides, with his having already acquired a reputation as something of a whiner, this would just make matters worse. He would be better off racing to the scene of the crime, gathering as many facts in as little time as possible, then hurrying back to the newsroom and handing over his notes to the associate editor, after which he would do his best to carry out the initial plan. He would not be able to see thirty minutes of each play, but if he could manage fifteen or even ten, he would probably be able to write an authentic-sounding, if not totally accurate, review. And since the three theaters were practically next door to one another, he might just be able to manage it.

Not a bad idea, he thought, all things considered—and it wasn't. But it did not work out. By the time he reached his destination, found a policeman who could tell him what he needed to know, tried with less success to find a witness or two, then got a ride back to the *Globe-Democrat*, it was after eleven. The plays were over, the theaters dark. Not only had he failed to see so much as a single minute of any of them, but what little he had discovered about the streetcar holdup indicated that it was a far less important story than the associate editor had believed. His coworker would be disappointed, and would probably blame him, accusing him of not devoting enough time to the story because he cared more about the plays. Which, he supposed, he did.

"Where are my reviews?" the reporter asked the associate editor, after discussing the holdup.

"They've gone to composing," he was told, meaning that the deadline had passed and they were now being set to run in the following day's paper.

Of course, the reporter thought. But maybe it wouldn't be so bad. He had parroted the opinions of critics in other cities and there was no reason to think that they didn't know what they were talking about. Still: "I went home," he later wrote, "and

went to bed but slept poorly, troubled by the thought that something might be wrong." It was. Terribly wrong:

> The next morning I arose and went through the two morning
> papers very eagerly and nervously the first thing. To my utmost
> horror and distress, there in the *Republic* on the first page was an
> announcement to the effect that owing to various washouts [on
> rail lines] in several states, not one of the three shows which had
> been scheduled to arrive the night before, and which I had written
> up as having appeared, had arrived! And in my own paper, to my
> great pain and distress, on an inside page was a full account of their
> having been staged and of the agreeable reception accorded them!

The reporter forced himself to read one of the encomiums
he had written about last night's nonexistent performances in
St. Louis. It seemed that "a large and enthusiastic audience had
received [the actor] Mr. Sol Smith Russell" at the Grand The-
atre. "Great God!" the reporter said.

Certain that he would be fired, no less certain that he deserved
to be, the reporter went to his office and began cleaning it out.
When he finished, he wrote a letter to Joseph McCullagh, who
was out of the office that day, explaining precisely what had happened the night before. He blamed himself for everything, especially for not calling the theaters after he had returned from the
streetcar stickup scene to confirm that the plays had been performed as scheduled. He put the letter in McCullagh's office,
then returned to his own desk to wait for the afternoon papers
like a man awaiting the executioner's ax. What would the competition make of his gaffe?

The *St. Louis Post-Dispatch* made plenty:

> To see three shows at once and those three wide separated by miles
> of country and washed-out sections of railroad in three different
> states (Illinois, Iowa and Missouri) is indeed a triumph, but to see
> them as having arrived and displaying their individual delights
> to three separate audiences of varying proportions assembled for

the purpose is truly amazing—one of the finest demonstrations of mediumistic, or perhaps we had better say materializing, power yet given to science to record. Indeed, now that we think of it, it is an achievement so astounding that even the *Globe* itself may well be proud of it—one of the finest flights of which the human mind or its great editor's psychic strength is capable.

The reporter was horrified. Sweat rolled down his forehead, he said, and his nerves shook from the shame of it all. Not only had the *Post-Dispatch* ridiculed the *Globe-Democrat*, but it had blamed the paper's editor, the estimable Joseph McCullagh, rather than the reporter who was really at fault. Things could not have been worse. The reporter had made his benefactor, the man who gave him a job when so many others had been unwilling, the laughingstock of the entire city, and it was more than he could bear.

He walked out of his office and for the next few days wandered the city from one end to the other, lost in the streets of a place he knew so well. He never returned to the *Globe-Democrat* or saw Joseph McCullagh again. Soon he left St. Louis. He was convinced he would never amount to anything.

The reporter's name was Theodore Dreiser, and in the years to come he would turn out to be the worst of the great American novelists.

His sentences are long and awkward and graceless. Stacked side by side, one following another in one of his lengthy novels like *Sister Carrie* or *An American Tragedy* or *Jennie Gerhardt*, they are like building blocks that don't quite fit; you can see the spaces between them, the unevenness that separates the rows. But there is an undeniable power to the structure as a whole, a power that most novels of more artful construction somehow do not achieve. Dreiser moves the reader more than he should, inflames him, stays with him. His passion for social justice overwhelms his inability to convey that passion with more conventional literary skills.

To his great frustration, though, despite the support of H. L. Mencken and a few other far-seeing critics, Dreiser's books did not sell well during his lifetime and were excoriated by a number of critics for carrying realism to a sordid extreme. He was no more successful a hundred years ago as a novelist than he had been as a theater critic.

On the other hand, and much more recently, there is the tale of Mitch Albom, a sports columnist for the *Detroit Free Press*. Fifty-one years old in 2009, Albom is an astonishing success in the publishing world, having produced nine books that have sold more than twenty million copies and been translated into forty-three languages. One of his books has been turned into a play, three into made-for-television movies. And he is still at it.

He is not a great author by any means, but he is a fluid one, and his books have a gift for stirring emotions in people about subjects that matter to them very much. What he shares with Dreiser is having written for his newspaper a column that, despite his best efforts to the contrary, turned out to be fiction.

In April 2005, Albom published a piece about the NCAA basketball tournament's Final Four game between Michigan State and North Carolina that began as follows:

> In the audience Saturday at the Final Four, among the 46,000 hoop junkies, sales executives, movie producers, parents, contest winners, beer guzzlers, hip-hop stars and lucky locals who knew somebody who knew somebody, there were two former stars for Michigan State, Mateen Cleaves and Jason Richardson. They sat in the stands, in the MSU clothing, and rooted for their alma mater. They were teammates in the magical 2000 season, when the Spartans won it all. Both now play in the NBA, Richardson for Golden State, Cleaves for Seattle. And both made it a point to fly in from wherever they were in their professional schedule just to sit together Saturday. Richardson, who earns millions, flew by private plane. Cleaves, who's on his fourth team in five years, bought a ticket and flew commercial.

It was loyalty, sure. And it was exciting, no doubt. But talking to both players, it was more than that. It was a chance to do something almost all of us would love to do: recapture, for a few hours, the best time of their lives.

Albom quoted Cleaves as telling him, "You gotta miss those college days. We were a family at Michigan State. In the NBA, you're just not as close." And he quoted Richardson as saying, "In the pros, you don't hang out with your teammates."

Albom did interview both Cleaves and Richardson. But he talked to them a day or two before the game, which was just enough time for both men to change their minds about attending. When Michigan State and North Carolina played against each other on a Saturday in April 2005, neither Cleaves nor Richardson was sitting in the stands, wearing MSU gear.

And for more than a week afterward, much was made of this on talk shows on all-news cable networks, including one hosted by me. It was a source of embarrassment to Albom, who, although apologizing promptly and effusively, was suspended by the *Detroit Free Press* as soon as his behavior was discovered.

But Barbara Stewart, a freelance reporter working at the time for the *Boston Globe*, might have been delighted with Albom's shortcut. It seems she had just taken one of her own. A few days after the Final Four, Stewart described for the *Globe*, in precise and graphic detail, the results of a seal hunt near Prince Edward Island in Canada and the protests that followed. It was a bloody account, and animal rights activists were predictably incensed.

But there was no hunt. There were no protests. The weather was so bad that the slaughter had to be canceled.

The storm over Albom, however, wiped out most of the coverage of Stewart. She did not have to suffer nearly as much public embarrassment as he did. On the other hand, Albom was a star; he soon returned to the *Free Press* payroll at his previous level of compensation. Stewart was a part-timer who never cashed another check from the *Boston Globe* for the rest of her life. He was a sports columnist who was not writing about an important topic. She was a news reporter whose topic, a much more serious one, was not to be trifled with.

Which leads us to, and leaves us with, a final faking of the truth in journalism, a faking so accidental that the person who did it does not even know he did it. Or she did it. In fact, he or she might not even have done it. If this reporter did do it, he or she probably did not do it deliberately; it happened because he or she is a human being and therefore subject to subjectivity, the curse of the reporter's craft and the stock-in-trade of human nature. Even now, more than a decade and a half after the fakery, it is just as certain as it was back then that the fakery was accidental. If, in fact, it was fakery to begin with.

On July 24, 1992, newspapers all over the country reported on findings about the difference in earning power between whites and blacks in the previous decades. The sources for the reports were the same census data, the exact same numbers and words. The interpretations, however, were different.

In the *New York Times* version:

WHITE-BLACK DISPARITY IN INCOME NARROWED IN 80s, CENSUS SHOWS

As *USA Today* put it:

INCOME EQUALITY GAP WIDENS FOR MINORITIES

For one reason or another, of one kind or another, it is certain that journalism will never be able to escape the occasional mangling of the truth into unrecognizable forms.

A Note to Readers

Most of the material in chapters two and three appeared in a different form in a previous book of mine, *Infamous Scribblers: The Founding Fathers and the Rowdy Beginnings of American Journalism.*

As for this book, it is a collection of aberrations. Most journalists do not perform their duties as did those in the preceding pages.

Nor do they behave like Dave Kindred, a columnist for the *Atlanta Journal and Constitution,* one of several reporters who pronounced a man guilty of a terrible crime even though he had not even been arrested and in fact never would be.

On July 27, 1996, three pipe bombs exploded at the Olympics, held in Atlanta that year, and two people were killed, with 111 more injured. Richard Jewell, a security guard, discovered the bombs in a knapsack at Olympic Centennial Park shortly after one in the morning. He had no idea what was in the knapsack at the time, but it looked suspicious to him and he immediately called for help. As he waited for it to arrive, he assisted in the evacuation of the area, still crowded at such a late hour because of a rock concert. There is no way of knowing how many lives he saved, how much pain he prevented. He was, for two or three days, considered a hero.

Then, with no evidence other than Jewell's proximity to the crime scene, and the assistance of a so-called profiler who found

Jewell something of a loner, the FBI told the press that he was now a "person of interest" in the case, and to a number of news outlets, rabid about the story, this meant he was not only a suspect, but was probably guilty of planting the knapsack himself.

Numerous television and print outlets either suggested or declared Jewell's guilt, but no one reported more irresponsibly about Jewell than Kindred, who wrote several columns about the crime, comparing Jewell—who, I repeat, was never arrested or charged with even the most minor of offenses—with a convicted mass murderer named Wayne Williams.

"As the FBI searched Jewell's house," wrote Kindred in one of the columns, Jewell "sat in the shadows with his back to the world. . . . He sat there, waiting [presumably for the authorities to turn up evidence of his guilt]. He sat seven miles from Centennial Park." Kindred concluded his column as follows: "Richard Jewell sits in the shadows today. Wayne Williams sits in prison forever."

Jewell escaped from some of the shadows later in the year, when the U.S. Attorney in Atlanta informed Jewell's attorneys via mail that their client was no longer a suspect. At a press conference a few days later, Jewell expressed his gratitude. But, obviously still troubled, he also criticized the FBI and the media for their treatment of him. He knew that the accusations of journalists have a longer life span than the acquittals of law enforcers.

From Kindred, who attended the press conference, came another column, this one describing Jewell's departure. Jewell, said Kindred,

> took no questions and walked from the dais immediately, his left hand on his mother's elbow, but how good it must have felt for Richard Jewell to say those words. Hero or fool? Such had been the question. If 88 days of federal investigation had led not to his arrest but to a government letter declaring him free from suspicion, then the answer seems to be Richard Jewell, hero.

It was as close as Kindred ever came to an apology. The *Atlanta Journal and Constitution* never even came that close.

On April 12, 2005, after a long search by various agencies, Eric Rudolph was arrested for the Olympic bombings. Rudolph, who had also set off explosive devices at an abortion clinic and a gay night club, confessed immediately.

Two years later, on April 28, 2007, Richard Jewell, still not completely out of the shadows as far as some people were concerned, died of complications from diabetes and kidney disease. He was forty-four years old and had never gotten over his media-inflicted shame.

Most journalists do not behave like Stephen Glass, who, in the 1990s, wrote fiction for the *New Republic*, insisting it was fact even though the magazine could not find the people, the places, or in some cases the organizations about which Glass reported in some of his stories.

They do not behave like Jayson Blair of the *New York Times*, who, a decade later, embellished his tales with fictional frills and plagiaristic frou-frous, which were apparently necessary because he did not even show up for a number of his assignments, instead relying for information on newspapers from the cities in which the events took place and then rewriting the articles from those papers. He first alerted at least a few of the *Times* employees to his misdeeds by his unwillingness, which turned out to be an inability, to file expense accounts. How could he? He had no airline receipts. He had no hotel receipts. He had no restaurant receipts. He had not *gone* anywhere! The accountants must have loved this guy. He had been a very cheap hire.

Most journalists do not behave like Jack Kelley, whose long-time status as a star political reporter at *USA Today* enabled him to make up sources for almost a decade and a half without serious challenge from any of his colleagues. This, in turn, gave him license to say almost anything he wanted to say about almost any subject, and to attribute the sentiments to almost anyone on the planet.

And most journalists do not behave like Ramiro Burr, a music writer for the *San Antonio Express-News*, who brought a new dimension to journalistic malfeasance that was not discovered until the summer of 2008. It seems that Burr had hired a ghost-writer for his columns, that the ghostwriter claimed to have written more than one hundred columns for Burr since 2001, and that he was tired of doing all that work without so much as a single byline, or even a farthing, to show for it. When the ghostwriter, Douglas Shannon, told the *Express-News* editors he wanted his name in print, Burr was told to clean out his desk and hit the pavement.

Most journalists behave like most other people in most other occupations. They do their jobs well or better than well. They realize that others depend on them and are stimulated by the need to meet their responsibilities. They want to succeed and to be rewarded for their success by gratitude, money, and maybe a few plaques at a few dinners in their honor. They believe that their chances of achieving these rewards are better if they follow the rules. By reporting news rather than making it up, journalists adhere to the norm. It is by contrasting them with the aberrant that we appreciate them more.

I also acknowledge that not all of the journalists about whom I have written were guilty of grievous misdeeds. Certainly Thomas Edison, Theodore Dreiser, and Mitch Albom were not. Neither was I, in my early days at NBC. (See my confession of skullduggery on the bayou in *Broadcast Blues*, published by HarperCollins in 1993, pp. 85–103.)

I chose to include these examples, and several others, to demonstrate the range of journalistic finagling that is possible and, more important, to illustrate the multitude of reasons for them. There are enough people in this book who serve as object lessons of more serious offenses and less forgivable motives; I thought I could afford a few lighter touches and different angles.

One of the more serious offenders would seem to be Janet Cooke. And she was, but I would put an asterisk by her name. After I read Mike Sager's interview with her, I decided that the circumstances of her childhood were such that she deserves a degree of forgiveness. In Sager's book, *Scary Monsters and Super Freaks*, the publisher introduced the chapter on Cooke with this note: "Janet Cooke caused the biggest scandal in the history of journalism when her Pulitzer Prize–winning article about an eight-year-old heroin addict turned out to be a fake." *The biggest scandal in the history of journalism?*

I hardly think so. Somewhere in a ghetto in Washington, D.C., there was a Jimmy. His name might have been Joey rather than Jimmy. He might have been nine, not eight. His fetish might have been for a consumer good other than sneakers. His drug of choice might have been something other than heroin. But he was real, at least in his broad strokes, and there were a lot of boys like him in Washington and other places, and there still are.

To contrast what Janet Cooke did with what Walter Duranty did and find Cooke's trespass the more vile is to carry sensationalism to the point of ignorance.

At any rate, it is because I came to feel a degree of sympathy for Janet Cooke that I did not seek to update her story. The most recent information I included about her in chapter fifteen will be, when this book is published, thirteen years old. So be it. Whatever has happened to her since then is her business. As far as I am concerned, invading privacy can be as serious a journalistic outrage as telling a lie.

But that sounds like the introduction to a new book. It is not. It is the end of this one.

Acknowledgments

As usual, my expressions of gratitude begin with Debbie Celia of the Westport Public Library in Westport, Connecticut. Difficult questions cannot dismay her, nor can information exceed her reach. Working with her is like having a genie who grants a limitless number of wishes without even requiring a bottle to be rubbed.

Among other librarians in Westport who helped me greatly were Marta Campbell, Marjorie Freilich-Den, Sylvia Schulman, Nancy Kuhn-Clark, Carolyn Zygmont, Lynn Hudock, and Susan Madeo, the last of whom arranged for my numerous interlibrary loans, and then arranged for them a second time when I found I had not studied the books sufficiently the first time.

I also wish to thank people and institutions from all over the country who sent me copies of hard-to-find documents or directed me down a path I would not have seen without them: Alison Beck, Center for American History, University of Texas, Austin; Barbara Buss, Fairfield Public Library, Fairfield, Connecticut; Nancy DelVecchio, Sacred Heart University, Fairfield, Connecticut; Hoyt Fields, Museum Director, Hearst Castle, San Simeon, California; Louisiana Division/City Archives, New Orleans Public Library, New Orleans; Suzanne Pichler, Andrew W. Mellon Foundation, New York City; Holly Snyder, John Hay

Library, Brown University, Providence, Rhode Island; Margaret Tufts Tenney, Harry Ransom Center, University of Texas, Austin; Claudia Stone Weisberg, the Pulitzer Prizes, Columbia University, New York City.

I also appreciate the quotations, insightful in all cases, that were provided for the text by Dr. Jeffrey Bass of Quinnipiac University, Hamden, Connecticut; Dr. William Stueck Jr. of the University of Georgia, Athens; and former NBC newsman Sander Vanocur.

The highest praise an author can give to the editor of his book is to say that the book is better because of the editor's perceptions. I am delighted I can say that about Stephen S. Power of John Wiley & Sons. To his assistant, Ellen Wright, I say thank you for a variety of services and a patient attitude, which I require whenever the subject is operating a computer, no matter how simple the task. My gratitude is no less for the book's senior production editor, Lisa Burstiner, and its publicist, Matt Smollon.

Among the clients represented by my agent, Timothy Seldes of Russell & Volkening, are the estates of Barbara Tuchman, Eudora Welty, A. J. Liebling, and Bernard Malamud. That I am among Tim's many living clients means that I can talk to him on the phone whenever I need to, or in fact whenever I feel like it, and those conversations are always among my life's small—and sometimes large—pleasures.

Finally, I thank my wife, son, and daughter, to whom this volume is dedicated. The truth is that none of them did anything to help me write the book; writing is of necessity a solitary business, even more solitary for me than for others, because I have never been the kind of author who likes to show early drafts of his work to family and friends for their comments. It is my life to which Dianne, Toby, and Cailin make their contributions, not my work, and I would be lost without them.

Notes

1. How Journalists Got the Idea

5 *"Who ate my apple?"* Bruce Deachman, www.canada.com/ottawacitizen/
   story.html?id=23cad17c-2fa0–4fd3-a56f-7dd90701889c.

6 *"Slight accident on way"* Huxley, p. 221.

6 *"To get out of a tedious social obligation"* Evelin Sullivan, pp. 64–65.

8 *"Lies of Vanity"* Quoted in ibid, p. 83.

8 *"The fear of losing something"* Ibid., p. 57.

10 *"Word of Gutenberg's achievement"* Koscielniak, unpaginated.

10 *"Within a short time"* Ibid.

2. Journalism from Afar

12 *"a sad Spectacle"* quoted in Bate, p. 125.

12 *"These obsessional traits"* Ibid., pp. 125–126.

12 *"they usually tend"* Ibid., p. 126.

12 *"inherited from his Father"* Ibid.

13 *"one of the most fascinating"* Ibid., p. 366.

13 *"bear"* and following definitions from *SJD*, pp. 90, 100, 144, 344, 419.

16 *"To encourage our Seamen"* *PD*, December 1740, p. 580.

16 *"My Lords"* Ibid., April 1741, unnumbered page before p. 172.

16 *"Let us not add"* Ibid., March 1742, unnumbered page before p. 116.

17 "The Parliamentary Debates *remain*" Bate, p. 203.

18 *"the best he had ever read"* Ibid, p. 203.

18 *"That speech I wrote"* Ibid., p. 203.

19 *"would not be accessory"* Ibid., p. 204.

19 *"he did not think"* Ibid., p. 204.
19 *"persons of enlarged views"* and *"Writing for money"* Brewer, p. 144.

3. A Woman Who Never Was

21 *"to expand the very definition"* Eric Burns, *Infamous Scribblers*, p. 86.
22 *"A raging passion"* BF, p. 23.
24 *"as sassy a lass"* Eric Burns, *Infamous Scribblers*, p. 88.
24 *" 'This is the fifth time' "* BF, pp. 127–129.
24 *" 'What must poor young women do' "* Ibid.
25 *"teaching a lesson"* Eric Burns, *Infamous Scribblers*, p. 89.
26 *"this burning torture"* Hawthorne, p. 273.

4. Lies against the British

28 *"some British banks"* Eric Burns, *Infamous Scribblers*, p. 138.
28 *"beseeching Parliament"* Ibid.
29 *"Oliver was burned in effigy"* Ibid., p. 144
30 *"He was highly regarded"* Ibid., p. 145.
30 *One night some of them did just that* Ibid., p. 146.
30 *The hellish crew remained* Ibid.
32 *"What shewed a degree"* BF, March 12, 1770.
33 *"hirelings, pimps, parasites"* Quoted in Eric Burns, *Infamous Scribblers*, p. 158.
34 *"Franklin perpetrated one of the practical jokes"* Dos Passos, p. 45.
34 *"indefinite frontiers to the westward"* Ibid., p. 47.
35 *"In establishing American independence"* Ramsay, p. 634.

5. Lies against Americans

37 *"Political Christmas!"* TA, March 7, 1797, p. 3.
39 *"some* compassionate *human being"* CC, July 7, 1800.
39 *"beautifully molded form"* Quoted in Brands, *Andrew Jackson*, p. 57.
40 *"We are content"* NHS, January 17, 1829.
44 *"a flurry of speculation"* Donald, p. 501.
45 *"[took] possession by military force"* Quoted in ibid., p. 502.
46 *"We will never permit"* Quoted in Harper, p. 67.
46 *"We do not mean to rebel"* Ibid., p. 68.
46 *"The Despotism of Lincoln and Co."* Ibid., p. 159.
46 *"Lincoln the beast"* Ibid., p. 92.
46 *"Newspapers are valuable organs"* Ibid., p. 132.
47 *"God Almighty"* Quoted in Oates, p. 166.
48 *"Rebels have slain"* DT, April 16, 1865, p. 3.
48 *"There was not the outward excitement"* LRUU, April 20, 1865, p. 2.

48   *"the biggest and most powerful newspaper"*   Thomas Fleming, "Fakery in American Journalism," History News Network (George Mason University), http://hnn.us/articles/1474.html.

6. The Boss

51   *"who looked like something"*   Callow, p. 10.

51   *"A craggy hulk of a man"*   Ibid., pp. 10–11.

52   *"The cuspidors . . . were priced"*   Connable and Silberfarb, p. 159.

53   *"A fictitious resolution"*   Allen, p. 163.

53   *"I never saw so many people"*   Quoted in Ackerman, p. 64.

54   *"also subsidized reporters"*   Callow, p. 178.

55   *"could barely leave his home"*   Ackerman, p. 129.

55   *"Is it a hopeless fight?"*   Ibid.

55   *"a gross, half-comic character"*   McCullough, p. 126.

55   *"I don't care a straw"*   Quoted in Allen, p. 171.

56   *"If a story was particularly damaging"*   King, p. 411.

57   *"a check changed hands"*   Quoted in ibid., p. 411.

57   *"My ambition"*   Ibid., p. 409.

7. The Epoch of the Hoax

60   *"When whole races"*   Mark Twain, aka Samuel Clemens, "My First Lie, and How I Got Out of It, " About.com Classic Literature, http://classiclit.about.com/library/bl-etexts/mtwain/bl-mtwain-myfirstlie.htm.

60   *"very well"*   Ibid.

60   *"It was human nature"*   Ibid.

61   *"Every limb and feature"*   WMT, October 4, 1862, p. 159.

61   *"for a lie to work"*   Hoffer, *The Historian's Paradox*, p. 89.

62   *"five Indians [being] smothered"*   WMT, April 16–18, 1863, pp. 246–47.

62   *"The whole country"*   Quoted in Brands, *The Age of Gold*, pp. 43–44.

64   *"It seems that"*   "A Bloody Massacre Near Carson," WMT, October 28, 1863, pp. 324–326.

65   *"a storm of denunciation"*   Lauber, p. 13.

65   *"To find a petrified man"*   "Virginia City Territorial Enterprise, 1862–1868," www.twainquotes.com/teindex.html.

66   *"stout, good-looking man"*   Fred Kaplan, p. 230.

67   *"unreasonable demands"*   Quoted in ibid., p. 252.

67   *"Although he is wealthy"*   Quoted in ibid., p. 253.

68   *"averaged four feet in height"*   "Great Astronomical Discoveries Lately Made by Sir John Herschel, L.L.D., F.R.S., &c, At The Cape of Good Hope. [From Supplement to the Edinburgh Journal of

Science], [Continued from yesterday's Sun]," August 28, 1835, www .museumofhoaxes.com/moonhoax4.html.

68 "*an elegant quadruped*" Ibid., August 27, 1835.

68 "*From the epoch of the hoax,*" *New York Sun*, April 13, 1844, p. 1, www.apoe.org/works/tales/ball/hxa.htm.

69 "*Let no one who wishes*" Trollope, pp. 15–16.

70 "*Therefore, the wise thing*" Mark Twain, "On the Decay of the Art of Lying," the Literature Network, www.online-literature .com/twain/1320/.

8. Furnishing a War

72 "*He likes his books*" Quoted in Swanberg, *Citizen Hearst*, p. 10.

74 "*THE WORST INSULT*" *NYJ*, February 9, 1898.

74 "*Everything is quiet*" Quoted in Swanberg, *Citizen Hearst*, p. 107.

74 "*Please remain*" Ibid., p. 108.

75 "*the backbone of a chocolate éclair*" Quoted in Brian, p. 233.

76 "*Anyone advocating peace*" Swanberg, *Citizen Hearst*, p. 140.

76 "*undoubted proof of Spanish treachery*" *NYJ*, February 17, 1898.

76 "*Hearst's coverage of the* Maine" Swanberg, *Citizen Hearst*, p. 137.

77 "*CRUISER MAINE BLOWN UP*" *NYJ*, February 16, 1898.

77 "*THE WARSHIP MAINE*" Ibid., February 17, 1898.

77 "*THE WHOLE COUNTRY THRILLS*" Ibid., February 18, 1898.

77 "*HOW THE MAINE ACTUALLY LOOKS*" Ibid., February 20, 1898.

77 "*HAVANA POPULACE INSULTS*" Ibid., February 21, 1898.

77 "*THE MAINE WAS DESTROYED*" Ibid., February 23, 1898.

77 "*SUICIDE LAMENTED THE MAINE*" Ibid., April 18, 1898.

77 "*Two contestants would portray*" Swanberg, *Citizen Hearst*, p. 139.

78 "*can stake its reputation*" Quoted in ibid., p. 141.

78 "*CONGRESS DECLARES WAR*" *NYJ*, April 25, 1898.

78 "*HOW DO YOU LIKE*" Ibid., April 27, 1898.

78 "*It is cheering*" and "*invention*" Quoted in Swanberg, *Citizen Hearst*, p. 141.

79 "*finds that Spanish government officials*" Ibid., p. 141.

79 "*the* Maine *was destroyed*" Ibid., p. 142.

80 "*His powers of observation*" Quoted in Lubow, p. 3.

80 "*a star reporter*" Ibid., p. 2.

80 "*His costume was an ulster*" Ibid., p. 3.

80 "*an aristocratic drawl*" Ibid., p. 3.

81 "*Certainly like to see Europe*" Sinclair Lewis, p. 4.

81 "*and Richard Harding Davis*" Quoted in Lubow, p. 1.

81 *"the reporter who brings"* Ibid., p. 3.

82 *"ran reports on the front page"* Swanberg, *Pulitzer*, p. 251.

82 *"undoubtedly semi-neurasthenic"* Quoted in Juergens, p. 4.

83 *"a coarse, bloated millionaire"* Quoted in Brian, pp. 175–176.

83 *"Pity Lucille!"* Ibid., p. 176.

84 *"a newspaper should be"* Quoted in Juergens, p. 73.

84 *"THE RIOTS IN HAVANA"* Quoted in Brian, p. 226.

85 *"nobody outside of a lunatic asylum"* Quoted in Swanberg, *Pulitzer*, p. 247.

85 *"MAINE EXPLOSION CAUSED"* Quoted in Brian, p. 229.

85 *"While lying off the Battery"* Quoted in Swanberg, *Pulitzer*, p. 247.

85 *"Spain is a decaying"* NYW, April 10, 1898, p. 4.

86 *"SLURS ON THE BRAVERY"* Quoted in Brian, p. 236.

86 *"Joy was unrestrained"* Quoted in Swanberg, *Pulitzer*, p. 252.

86 *"a contest of madmen"* Quoted in Brian, p. 2.

87 *"regain[ed] its former glowing reputation"* Ibid., p. 3.

89 *"spate of U.S. interventionism"* Author interview with Dr. Jeffrey Bass, via e-mail, June 18, 2008.

89 *"It is highly unlikely"* Author interview with Dr. William Stueck Jr., via e-mail, June 18, 2008.

90 *"Brixton D. Allaire, dear reader"* Quoted in Swanberg, *Citizen Hearst*, p. 299.

90 *"Paris, August 23"* NYJ, August 23, 1917, p. 1.

91 *"routinely invented sensational stories"* Lee and Solomon, p. 93.

9. L'Affaire

94 *"saddened and angry"* Michael Burns, p. 68.

96 *"reserved, highly controlled"* Ibid., p. 98.

96 *"an agent of international Jewry"* Halasz, p. 44.

96 *"entered the army"* Michael Burns, p. 117.

96 *Tending goats* Ibid., p. 166.

97 *"Until now"* Quoted in David L. Lewis, p. 107.

97 *"Blow his brains out"* Quoted in Michael Burns, p. 167.

98 *"My heart bleeds so"* Quoted in David L. Lewis, p. 112.

98 *"When occasionally he did sleep"* Ibid., pp. 109–110.

99 *"When storms stirred up the sea"* Halasz, p. 63.

100 *"hot word"* Ibid., p. 63

100 *"savage energy"* Quoted in Michael Burns, p. 91.

100 *"hooknose tribe"* Ibid., p. 92.

101 *"special correspondent"* Quoted in Halasz, p. 64.

101   *"Stirring up emotions'"*   Michael Burns, p. 180.
102   *"an iron band"*   Halasz, p. 63.
102   *"The torture was hardly bearable"*   Ibid., p. 64.
103   *"received orders to report"*   Ibid., p. 64.

10 Speeding Up a War

108   *"There is something about a national convention"*   Quoted in Hobson, p. 254.
108   *"The college professor"*   GM, p. 95.
108   *"a string of wet sponges"*   Quoted in Hobson, p. 217.
109   *"It is the close"*   Quoted in Rodgers, p. 246.
109   *"the nearest thing to Voltaire"*   Quoted in Hobson, p. 251.
111   *"The vast majority"*   Ibid., p. 248.
111   *"buoyed up, exhilarated"*   Quoted in ibid., p. 249.
112   *"I believe that [Jews]"*   Ibid., p. 454.
113   *"The revival of literary controversy"*   GM, p. 6. From "The Embattled Literati," *AMM*, June 1930, p. 154.
114   *"My own talent for faking"*   Mencken, p. 219.
114   *"synthetic war dispatch"*   Ibid., pp. 219–222.
115   *"Years later"*   Ibid., p. 222.
116   *"pestered me with unanswerable questions"*   Quoted in Rodgers, p. 67.
117   *"The Colonel glared at me"*   Ibid., p. 67.
118   *"my masterpiece of all time"*   Mencken, p. 219.
118   *"On December 20"*   Quoted in Hobson, p. 186.
118   *"What ails the truth"*   Quoted in Gilovich, p. 88.

Part Two: Hiding the Truth

122   *"We shall endeavor"*   Quoted in Stephens, p. 226.

11. *Their* Man in Moscow

123   *"fancied himself a Citizen"*   Taylor, p. 9.
124   *"only acknowledgment of his family"*   Ibid., p. 27.
124   *"ten years old"*   Duranty, p. 1.
124   *"One may think"*   Ibid., p. 131.
126   *"Stalin is giving the Russian people"*   NYT, June 14, 1931, p. 14.
126   *"RED ARMY IS HELD"*   Ibid., June 25, 1931, p. 7.
127   *"Every nationality"*   Ibid., June 26, 1931, p. 8.
128   *"You have done a good job"*   Quoted in Taylor, p. 192.
129   *"made sweeps through private homes"*   Quoted in Woods, p. 164.
129   *"the famine was an organized one"*   Quoted in Taylor, p. 205.
129   *"the only creatures"*   Ibid., p. 194.

129   *"horrible sight"*   Ibid., p. 195.

130   *"embryos out of alcohol bottles"*   Quoted in Taylor, p. 202.

131   *"delicate, ascetic features"*   Quoted in Wolfe, p. 280.

132   *"I didn't quite like it"*   Ibid., p. 200.

132   *"I mean starving"*   Quoted in Wolfe, p. 205.

133   *"Russia today is in the grip"*   Quoted in Dana G. Dalrymple, *Soviet Studies* 15, no. 3 (January 1964): 254.

133   *"The struggle for bread"*   Ibid., p. 253.

133   *"The children had fallen asleep"*   Muggeridge, *Winter in Moscow*, pp. 43–44.

134   *"Unlike the children"*   Ibid., p. 44.

134   *"The famine is mostly bunk"*   Quoted in Taylor, p. 210.

134   *"any report of a famine"*   Quoted in Woods, p. 165.

134   *"apple-cheeked dairymaids"*   Muggeridge, *The Green Stick*, p. 258.

134   *"food shortages"*   Quoted in Taylor, p. 215.

135   *"The blunt truth,"*   *NYT*, September 16, 1933, p. 14.

135   *"the harvest is so good"*   Ibid.

135   *"BIG SOVIET CROP"*   Ibid.

136   *"a triumph, one might say"*   Ibid., p. 14.

136   *"covered up the horrors"*   Quoted in Taylor, p. 244.

137   *"the greatest liar"*   Quoted in Woods, p. 165.

137   *"admired Stalin and his regime"*   Muggeridge, *The Green Stick*, p. 255.

137   *"I had the feeling"*   Ibid., p. 256.

138   *"Whatever Stalin's apologists may say"*   Quoted in Woods, p. 239.

12. Sins of Omission

142   *"No word of this activity"*   Barry, p. 225.

143   *"the papers helped"*   Ibid.

144   *"had worked in several presidential campaigns"*   Ibid., p. 167.

144   *"the most insatiable patronage grabber"*   Ibid., p. 225.

145   *With the weather bureau*   NOMT, April 9, 1927, p. 1.

148   *"Neither of the planes"*   *NYT*, March 28, 1977, p. 1.

149   *"Flying after the start"*   Brafman and Brafman, p. 12.

151   *"Five Hundred Eighty-three Die"*   Quoted in James Randi, "The Media and Reports on the Paranormal," *Humanist* 37 (July–August 1977): 45.

151   *"I have in my possession"*   Ibid., p. 45.

152   *"I don't claim"*   Ibid., p. 45.

153   *"Fried says"*   Ibid., p. 45.

155   *"killing free enterprise"*   William S. White, p. 117.

156   *"rough-hewn, benignly ursine"*   Black, p. 586.

156   *"a crippled imbecile"*   Quoted in Farr, p. 286.

157   *"A reshuffling of the personnel"*   *WSJ*, November 7, 1940.

13. The Same Team

162   *"hoping the chop"*   Berg, p. 203.

162   *"furious, [they] simply backed their car off"*   Amory, p. 243.

163   *"thin-voiced, thin-bodied"*   Quoted in Cannadine, p. 57.

163   *His most thorough biographer*   Ibid., p. 114.

163   *"rarely looked them in the eye"*   Ibid.

165   *"In her presence"*   Ibid., p. 143.

165   *"I never can understand"*   Ibid., p. 187.

167   *"Why waste a reporter's time"*   George Seldes, p. 18.

167   *"But the moment"*   Ibid., p. 19.

167   *"I gave him my notes"*   Ibid.

168   *"done everything with the Pennsylvania legislature"*   Quoted in Weinberg, p. 198.

168   *"Surely it was not mere coincidence"*   George Seldes, p. 18.

168   *"a sort of family gathering"*   Quoted in Lubow, p. 145.

169   *"Mrs. McKinley has epileptic fits,"*   Ibid.

169   *"not saying anything"*   Ibid.

169   *"For much of this century"*   Kurtz, p. 239.

171   *"Mind, this is private"*   Quoted in Thayer, p. 300,

171   *"He was the earliest American"*   Mark Sullivan, vol. 3, p. 74.

172   *"I made a bet today"*   Quoted in Greenberg, p. 10.

172   *"could be silent in five languages"*   Ibid., p. 9.

172   *"much like a wooden Indian"*   Ibid., p. 8.

172   *"How could they tell?"*   Ibid., p. 9.

173   *"The words of the President"*   Ibid., p. 63.

173   *"at the constant correctness"*   Ibid.

174   *"Churchill had intended"*   Goodwin, p. 408.

175   *recalled traveling with a small White House press corps*   Smith, p. 28.

177   *"youthful energetic"*   Caro, p. 505.

177   *"one of the keenest"*   Ibid., p. 572.

178   *"I remember as a kid reporter"*   Quoted in Sabato, p. 32.

178   *"When I first came to Washington"*   Ibid.

178   *"In 1962 Senator Pete Williams"*   Ibid., p. 32.

179   *"Newspapers are read"*   Quoted in Lipstadt, p. 133.

179   *"Three newsmen invited to dine"*   Quoted in Boardman, p. 4.

180   *"like all Negroes"*   Ibid., p. 4.

180 *"If it can be avoided"* Quoted in Mark Sullivan, vol. 6, p. 94.

181 *"was not pretty"* Quoted in Neal, p. 38.

182 *"reporters sometimes called"* Kurtz, p. 144.

182 *"Everybody knows about us"* Quoted in Neal, pp. 43–44.

182 *"I never even heard the rumors"* Author interview with Sander Vanocur, via telephone, April 19, 2008.

183 *"kiddo"* and *"sweetie"* Quoted in Collier and Horowitz, p. 175.

183 *"Let's sack with Jack"* Quoted in Sabato, p. 37.

183 *"Bobby Baker, Senator Lyndon Johnson's aide"* Collier and Horowitz, p. 175.

184 *"News of the President's indiscretions"* Kaiser, p. 127.

185 *"Where did these men"* Ibid., p. 415.

186 *"The reason we didn't follow up"* Quoted in Sabato, p. 39.

186 *"Even if I did know about Kennedy"* Author interview with Sander Vanocur via telephone, April 19, 2008.

14. Rejecting the Faith

192 *"it seemed, forgot to blossom"* Theodore White, pp. 67–88.

192 *"manipulate American public opinion"* Ibid., p. 76.

192 *"dwarf bandits"* Ibid., p. 77.

193 *"the guerrilla chieftain"* Ibid, p. 78.

194 *"Pistol-Packing Miss Golden Flowers"* Ibid.

195 *"Three years later"* Ibid., p. 79.

196 *"Chiang Conquers All"* TM, January 3, 1938, p. 15.

196 *"a pathetic man"* and *"did not know"* Theodore White, p. 160.

196 *Chiang fumbled and bumbled at his tasks* Ibid., pp. 160–161.

197 *"In Chungking you are"* Quoted in Halberstam, p. 78.

198 *"I'm not sure"* Quoted in Swanberg, *Luce and His Empire*, p. 243.

15. Janet's World

203 *"sashayed"* and *"wearing a red wool suit"* Sager, p. 103.

204 *"was very hard to live with"* Quoted in http://academics.smcvt.edu/ dmindich/Jimmy's%20World.htm.

204 *"Jimmy is 8 years old"* From "Jimmy's World," www.uncp.edu/home/ Canada/work/markport/lit/litjour/spg2002/cooke.htm.

205 *"Janet had written a great piece"* Quoted in http://academics.smcvt .edu/dmindich/Jimmy's%20World.htm.

205 *"We were supposed to"* Ibid.

206 *"It didn't take long"* Ibid.

206 *"They're just jealous"* Ibid.

206 *"Say two words"* Quoted in Sager, p. 120.
207 *"spent her life on the run"* Ibid., p. 106.
208 *"I want my life back"* Quoted in ibid, p. 105.
208 *"What I did was horrible"* Quoted in ibid., p. 108.

16. What a Picture Is Worth

210 *"The only value ever claimed"* AHM, "The True Story of Bernarr McFadden," December 1981, p. 28.
210 *"the Kip Rhinelander trial"* Gabler, p. 73.
210 *"one of the low points"* AHM, "The True Story of Bernarr MacFadden," p. 28.
211 *"Honk, Honk. It's the Bonk"* Quoted in Gabler, p. 76.
213 *"End Poverty"* Quoted in Manchester, p. 101.
213 *"Empty Promises"* Ibid.
213 *"MGM employees were invited"* Hamilton, p. 87.
213 *"leaflets, radio broadcasts"* Ibid., p. 87.
214 *"sturdy, decent workmen"* Gilbert Seldes, p. 93.
214 *"elderly bit actress"* Manchester, p. 101.
214 *"get out of the shadow of states' rights"* Hubert H. Humphrey 1948 Democratic National Convention Address, www.americanrhetoric.com/speeches/huberthumphey1948dnc.html.
215 *"And all the laws of Washington"* Quoted in Bass and Thompson, p. 106.
217 *"and found evidence"* "NBC Go Boom!" www.whatreallyhappened.com/RANCHO/LIE/nbc.html.
217 *"This is the worst black eye"* Ibid.
217 *"First, and most importantly"* Quoted in "Excerpts from Statement," http://query.nytimes.com/gst/fullpage.html?res=9F0CEFD6163AF933A25755C0A965958260.
219 *"critics contend that at least 300 people"* NYT, February 15, 1993, p. D5.

17. The Most Hated Man in American Newsrooms

223 *"Anne," he said, " they have stolen our baby"* Quoted in Berg, p. 240.
224 *"the Crime of the Century"* Quoted in Jon Blackwell, "1932: Crime of the Century," www.capitalcentury.com/1932.html.
224 *"the Trial of the Century"* Quoted in www.nj.com/lindbergh/hunterdon/index.ssf?/lindbergh/stories/trial.html.
224 *"the Most Hated Man in the World"* Quoted in "1936: Bruno Richard Hauptman, the Most Hated Man in the World," www.executedtoday.com/2008/04/03/1936-bruno-richard-hauptmann-lindbergh-baby/.

225 *"The worst offender"*   Ludovic Kennedy, pp. 208–9.

226 *"I said that in October"*   Quoted in Gabler, p. 212.

226 *"How do they let a fucking child"*   Ibid.

18. What Haste Makes

230 *"Down in Virginia"*   Quoted in Clark, p. 21.

232 *"Urgent"*   Quoted in David Kennedy, p. 231.

233 *"Armistice Allies Germany"*   Ibid.

233 *"all the joyful enthusiasm"*   *NYT*, November 8, 1918, p. 1.

233 *"carnival of noise and ribaldry"*   Quoted in David Kennedy, p. 231.

234 *"was deliciously caught up"*   Daniels, p. 1.

234 *"understood that America now"*   Ibid., p. 2.

234 *"The Thief of Joy"*   Quoted in Mark Sullivan, vol. 5, p. 516.

Epilogue: A Few Final Mistakes

238 *"private rages and despairs"*   Dreiser, p. 248.

239 *"I went home"*   Ibid., p. 250.

240 *"The next morning I arose"*   Ibid., p. 251.

240 *"a large and enthusiastic audience"*   Ibid.

240 *"Great God!"*   Ibid.

240 *"To see three shows at once"*   Ibid., p. 252.

242 *"In the audience Saturday"*   James Joyner, "The Mitch Albom Scandal: Much Ado about Nothing," http://outsidethebeltway .com/archives/2005/04/the_mitch_albom_scandal/.

244 *"WHITE-BLACK DISPARITY"*   *NYT*, July 24, 1992, p. 1.

244 *"INCOME EQUALITY GAP WIDENS"*   *USA*, July 24, 1992, p. 3.

A Note to Readers

246 *"As the FBI searched"*   Dave Kindred, "Park Bombing: The Scene on Buford Highway," *AJC*, August 1, 1996, p. 14A.

246 *"took no questions"*   Quoted in "Teaching Notes: Richard Jewell and The Olympic Bombing, www.concernedjournalists.org/node/428.

249 *"Janet Cooke caused the biggest scandal"*   Sager, p. 103.

Bibliography

Newspapers and Magazines

AHM	*American Heritage* magazine
AJC	*Atlanta Journal-Constitution*
AMM	*American Mercury* magazine
BG	*Boston Gazette*
CC	*Connecticut Courant*
DT	*Daily Times* (Leavenworth, KS)
LRUU	*Little Rock Unconditional Union*
NHS	*New Hampshire Statesman and Concord Register*
NOMT	*New Orleans Morning Tribune*
NYJ	*New York Journal*
NYT	*New York Times*
NYTM	*New York Times Magazine*
NYW	*New York World*
TA	The *Aurora*
TM	*Time* magazine
TT	*Tulsa Tribune*
USA	*USA Today*
WP	*Washington Post*
WSJ	*Wall Street Journal*

Collected Works

BF   *A Benjamin Franklin Reader*. Edited by Walter Isaacson. New York: Simon and Schuster, 2003.

GM   *The Gist of Mencken: Quotations from American's Critic*. Edited by
        Mayo DuBasky. Metuchen, NJ: Scarecrow Press, 1990.
PD   *The Parliamentary Debates*. Samuel Johnson. Internet Library of
        Early Journals.
SJD   *Samuel Johnson's Dictionary: A Modern Selection*. Edited by
        E. L. McAdam Jr. and George Milne. New York: Pantheon, 1964.
WMT   *The Works of Mark Twain: Early Tales and Sketches*. Vol. 1,
        1851–1864. Edited by Edgar Marquess Branch and Robert H.
        Hirsh. Berkeley: University of California Press, 1979.

Books

Ackerman, Kenneth D. *Boss Tweed: The Rise and Fall of the Corrupt Pol Who
    Conceived the Soul of Modern New York*. New York: Carroll & Graf, 2005.

Allen, Oliver E. *New York, New York: A History of the World's Most Exhilarating
    and Challenging City*. New York: Atheneum, 1990.

Amory, Cleveland. *Who Killed Society?* New York: Harper & Brothers,
    1960.

Barone, Michael. *Our Country: The Shaping of America from Roosevelt to
    Reagan*. New York: Free Press, 1990.

Barry, John. *Rising Tide: The Great Mississippi Flood of 1927 and How It
    Changed America*. New York: Simon & Schuster, 1997.

Bass, Jack, and Marilyn W. Thompson. *Ol' Strom: An Unauthorized Biography
    of Strom Thurmond*. Atlanta: Longstreet Press, 1998.

Bate, W. Jackson. *Samuel Johnson*. New York: Harcourt Brace Jovanovich,
    1977.

Bauer, Nancy W. *The American Way*. Annotated Teacher's Edition. New
    York: Holt, Rinehart and Winston, 1979.

Behn, Noel. *Lindbergh: The Crime*. New York: Atlantic Monthly Press,
    1994.

Berg, A. Scott. *Lindbergh*. New York: G.P. Putnam's Sons, 1998.

Bernstein, Burton. *Thurber: A Biography*.New York: Dodd, Mead, 1975.

Black, Conrad. *Franklin Delano Roosevelt: Champion of Freedom*. New York:
    PublicAffairs, 2003.

Boardman, Barrington. *Isaac Asimov Presents from Harding to Hiroshima:
    An Anecdotal History of the United States from 1923 to 1945*. New York:
    Dembner, 1988.

Bok, Sissela. *Lying: Moral Choice in Public and Private Life*. New York:
    Vintage, 1989.

Brafman, Ori, and Rom Brafman. *Sway: The Irresistible Pull of Irrational
    Behavior*. New York: Doubleday, 2008.

Brands, H. W. *The Age of Gold: The California Gold Rush and the New American Dream*. New York: Doubleday, 2002.

———. *Andrew Jackson: His Life and Times*. New York: Doubleday, 2005.

———. *T.R.: The Last Romantic*. New York: Basic Books, 1997.

Brewer, John. *The Pleasures of the Imagination: English Culture in the Eighteenth Century*. New York: Farrar, Straus & Giroux, 1997.

Brian, Denis. *Pulitzer: A Life*. New York: John Wiley & Sons, 2001.

Brooks, John. *The Great Leap: The Past Twenty-Five Years in America*. New York: Harper & Row, 1966.

Burns, Eric. *Infamous Scribblers: The Founding Fathers and the Rowdy Beginnings of American Journalism*. New York: PublicAffairs, 2006.

———. *The Smoke of the Gods: A Social History of Tobacco*. Philadelphia: Temple University Press, 2007.

Burns, James MacGregor. *Roosevelt: The Lion and the Fox; The First Political Biography of F.D.R.* New York: Harcourt, Brace & Company, 1956.

Burns, Michael. *Dreyfus: A Family Affair, 1789–1945*. New York: HarperCollins, 1991.

Burstein, Andrew. *The Passions of Andrew Jackson*. New York: Knopf, 2003.

Callow, Alexander B., Jr. *The Tweed Ring*. Norwalk, CT: Easton Press, 1990.

Cannadine, David. *Mellon: An American Life*. New York: Knopf, 2006.

Caro, Robert A. *The Years of Lyndon Johnson: Master of the Senate*. New York: Knopf, 2002.

Clark, Ronald W. *Einstein: The Man Who Made the Future*. New York: Putnam, 1977.

Collier, Peter, and David Horowitz. *The Kennedys: An American Drama*. New York: Summit Books, 1984.

Connable, Alfred, and Edward Silberfarb. *Tigers of Tammany: Nine Men Who Ran New York*. New York: Holt, Rinehart and Winston, 1967.

Crossen, Cynthia. *Tainted Truth: The Manipulation of Fact in America*. New York: Simon & Schuster, 1994.

Dallek, Robert. *An Unfinished Life: John F. Kennedy, 1917–1963*. Boston: Little, Brown, 2003.

Daniels, Jonathan. *The Time Between the Wars: Armistice to Pearl Harbor*. Garden City, NY: Doubleday, 1966.

Davis, Kenneth. *Don't Know Much about History: Everything You Need to Know about American History but Never Learned*. New York: Crown, 1990.

Donald, David Herbert. *Lincoln*. New York: Simon and Schuster, 1995.

Dos Passos, John. *The Men Who Made the Nation: The Architects of the Young Republic, 1782–1802*. Garden City, NY: Doubleday, 1957.

Dreiser, Theodore. *Newspaper Days*. Edited by T. D. Nostwich. Philadelphia: University of Pennsylvania Press, 1991.

Duranty, Walter. *Search for a Key*. New York: Simon and Schuster, 1943.

Farr, Finis. *FDR*. New Rochelle, NY: Arlington House, 1972.

Gabler, Neal. *Winchell: Gossip, Power and the Culture of Celebrity*. New York: Knopf, 1994.

Gilovich, Thomas. *How We Know What Isn't So: The Fallibility of Human Reason in Everyday Life*. New York: Free Press, 1991.

Goodwin, Doris Kearns. *No Ordinary Time: Franklin and Eleanor Roosevelt; The Home Front in World War II*. New York: Simon & Schuster, 1994.

Green, Robert P., Jr., Laura L. Becker, and Robert E. Coviello. *The American Tradition: A History of the United States*. Annotated Teacher's Edition. Columbus, OH: Charles E. Merrill Publishing Co., 1986.

Greenberg, David. *Calvin Coolidge*. New York: Times Books, 2006.

Halasz, Nicholas. *Captain Dreyfus: The Story of a Mass Hysteria*. New York: Simon & Schuster, 1955.

Halberstam, David. *The Powers That Be*. New York: Knopf, 1979.

Hamilton, Ian. *Writers in Hollywood, 1915–1951*. New York: Carroll & Graf, 1991.

Harper, Robert S. *Lincoln and the Press*. New York: McGraw-Hill, 1951.

Harris, Brayton. *Blue and Gray in Black and White: Newspapers in the Civil War*. Washington, DC: Brassey's, 1999.

Hawthorne, Nathaniel. *The Scarlet Letter*. Norwalk, CT: Easton Press, 1975.

Hobson, Fred. *Mencken: A Life*. New York: Random House, 1994.

Hoffer, Peter Charles. *The Historian's Paradox*. New York: New York University Press, 2008.

———. *Past Imperfect: Facts, Fictions, Fraud—American History from Bancroft and Parkman to Ambrose, Bellesiles, Ellis, and Goodwin*. New York: PublicAffairs, 2004.

Huxley, Aldous. *Antic Hay*. Normal, IL: Dalkey Archive Press, 1997.

Isaacson, Walter, ed. *A Benjamin Franklin Reader*. New York: Simon & Schuster, 2003.

Juergens, George. *Joseph Pulitzer and the New York World*. Princeton, NJ: Princeton University Press, 1966.

Kaiser, David. *The Road to Dallas: The Assassination of John F. Kennedy*. Cambridge, MA: Belknap Press of Harvard University Press, 2008.

Kaplan, Fred. *The Singular Mark Twain*. New York: Doubleday, 2003.

Kaplan, Justin. *Mr. Clemens and Mark Twain: A Biography*. New York: Simon and Schuster, 1966.

Kennedy, David M. *Over Here: The First World War and American Society*. New York: Oxford University Press, 1980.

Kennedy, Ludovic. *The Airman and the Carpenter: The Lindbergh Kidnapping and the Framing of Richard Hauptmann*. New York: Viking, 1985.

King, Greg. *A Season of Splendor: The Court of Mrs. Astor in Gilded Age New York*. Hoboken, NJ: John Wiley & Sons, 2008.

Koestler, Arthur. *Darkness at Noon*. Translated by Daphne Hardy. New York: Macmillan, 1963.

Koscielniak, Bruce. *Johan Gutenberg and the Amazing Printing Press*. Boston: Houghton Mifflin, 2003.

Kurth, Peter. *American Cassandra: The Life of Dorothy Thompson*. Boston: Little, Brown, 1990.

Kurtz, Howard. *Media Circus: The Trouble with America's Newspapers*. New York: Times Books, 1993.

Lauber, John. *The Inventions of Mark Twain: A Biography*. New York: Hill & Wang, 1990.

Lee, Martin A., and Norman Solomon. *Unreliable Sources: A Guide to Detecting Bias in News Media*. New York: Carol Publishing (A Lyle Stuart Book), 1990.

Lewis, David L. *Prisoners of Honor: The Dreyfus Affair*. New York: William Morrow, 1973.

Lewis, Sinclair. *Dodsworth*. New York: Harcourt, Brace & Company, 1929.

Lipstadt, Deborah. *Beyond Belief: The American Press and the Coming of the Holocaust, 1933–1945*. New York: Free Press, 1986.

Loewen, James. *Lies My Teacher Told Me: Everything Your American History Textbook Got Wrong*. New York: New Press, 1995.

Lubow, Arthur. *The Reporter Who Would Be King: A Biography of Richard Harding Davis*. New York: Charles Scribner's Sons, 1992.

Man, John. *Gutenberg: How One Man Remade the World with Words*. New York: John Wiley & Sons, 2002.

Manchester, William. *The Death of a President: November 1963*. New York: Harper & Row, 1967.

———. *The Glory and the Dream: A Narrative History of America, 1932–1972*. Boston: Little, Brown, 1974.

McCullough, David. *The Great Bridge: The Epic Story of the Building of the Brooklyn Bridge*. New York: Simon and Schuster, 1972.

Mencken, H. L. *A Choice of Days: A One-Volume Abridgement of the Author's Classic Autobiographic Works, Happy Days, Newspaper Days, and Heathen Days*. New York: Knopf, 1980.

Miller, Douglas T., and Marion Nowak. *The Fifties: The Way We Really Were*. Garden City, NY: Doubleday, 1977.

Miller, Nathan. *New World Coming: The 1920s and the Making of Modern America*. New York: Scribner, 2003.

———. *Theodore Roosevelt: A Life*. New York: William Morrow, 1992.

Morris, Edmund. *Theodore Rex*. New York: Random House, 2001.

Muggeridge, Malcolm. *Chronicles of Wasted Time, Chronicle I: The Green Stick*. New York: William Morrow, 1973.

———. *Winter in Moscow*. Boston: Little, Brown, 1934.

Neal, Steve. *Dark Horse: A Biography of Wendell Willkie*. Garden City, NY: Doubleday, 1984.

Oates, Stephen B. *Abraham Lincoln: The Man behind the Myths*. New York: Harper & Row, 1984.

Ramsay, David. *The History of the American Revolution*. 2 vols. Indianapolis: Liberty Fund, 1900.

Reeves, Thomas C. *A Question of Character: A Life of John F. Kennedy*. New York: Free Press, 1991.

Remnick, David. *King of the World: Muhammad Ali and the Rise of an American Hero*. New York: Random House, 1998.

Rodgers, Marion Elizabeth. *Mencken: The American Iconoclast; The Life and Times of the Bad Boy of Baltimore*. New York: Oxford University Press, 2005.

Sabato, Larry. *Feeding Frenzy: How Attack Journalism Has Transformed American Politics*. New York: Free Press, 1991

Sager, Mike. *Scary Monsters and Super Freaks: Stories of Sex, Drugs, Rock 'n' Roll and Murder*. New York: Thunder's Mouth Press, 2003.

Seldes, George. *Witness to a Century: Encounters with the Noted, the Notorious, and the Three SOBs*. New York: Ballantine, 1987.

Seldes, Gilbert. *The Great Audience*. New York: Viking, 1951.

Shenkman, Richard. *"I Love Paul Revere, Whether He Rode or Not."* New York: Harper Perennial, 1991.

———. *Legends, Lies and Cherished Myths of American History*. New York: William Morrow, 1988.

Smith, Hedrick. *The Power Game: How Washington Works*. New York: Random House, 1988.

Stephens, Mitchell. *A History of News: From the Drum to the Satellite*. New York: Viking, 1988.

Sullivan, Evelin. *The Concise Book of Lying*. New York: Farrar, Straus & Giroux, 2001.

Sullivan, Mark. *Our Times: The United States, 1900–1925*. Vol. 3, *Pre-War America*. New York: Charles Scribner's Sons, 1930.

———. *Our Times: The United States, 1900–1925*. Vol. 5, *Over Here*. New York: Charles Scribner's Sons, 1933.

———. *Our Times: The United States, 1900–1925*. Vol. 6, *The Twenties*. New York: Charles Scribner's Sons, 1935.

Swanberg, W. A. *Citizen Hearst: A Biography of William Randolph Hearst.* Norwalk, CT: Easton Press, 1988.

———. *Luce and His Empire.* Norwalk, CT: Easton Press, 1989.

———. *Pulitzer.* New York: Charles Scribner's Sons, 1967.

Taylor, S. J. *Stalin's Apologist: Walter Duranty; The New York Times's Man in Moscow.* New York: Oxford University Press, 1990.

Thayer, William Roscoe. *Theodore Roosevelt: An Intimate Biography.* Boston and New York: Houghton Mifflin, 1919.

Trollope, Frances. *Domestic Manners of the Americans.* New York: Knopf, 1949.

Tuchman, Barbara. *Stilwell and the American Experience in China, 1911–1945.* New York: Macmillan, 1971.

Weinberg, Steve. *Taking on the Trust: The Epic Battle of Ida Tarbell and John D. Rockefeller; How an Investigative Journalist Brought Down Standard Oil.* New York: W. W. Norton, 2008.

White, Theodore H. *In Search of History: A Personal Adventure.* New York: Harper & Row, 1978.

White, William S. *Majesty and Mischief: A Mixed Tribute to F.D.R.* New York: McGraw-Hill, 1961.

Wolfe, Gregory. *Malcolm Muggeridge: A Biography.* Grand Rapids, MI: William B. Eerdsmans Publishing, 1995.

Woods, Thomas E., Jr. *The Politically Incorrect Guide to American History.* Washington, DC: Regnery, 2004.

Index